MOSQUITO

The Original Multi-Role Combat Aircraft

Graham M Simons

First published in 1990 by Arms and Armour Press

Revised and expanded in 2011
and reprinted in 2013 by
PEN & SWORD AVIATION
An imprint of
Pen & Sword Books Ltd
47 Church Street, Barnsley
South Yorkshire
S70 2AS

ISBN 978 1 84884 426 1

A CIP catalogue record for this book is available from the British Library

Printed and bound in England
By CPI Group (UK) Ltd, Croydon, CR0 4YY

Pen & Sword Books Ltd incorporates the Imprints of Pen & Sword Aviation,
Pen & Sword Family History, Pen & Sword Maritime, Pen & Sword Military,
Pen & Sword Discovery, Pen & Sword Politics, Pen & Sword Atlas,
Pen & Sword Archaeology, Wharncliffe Local History, Wharncliffe True Crime,
Wharncliffe Transport, Pen & Sword Select, Pen & Sword Military Classics,
Leo Cooper, The Praetorian Press, Claymore Press, Remember When,
Seaforth Publishing and Frontline Publishing

For a complete list of Pen & Sword titles please contact
PEN & SWORD BOOKS LIMITED
47 Church Street, Barnsley, South Yorkshire, S70 2AS, England
E-mail: enquiries@pen-and-sword.co.uk
Website: www.pen-and-sword.co.uk

CONTENTS

ACKNOWLEDGEMENTS

A project of this nature could not be undertaken without considerable help from many organizations and individuals. My thanks are due to: A large number of people at British Aerospace, Hatfield, in particular Darryl Cotts, their Chief Photographer who not only combed the Hatfield archives, for every Mosquito-related image and document he could find, but also painstakingly stamped the reverse of so many prints *'Photograph Courtesy of British Aerospace Hatfield - this photograph may be published without payment of any fee'*. To Barry Guess and Trevor Friend, BAE SYSTEMS Farnborough; Kelly Merriman at Molins PLC Milton Keynes, the Royal Air Force Museum, Hendon; the A & AEE Science Library, Boscombe Down; the RAE Library, Farnborough; the Imperial War Museum, Lambeth; the Air Historical Branch of the Ministry of Defence; the Public Records Office, now the National Archives Kew; the Fleet Air Arm Museum, Yeovilton; The National Museum of the United States Air Force, Dayton, Ohio; the National Canadian Aviation Museum, Toronto; the Royal Australian Air Force Museum, Point Cook; the late Desmond Molins; the late 'Paddy' Porter; Tom Brewer; Dr Harry Friedman, John Stride; Squadron Leader Mike Deans, RAF; David Lee; John Hamlin: Peter Green; Martin Bowman; Simon Peters; the late Roger Wastell; and especially my wife Anne, for suffering so long having books, papers, photographs and notes scattered around the house in 1990, and then went through it all again in 2010!

Graham M Simons
Peterborough
May 2010

INTRODUCTION

Throughout the history of aviation there have been very few aircraft designs that have achieved immediate success when entering front-line service. The de Havilland DH.98 Mosquito was one such machine: it proved to be a winner from the start.

The concept of an unarmed wooden bomber possessing the performance to out-fly all contemporary fighters originated in a progressive company, blessed with a design office made up of extremely gifted designers and highly talented engineers. All were prepared to demonstrate supreme faith in their ideas and incorporate into them a far-sighted understanding of the forthcoming conflict that was unmatched by others. Their efforts resulted in a completely radical private venture design, totally against the thinking of many members of the Air Ministry who were only prepared to consider metal machines bristling with defensive armament.

The battle to get the design into production continued until the last few days of 1939 when, due to the foresight and support of Sir Wilfred Freeman - the Air Council's Member for Research, Development and Production - a single machine was sanctioned as a light bomber with the ability to carry a 1,000 lb bomb load over a range of 1,500 miles. Such was the drive and determination within the company, that less than eleven months later the prototype Mosquito took to the air.

Flight tests soon established the machine as the world's fastest operational aircraft, a distinction that the type enjoyed for the next two and a half years. Being small and with the manoeuvrability of a fighter, the Mosquito was rapidly developed into a multi-purpose aircraft, a factor which allowed an increased economy of tooling in the factories of Britain, Canada and Australia. The bomber version increased its load and was eventually able to carry a single 4,000 pound 'Blockbuster' bomb, two 'Highball' bouncing bombs or a myriad of other explosive stores. It could also be used as a specialized target-marker from almost ground level to six miles high.

Although originally conceived as an unarmed bomber, fighter variants were rapidly developed. Armed with four 0.303 inch machine-guns in the nose and four 20mm Hispano cannon under the cockpit floor, the Mosquito took on the role of night-fighter defence of Great Britain during 1943. With minimal modification, the basic airframe was adapted to take airborne radar, thereby creating a formidable night-fighter version that prevented virtually any night intrusion by the enemy. Mosquitos had accounted for nearly 660 enemy aircraft destroyed by the end of November 1944 and brought down over 600 flying bombs during the first 60 nights of this new threat. The aircraft's armament became increasingly sophisticated: rocket projectiles slung under the wings allowed the Mosquito to pound ships, U-boats, harbour installations and other ground targets; and one variant was equipped with a 57mm cannon which automatically fired a six pound shell every one and a half seconds.

A combination of the two main aircraft requirements resulted in the creation of the fighter-bomber in 1941, a variant which was used extensively against the V-weapon sites and was later active in support of the D-Day landings. Of the more bizarre tasks performed, was that some machines were supposed to have delivered beer to the invasion beachhead!

Towards the end of the war the Mosquito was given a hook and folding wings to become the world's first twin-engined deck-landing aircraft - along with the ability to carry a eighteen-inch torpedo. The Mosquito was also the Allies' only real and effective long-range photo-reconnaissance and weather-reporting aircraft. It photographed and surveyed the whole of Europe to the borders of Russia, along with much of Africa and Asia. Urgent combat requirements consistently led from variant to variant as the war progressed. During the latter stages of the production run, the Air Ministry changed the mark designation system from Roman to Arabic, producing a much clarified system. However, in the interest of historical accuracy, both systems are used throughout this book.

From bomber to fighter, to photographic and weather reconnaissance, and also as a high-speed emergency airliner, the Mosquito airframe was easily modified to suit all needs. The combination of a superb airframe structure, coupled with a parallel effort to increase the power of the Rolls-Royce Merlin engines, meant that no matter what the requirement, whether it be increase in weight, or change in equipment, the DH.98 design could accommodate it; it was truly a multi-role combat aircraft.

This book takes the reader from conception - including the thinking behind the project - through the somewhat protracted birth and on into the development of what must be one of the most versatile aerial weapons systems ever devised.

This edition is not so much a revision as a 'jack up the title and slide a new book underneath! The original 1990 book had been written to a much larger size, but was edited down to suit that publishers requirements. This edition has restored the work to its original what it was supposed to be and then revised to bring things up to date with current research.

Throughout the book the reader should be aware that 'de Havilland' refers to the man - either Captain (later Sir) Geoffrey or his son Geoffrey Jnr, whereas 'De Havilland' refers to the company.

It also should be understood that as the subject of this book covers a time frame from the late 1930s through to the 1950s when Imperial dimensions was the standard unit of measurement in use, so those are the figures used. This means that if a statement of '*a range of 3,000 miles with a 4,000 lb bomb load*' is used, it makes much more sense than the ridiculous-looking metric equivalent of '*a range of 4828.032 kilometres with a 1814.369 kilogram bombload*'.

For those wishing to convert:

       1 inch = 25.4 millimetres
       1 foot = 0.3 metres
       1 mile = 1.6 kilometres
       1 pound = 0.45 kilograms
       1 Imperial gallon = 4.54 litres

PROJECT

'Germany is already well on her way to becoming, and must become, incomparably the most heavily armed nation in the world and the nation most completely ready for war... We cannot have any anxieties comparable to the anxiety caused by German rearmament'.

So spoke Winston Churchill when addressing the House of Commons on 21 October 1933. Churchill may have over-estimated Hitler's readiness for war at that time, but he had correctly judged the scale of things to come.

At the end of World War One the Royal Air Force was, without doubt, the most powerful air arm in the world, but within a few short years it had shrunk to a shadow of its former self. Re-trenchment was the order of the day. In addition, the RAF suffered from internal battles to decide its exact composition; these in turn created a lack of urgency to modernize and rearm. The League of Nations disarmament commission, which had begun work in 1925, did little to help matters by conducting a series of unsuccessful negotiations which dragged on until 1933 and contributed to the negative mood pervading the Air Force. A change of mood from 1934 onwards brought forth a series of RAF expansion plans, each one quickly overtaking the previous plan, after the Air Ministry discovered that both the quality and quantity of its aircraft were generally below international standards, with many of the newer technical aspects sadly missing. It was not until the inception of Expansion Scheme F, during 1936, that the Air Ministry finally began to take the threat from Adolf Hitler's new Germany seriously.

The De Havilland team: Left to right: Charles C Walker, Capt Geoffrey de Havilland, Richard M Clarkson and Ronald E Bishop.
(©BAE SYSTEMS)

First Air Ministry Requirement

Of the many specifications drawn up for new aircraft. Air Ministry Specification P. 13/36 - which itself stemmed from Operational Requirement 41 - issued on 8 September 1936 by Air Commodore R H Verney on behalf of the RAF Directorate of Technical Development (DTD), was one of the most significant. It called for a '*...twin-engined medium bomber for world-wide use ...an aircraft that could exploit the alternatives between long range and very heavy bomber load which are made possible by catapult launching in heavily loaded condition. During all operations it is necessary to reduce time spent over enemy territory to a minimum. Therefore the highest possible cruising speed is necessary. It appears there is a possibility of combining medium bomber, general reconnaissance and general purpose classes into one basic design, with possibly two 18-inch torpedoes carried.*'

The DTD requirement called for two forward- and two rearward-firing Browning machine-guns; horizontal bomb stowage, in tiers if necessary; suitability for outdoor maintenance at home or abroad; consideration of remotely controlled guns; and a top speed of not less than 275 mph at 15,000 ft on two-thirds engine power and a range of 3,000 miles with a 4,000 lb bomb load. From this eventually came the Avro Manchester, the Handley Page H.P. 56 (which in turn evolved into the Handley Page Halifax and the Vickers Warwick powered by a pair of Rolls-Royce Vulture engines.

The first reaction from De Havilland to Specification P. 13/36 was to propose an adapted DH.91 Albatross. This machine had originated as a fast airliner and was based on the clean form of the DH.88 Comet racer which had won the 1934 MacRobertson Air Race from Mildenhall in England to Melbourne in Australia. The Albatross had not been allowed to realize its full potential until 1937 when it emerged as a North Atlantic mail carrier. Powered by four 525 hp De Havilland Gipsy Twelve inverted-vee twelve-cylinder engines, it had an all-up weight of 32,000 lb, which allowed the carriage of a 1,000 lb payload over a range of 2,500 miles against a 40 mph headwind. For a shorter range it was calculated that the aircraft could carry a payload of 6,000 lb to Berlin and back at 11,000 ft - a suggestion that raised cries of horror from appeasers and pacifists when it was mentioned in Parliament. De Havilland were wary of competing for Government military contracts due to unfortunate experiences in the 1920s, preferring instead to build civil aircraft for the open market. They felt on this occasion, however,

The DH.88 Comet Racer. The DH.98 Mosquito design can be traced back to this design.
(©BAE SYSTEMS)

The DH.91 Albatross *'Fortuna'* in the colours of Imperial Airways. The Albatross was the second-generation forerunner to the Mosquito.

Captain Geoffrey de Havilland with Lois Butler, wife of the company Chairman. They are standing in front of one of the DH.91s under construction. Directly behind and above them is one of the DH Gipsy King inverted vee-twelve engines. *(both©BAE SYSTEMS))*

that a modified Albatross airliner would be the most effective way to make a positive contribution to re-armament. After all, it made as much sense to have a fast, aerodynamically clean aircraft for a bomber as it did for a civil airliner; furthermore, it was a time-saving possibility.

During April 1938 studies were made for a twin Rolls-Royce Merlin-powered version of the aircraft. On 7 July De Havilland sent a letter discussing the specification to Sir Wilfrid Freeman, the Air Council's Member for Research and Development. The letter contained two reasons why they thought that the eventual end result of all these discussions would be so good: wooden construction and the Merlin engine.

De Havilland felt that the use of wood was not as antiquated an idea as it first appeared. Indeed, wood offered a considerable number of advantages: the strength for weight (except in torsion) was as great as that of steel or duralumin; it was more readily available and placed less strain on the country's valuable metal resources; the technology of such structures was already developed and had been proved in the Comet racer and Albatross; the stiffness of a thick, stressed skin wooden fuselage did away with the need for much internal reinforcement, thus leaving many clear spaces for bombs, guns, fuel tanks and equipment; any shell or bullet holes would represent a much smaller percentage of mass lost in a bulky timber structure - a shell fragment that could destroy a strong metal member would hardly weaken a continuous wood shell or spar; wood offered natural buoyancy and no greater fire risk; its weathering properties were well known; finally, the surface smoothness required was easily manufactured into the aircraft during construction and could be exploited to the full to produce a reduction in drag.

When Geoffrey de Havilland and Charles C Walker first suggested the high-speed bomber in 1938 they suggested a load of four 250 lb bombs. At the time, this bomb load had seemed impressive. However, in 1940 it presented a new challenge.

Chief Designer for De Havilland, Ronald E. Bishop and his team studied the standard 250 lb bomb and decided that the tail fin was wasting too much weight and occupying too much space. Bombs may not have been De Havilland business, but they began to consider the problem. Bishop suggested that they cut down the fins - they did, and tested

Concerns about using plywood construction - and the need to provide reinforcement at all the stress concentration points - were clearly demonstrated during overload tests on the DH.91 Albatross E.3 G-AEVW during 1937. The aircraft was repaired and back flying again within weeks.*(©BAE SYSTEMS)*

the sawn-off bomb by dropping it on their own airfield at Hatfield - it worked. The new high-speed bomber's payload was therefore doubled 'at the cut of a hacksaw' and a first step had been taken towards the time when Mosquito bombers would carry 4,000-pounders.

Engine Development

The other important influence in the design lay in the choice of engines. To understand why the Merlin was chosen, one has to consider the development of this engine from its conception. The Rolls-Royce Merlin twelve-cylinder upright Vee in-line engine of 1,650 cubic inch (27 litre) capacity was a development of the company's PV.12 design, which in turn derived from previous engines dating back to 1925. The first of these was the 'F' with a modest capacity of 1,295 cubic inches, which was type-tested at 490 hp and broke with tradition by using cast-alloy monobloc banks of six cylinders, the pistons running within thin carbon steel liners.

In 1926, before it entered production as the Kestrel, Henry Royce had begun design work on a much larger engine intended for heavy aircraft. This was the 'H' which had a 2,240 cubic inch capacity; it evolved into the Buzzard, of which only 100 were built, mainly for flying-boats. Such developments served to illustrate the lines upon which Royce was thinking.

By late 1928 a new engine was required for the 1929 Schneider Trophy air

One of the few surviving Rolls Royce 'R' engines, the forerunner to the 'PV' that evolved into the magical Merlin.

race and Rolls-Royce were keen to develop one to power the Supermarine S.6 seaplanes. Their resultant design, the 'R' or racing engine, was based on the earlier Buzzard but few of the components were exactly alike for every part now had to be designed to withstand running at speeds and stresses that had never before been encountered. No existing light alloy could stand up to these stresses, so a whole new range of materials had to be developed in the company's metallurgical laboratories; these were eventually licensed to outside firms under the title of 'Hinduminium'.

The engine was first started up on 14 May 1929, by which time its power had been increased from 1,545 to 1,900 hp. With the 'R' engine fitted, the S.6 won the race. Following further development which took the power to 2,350hp, the 'R' was installed in the S.6B where it repeated the feat in 1931 - thus winning the Trophy outright for Great Britain. A 'sprint' engine, running on a specially developed 'cocktail' fuel was created, which was capable of a phenomenal 2,780 hp. This kind of power enabled Flt Lt George Stainforth AFC of the RAF's High Speed Flight to set a new world speed record of 407.5 mph.

So much progress had been made that it became obvious that either a complete redesign of the Kestrel was required, or a brand new engine would have to be produced. The Air Ministry stated that it had no money to fund such a powerplant, so the Rolls-Royce board of directors decided to finance the project themselves. Sir Henry Royce and A G Elliott studied a series of possible designs, before deciding, in 1933, upon a size bigger than the Kestrel but smaller than the 'R' to give a nominal 1.000 hp. This new twelve-cylinder engine was designated PV.12, the PV standing for Private Venture. All the design work had been completed by the end of April 1933 and the first engine was started up at Derby on 15 October 1933. It immediately ran into trouble; the main reduction drive gearbox, which was designed to use double helical gears, failed repeatedly and had to be replaced with plain spur gears.

To gain maximum strength for minimum weight, the entire body of the engine, both cylinder blocks and the upper part of the crankcase, had been manufactured from one large alloy casting. It was then discovered that this

The Rolls Royce Merlin. The difference between it and it's forerunner is noticeable.

The Rolls-Royce Merlin III that formed the basis for development from a basic 1,000 horsepower up to over 2,000 horsepower on the test bench that was an indicator of things to come.

method of production created a much more serious problem: the cylinder water jackets kept cracking. Eventually this fault was cured by casting the cylinder heads, blocks and crankcase top separately.

The result was a more definitive engine lying somewhere between the Kestrel and the 'R'. It retained the 5.4 inch bore and 6 inch stroke of 1,650 cubic inch capacity and created with room to spare for further development, the desired 1,000 horsepower as a normal combat power. It did all this while also maintaining minimum frontal area in order to reduce drag.

By 1936 the early examples of the engine had flown in the prototype Spitfire and F. 36/24 Hawker high-speed monoplane, forerunner to the Hurricane. It now carried the name 'Merlin', after a bird of prey and following in the tradition common to other Rolls-Royce aero-engines.

During 1937 the company began work on a special racing version of the Merlin to power the Supermarine 323 Speed Spitfire as it prepared to attack the world speed record. This engine was basically a Merlin III strengthened to take the extra loads; it produced a staggering 2,160 hp on the test-bench, thereby demonstrating the possibilities of what was to come. A year later production Merlins were fitted with a two-speed supercharger gearbox which gave better performance at all altitudes. A major change in cylinder head design had also been adopted by Rolls-Royce as a result of data gained from single cylinder tests. This innovation was the semi-penthouse combustion chamber which, although offering great promise, did not produce the expected results in engine tests and also suffered from cracking during manufacture. So, having designed a two-piece block to eliminate the internal coolant leaks to which the one-piece Kestrel type block was prone, the company found that the Merlin continued the problem in a much more serious form. The decision was therefore made to revert to the one-piece block with

The Union Flag flies proudly over the De Havilland Aircraft headquarters at Hatfield. *(©BAE SYSTEMS)*

a single plane combustion chamber in order to meet immediate production needs. Meanwhile, work was to begin without delay on the design of a two-piece block that would enable the Merlin to achieve major power increases with a reliable and intact cylinder assembly.

This then was the position of aero-engine development in the pre-war era. The Merlin engine offered good prospects for a powerful high-speed aircraft design, but no one could have been aware just how much actual future power development was to be gained from the engine.

A radical proposal from De Havilland

With the benefit of hindsight it becomes clear that the original specification laid before Britain's aircraft manufacturers was merely a 'catch-all' for any potentially good ideas that were floating around the Directorate of Technical Development at the time. Even then, the Ministry were evidently considering a form of 'multi-role aircraft'; this is borne out by the specification which read: '...*the aircraft was to be suitable for day and night operation, at home or abroad, and to combine the medium bomber, general reconnaissance, and general purpose classes into one basic design which could then be adapted during construction into a specific role'.*

The paper, however, was not clear enough in its requirements, nor was the accepted thinking of the Air Force and Air Staff conducive to such a machine being built using the technology then available.

A V Roe , however, did pick up the challenge, with a design that eventually became the ill-fated Rolls-Royce Vulture-powered Manchester bomber. The Vulture engine was, in effect, two Kestrel cylinder assemblies joined together by a common crankcase to create an 'X'-form powerplant. Problems abounded with this engine and it's associated steam evaporative cooling system that were never fully solved. The Manchester was later transformed into the highly successful Lancaster, but it took the loss of many valuable aircrew and a major redesign of the airframe - plus a change to four Merlin engines - to make this so.

De Havilland were certain that the targets laid out in Air Ministry Specification

Another picture showing more of the De Havilland management team.

From left to right: Frank R Hearle, Wilfred E. Nixon, Captain Geoffrey de Havilland Snr, Charles C Walker, Francis E N St. Barbe, Alan S Butler.
(both ©BAE SYSTEMS)

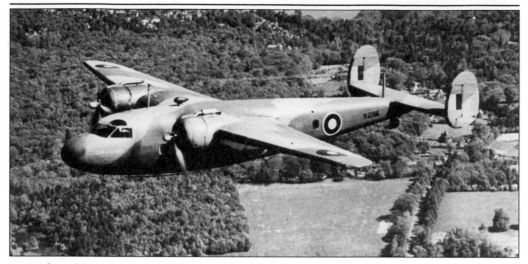

P. 13/36 would produce a mediocre aeroplane. Their further studies indicated that a wooden twin- Merlin-powered Albatross, redesigned to meet the specification, would require a minimum crew of three. It should also have six or eight forward-firing guns, along with one or two manually operated weapons, with provision for a rear turret. The weight would be 19,000 lb with a top speed of 300 mph and a cruising speed of 268 mph at 22,500 ft.

The DH.95 Flamingo - in this case R2766 - shown in RAF markings. It only ever flew in a transport form. (©BAE SYSTEMS)

The Hatfield firm therefore suggested a radically different approach to the specification requirement. It reasoned that a conventional bomber's defensive guns - along with the gunners, structure and fuel needed to both operate and carry them - could amount to around one-sixth the total weight of the aircraft. Escort fighters, for the purpose of offensive defence, would still be needed. Any guns fitted to the bomber were no real defence against anti-aircraft guns; it was only with speed and manoeuvrability, coupled with height, that an aircraft could take evasive action against fighters and ground- based guns. The larger armed aircraft would obviously take more man-hours to build, fly and service; whereas the unarmed, fast bomber would be a much smaller investment all round - taking less time to build, require fewer hours to maintain, and a smaller crew which, because of the higher speed, would be exposed to a smaller danger for less time. In turn this meant that an aircraft could make more trips and therefore deliver more bombs for a given period of time.

In a further letter, sent on 27 July, De Havilland concluded that the specification could not be met on two Merlins alone. If speed was of prime importance, then only half the load could be carried; if load was important, then a larger, slower machine would result. A compromise bomber design was arrived at during August, but again De Havilland disliked the results.

The Munich crisis of September 1938 suddenly brought the message home to everyone just how critical the world situation had become. Hatfield now felt that the most useful aircraft the company could contribute was a bomber that sacrificed everything for speed - it could not now be just an Albatross conversion. Geoffrey de Havilland considered that it should be a small machine, have a crew of two, and be powered by two Rolls-Royce Merlins. Thus the die was set, but how were they

The Service protagonists. Staunch supporter of the DH.98 - Air Chief Marshal Sir Wilfrid Rhodes Freeman, 1st Baronet, GCB, DSO, MC, RAF (18 July 1888 - 15 May 1953)

Air Chief Marshal Sir Edgar Rainey Ludlow-Hewitt GCB, GBE, CMG, DSO, MC, DL (9 June 1886 - 15 August 1973)

to convince the doubters at the Air Ministry?

De Havilland had always argued that in a future war all the metal industries would be overstretched, while wood workers would be under-employed. Geoffrey de Havilland and Charles C Walker went to the Ministry with this proposal in October. They wanted a timber construction, as with the Albatross conversion, for this would save a year of time in the prototype stage, and speed up development of every subsequent variant. The suggestion raised very little interest, for it was against all accepted thinking at the time and the project was set aside.

The DH.95 Flamingo twin-engined airliner remained a possibility. This all-metal aircraft had first flown in December 1938 and adaptation of the design into a heavily armed bomber, carrying four 500 lb bombs, was considered, but the proposed speed was uninteresting and the service ceiling was, at around 24,000 ft, too low. Consideration was also given to fitting Bristol Taurus radial engines of reduced diameter, and therefore drag, but the top speed was still only estimated at around 280-290 mph, which did not meet the De Havilland high-speed requirements. During December another new bomber specification, B. 18/38, appeared but this was of no interest to the company who continued to make efforts throughout 1939 to try to discover a formula that would be worthwhile and of interest to the Air Ministry.

Why did this continuing gulf exist between De Havilland and the Air Ministry? Basically the Air Council still wanted a metal aircraft, no matter how convincing a case the company could make. They regarded as highly suspect the estimates of speed provided by De Havilland for a clean aircraft based on the performance figures taken from the Comet and Albatross. Even if the manufacturers were correct, it was constantly in the back of Ministry minds that the Germans would develop and build even faster fighters than were at present expected, thereby placing the proposed unarmed bomber in great danger. Thus the novel design made absolutely no progress right up to the outbreak of war.

Once war was declared on 3 September 1939, there was no future for the company's civil aircraft designs and many of the civilian design staff were now freed for other duties. The following Wednesday Geoffrey de Havilland approached the Air Ministry again, finding them less sceptical but still by no means receptive. A long list of doubts were still expressed about the bomber out-running enemy fighters; it was thought that the crew of two would have too high a workload; the pilot would have no relief at the controls and the navigator would have not only to look after the radio and watch for enemy fighters, but aim, drop the bombs and watch out for their own vapour trails.

Still further studies and estimates were made during September and October, including versions powered by two Rolls-Royce Griffons, two Napier Daggers or one Sabre; but the design staff still kept coming back to Merlin powerplants, as these were now becoming readily available and offered good prospects for further development. Exhaust propulsion, drag and the effect of adding armament were all investigated, together with the effect of adding a two-gun turret - which would cause a speed reduction of at least 20 mph with a weight penalty of 500 lb. Weight and drag estimates for the larger armed aircraft were made in October, and plainly revealed a much reduced performance.

In a letter to Sir Wilfrid Freeman on 20 September Captain Geoffrey de Havilland wrote: *'We believe that we could produce a twin-engine bomber which would have a performance so outstanding that little defensive equipment would be needed'.* De Havilland continued to patiently explain that wood was very suited to really high speed as the surface was clean and free from rivets, overlapped plates and undulations, whilst its use would not impinge on labour and material already in use, or scheduled for the RAF's expansion programme.

Geoffrey de Havilland also stated that use of wood would lend itself to rapid production, for the company experience had shown that no weight penalty was expected using wood, while the simplified structure needed fewer drawings and it therefore needed less time to produce prototypes.

Although Freeman was a strong supporter of De Havilland design he nevertheless consulted Capt R N Liptrot of the Directorate of Scientific Research. Liptrot, who thought the firm was being overly-optimistic in suggesting a maximum 405 mph with Merlins, while the weak-mix cruise did not match the claimed maximum. Liptrot expressed his views with annoyance, saying it was: *"...ludicrous for a firm making such a far-reaching claim for a new aircraft type to*

Performance data from the turreted Airspeed Oxford (left) and the De Havilland Don (above) were used by De Havilland to justify their case for the DH.98 not to carry a gun turret which was considered (top) in mock-up form. *(©BAE SYSTEMS)*

Marshal of the Royal Air Force Arthur William Tedder, 1st Baron Tedder, GCB. (11 July 1890 - 3 June 1967)

present it in so meagre a way". He thought the firm's weight predictions as quoted were too low and the speeds quoted too high. He predicted 350 mph maximum and 19,500 lb weight (with extra fuel). Thus De Havilland were forced to revise its figures downwards to a more accurate 386 mph at 20,000 ft with a cruising speed of 315 mph at 15,000 ft.

To counter Liptrot's objections, and at the same time to back up the company's case for dropping the turret, data on drag from turrets fitted to the DH.93 Don and Airspeed Oxford were passed to the Royal Aircraft Establishment for comparison, together with models of the DH.98 (as the design was now designated) for wind-tunnel tests.

The case made by the company was that the two-crew unarmed wooden bomber powered by two Merlins could carry 1,000 lb for 1,500 miles and, with a wetted area twice that of the Supermarine Spitfire, would produce an aircraft some 20 per cent faster. This improvement would be gained by less back-pressure power loss, a higher altitude, faired propeller blade roots and cleverly designed ducted radiators which produced more thrust than drag. Chief Designer for De Havilland, Ronald E. Bishop, already had his eye on basic versatility, for all the while during these design studies he made sure that there was always enough space under the floor for four 20mm cannon.

The fundamental objection to an unarmed bomber was stated vehemently and repeatedly - predominately by ACM Sir Edgar Ludlow-Hewitt, AOC-in-C Bomber Command who insisted on the absolute necessity of rear defence. He based his objections mostly on the grounds of tactics in that he required his fast bombers to penetrate heavily defended territory singly to reach selected targets and, for reasons of morale if nothing else, it was necessary for the aircraft to be able to defend themselves against enemy attack.

Long-range and escort fighter development were reviewed in November, together with bomber, reconnaissance and fighter versions, all of which looked good to De Havilland. However, Air Vice-Marshals Arthur Tedder and William Sholto Douglas, respectively the Director General for Research and Development and Assistant Chief of the Air Staff, agreed on 1 November that this type would only be of interest as a bomber if it had effective rear defence, though they conceded that this would force a drop in performance, *"...but the speed of opposing fighters ... is such that we cannot hope to depend upon obtaining security by a margin of superior performance. If designed without effective rear defence, it could only be considered as a development aircraft for possible use on fast reconnaissance duties"*.

Air Marshal Sir Roderic Maxwell Hill KCB. (1 March 1894 - 6 October 1954)

A conference was called with Sir Wilfrid Freeman later in the month to consider the company's findings and its strong objections to the turret idea. Richard Clarkson was certain that the turret would spoil the design, since fighter speed could be obtained without it and almost all interceptions by the enemy could therefore be avoided. 'Scare guns' fitted to the rear of the

The Air Council of March 1941. Left to right: Captain Harold H Balfour, MC, MP, Parliamentary Under-Secretary of State for Air, ; Rt Hon Sir Archibald Sinclair Bt, PC, CMG, MP, Secretary of State for Air; Air Chief Marshal Sir Charles Portal KG, GCB, OM, DSO and Bar, MC, Chief of Air Staff. *(Authors Collection)*

engine nacelles were also considered, but again the penalty in range and/or payload was undesirable. Sir Wilfrid was very much in favour of the unarmed formula, a decision which virtually put an end to talk of a rear turret. There was still doubt about the De Havilland performance estimates and further pressure was applied for a third crew member.

At this point two cases had to be reconsidered before being resubmitted to the Ministry: The first was for a three-man bomber, with the third crew member sitting aft of the wing, the position having rearward and downward looking windows. The machine was to carry a load of four 250 lb or two 500 lb bombs. These could be replaced in the fighter version with four forward-firing 20mm cannon, the ammunition drums being changed by the third crew-member.

The second was a two-man reconnaissance or fighter aircraft equipped with three F.24 cameras or four 20mm cannon, the crew sitting in tandem, with the pilot overlooking the wing to ensure a good view.

The idea of a three-man bomber was still, to De Havilland's mind, over-manned; the proposed third crew position, with rear and downward windows, was an nothing else but an attempt to overcome the Air Ministry's desire for some kind of rearward armament, without resorting to fitting a turret. The reconnaissance/fighter version appeared to be about right, but perhaps the crew seating could be better if they were side-by-side.

The project was nearly halted again on 12 December during a further conference attended by the Assistant Chief of Air Staff, the Director-General of Research and Development, the Air Officer Commanding-in-Chief Bomber Command and a number of other high- ranking officers. The compromise armed bomber - as per the first case - was still not viewed in a favourable light, and phrases like 'no use for the unarmed bomber' were recorded. The AOC-in-C did, however, agree that there was a demand for a fast, unarmed reconnaissance aircraft.

 Contact with the Royal Aircraft Establishment (RAE) at Farnborough regarding model tests followed on November 18. However, for the Ministry there were other difficulties. H. Grinsted, the Deputy Director of Research and Development, noted that: *'Our experience of Messrs De Havilland is that they are extremely slow in producing anything for the RAF'*. It is clear that from all surviving records that during this period most technical and production experts within the Establishment had severe doubts of the firm's ability to achieve their performance and production promises.

On November 8 Grinsted heard from Charles Walker of De Havilland that the Griffon-powered design size had been increased, and that with a Frazer-Nash four-gun tail turret, 1,000lb of bombs and a crew of three it could still attain 390-400 mph at 20,000 ft.

Walker went on to explain that this aircraft could quickly be put into production, but the company acknowledged that the Air Ministry would not commit itself to large production of a type for which it had no experience. From the company's point of view they in turn were unable to expend all its design effort on producing a single prototype, so the idea of a small batch of aeroplanes was suggested as a solution. The Griffon design was now the favoured engine (but with provision for Merlins), and gentle persuasion seemed to work, as at a conference at Whitehall on November 12 it was decided to order about 50 DH.98s with Merlins. Tedder informed Geoffrey de Havilland on November 20 that it had been decided to build two prototypes with the four-gun turret, and asked him to construct a mock-up. As far as can be ascertained, no separate prototype order was ever placed.

A meeting at the Air Ministry in Harrogate on November 22, including William S. Farren, Freeman, Liptrot, plus from De Havilland, Clarkson and Bishop, brought matters together. The two designs were of similar size but the second had a rear turret giving a difference of 30-40 mph in speed. The De Havilland people stated that the first design was to demonstrate the main features of the type; the second was a development adapted for Service use as a bomber, but the overall main objective was to produce an aeroplane within about nine months without conflicting with production of other types. It was not the firm's intention to produce both aircraft simultaneously.

They claimed the design was four years ahead of the Spitfire, that its wooden construction was so perfected that the smooth skin would eliminate sources of drag and that the ducted internal radiators added 10 mph to the speed.

Freeman contended that introducing a turret tended to defeat the firm's objective to produce a bomber which would outpace contemporary fighters. The question was speed versus armament, and Freeman suggested that the firm should concentrate on producing an aeroplane which could not be overtaken by any contemporary enemy aircraft. Freeman said that if De Havilland could guarantee that they could provide a Merlin-powered aircraft having the highest possible speed with a maximum 1,500 miles range within the next nine months and they then would immediately start to build a modified type with Griffons capable of the same range at 375 mph within a further nine months and then start on a further modified type with Sabre engines capable of greater speed over the same range - he would recommend it to the Air Council purely as a gamble.

The men from De Havilland went away and did further work on their proposals. More talks were held either side of Christmas 1939, and a further meeting took place at the Air Ministry on 1 January 1940 with just four people present: Geoffrey de Havilland, Sir Wilfrid Freeman, John Buchanan, Deputy

Not the best of pictures, but one of the few located that shows the de Havilland family together - all were involved in Mosquito production in one form or another.

Left to right: Peter, Geoffrey Jnr, John, Hereward and Captain Geoffrey
(©BAE SYSTEMS)

Director-General of Aircraft Production, and John Connolly, Buchanan's staff officer. Geoffrey de Havilland had with him the outline drawings of the Mosquito. As he put them on the table he is reputed to have said. *'This is the fastest bomber in the world; it must be useful'.* Sir Wilfrid again fought for the cause, and as he was empowered to order single prototype aircraft, a decision was minuted to order a prototype of the unarmed bomber, with the official specification B.1/40/dh to Operational Requirement 70 was drawn up around the proposal at the meeting by John Connolly.

Specification B.1/40 was drawn up on the basis of an unarmed bomber aircraft (that could be used for photographic reconnaissance work if required), powered by two Rolls- Royce Merlins with ducted radiators, these engines to rate 1,280 bhp each at 12,250 ft and 1,215 bhp at 20,500 ft. The aircraft was to have a structural weight of 4,319 lb and total weight (with all normal equipment fitted) of 12,674 lb. Overload weight was to be 18,845 lb, but when used for PR duties the aircraft was to have a loaded weight of 17,150 lb. A level speed of 297 mph at 23,700ft was expected, together with a cruising speed of 327 mph at 26,600 ft. The range on full tanks of 555 gallons was to be 1,480 miles at 343 mph and 24,900 ft or 1,500 miles at full power. Service ceiling was to be 32,100 ft and the aircraft was to have a landing run of 637 yards.

The specification was approved by Roderick Hill on behalf of the DTD on 1 March 1940, and it was this bomber/reconnaissance variant that kept the project alive, but possibilities for pure bomber and fighter versions were not excluded. Within the Ministry, however, there was still ferocious opposition at almost at every turn, and without Freeman's constant support the project must surely have faltered. Nevertheless, the go-ahead for construction was given.

PROTOTYPES

The need for secrecy and protection from air attack caused the nucleus of the Mosquito design team to move out from the Hatfield factory on 5 October 1939 to the historic country house of Salisbury Hall, some five miles to the west, near London Colney. The Manor House, lying behind trees and surrounded by a moat, had previously been the discreet meeting place for King Charles II and Nell Gywnne (who is reputed to haunt the building), together with their son. It is rumoured that it was over this moat that Nell Gywnne held their son and threatened to drop him in unless the King enobled him. Just in time, the King is supposed to have cried out *'Don't drown the Duke of St. Albans!'*

Other important residents had included Edward VII, George VI and Sir Nigel Gresley, the London North-Eastern Railway locomotive designer. At the turn of the century the Hall was the home of Sir Winston Churchill's American-born mother, Jenny Jacobson Churchill. During his visits to the Hall the young Churchill often caught fish in the moat, one of which he had shot - it was said - with a rifle, to be stuffed and displayed for some strange reason on a lavatory wall. Some time during the early days of Mosquito design at the Hall, Charles T Wilkins, OBE FRAeS, Assistant Chief Designer of the Mosquito, claimed it was a study of the shape of this pike during periods of quiet contemplation that had influenced the design of the Mosquito's fuselage!

The main entrance to Salisbury Hall in 1940 - note the sandbags, sentry box and butler standing by the door!
(©BAE SYSTEMS)

The choice of Salisbury Hall came about as a recommendation from Rumball & Edwards, house agents in St Albans following a decision by Ronald Bishop and Richard M Clarkson, chief aerodynamicist at De Havilland, to set up a detachment of the design team away from the main works at Hatfield.

Above: The original hangar at Salisbury Hall. Access was severely restricted, the sign by the door states *'No admission without permit'* and the view inside is blocked by plywood sheeting...

...which was hiding this scene, as the fuselage of the prototype starts to come together. *(both ©BAE SYSTEMS))*

Bishop appreciated the Hall, for its rooms, which although dark, were large, and it contained a large Edwardian ballroom that might have been custom-built for the draughtsmen on the team. Bishop and his staff moved into the old house and soon the moat was encircling a self-contained cottage industry that became unique in the history of aviation.

Ronald Bishop's move to the old house paid off. The divorce of his design team from the production hub-bub at Hatfield was producing the desired effect. Very soon the first mock-up took shape. It was suspended, like some grotesque carcass, from the ceiling of the kitchen, which being vast and old-fashioned, provided space for a number of activities. The production men worked at the far end until their shop was ready. The switchboard girl sat in her earphone harness at the near end. The cooking area functioned under the command of Bishop's secretary, Mrs Ledeboer, who supervised the catering.

It was not long before a small hangar, disguised as a barn, was built in the grounds to house the prototype as it was built. Later the main design and drawing office staff moved into the Hall as well. By January 1940 there were no fewer than fourteen designers, aerodynamicists and stress men working on the project in the ballroom of the Hall, with twelve craftsmen in the prototype shop, under the control of Fred Plumb, the experimental shop superintendent. The mock-up, built to check the general arrangement of the aircraft and fitment of much of the controls and equipment, soon began to take shape in plywood and brown paper ahead of the prototype.

Construction

The prototype's wing, with a span of 55 feet 10 inches (slightly smaller than on later production machines), was manufactured in one piece from tip to tip. It was built up around two wooden box spars with laminated spruce flanges and plywood webs. To develop compression in the birch, plywood double skins were used, separated by spruce stringers. A false leading edge, built up of nose-rib formers and a D-skin, was attached to the front spar. The whole structure was screwed, glued and pinned before being finally covered with fabric over the plywood. The hydraulically operated slotted flaps, fitted between the fuselage, engine nacelles, and ailerons were also of wooden construction. Ailerons were metal framed and skinned, incorporating controllable trim tabs.

A mixture of prototype and mock-up parts are constructed in the hangar at Salisbury Hall in the first half of 1940. Visible is the one-piece wing and mock-up engine nacelle items.

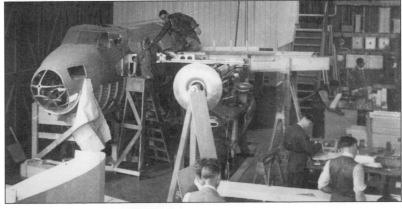

The Mosquito mock-up at Salisbury Hall on 16 June 1940. The view from the cockpit over the engines was considered important, and the value of a side blister to improve the view aft is being assessed in this picture. A Rolls-Royce Merlin is installed in the port engine position. Note also the segmented nose glazing.
(both © BAE SYSTEMS)

Accommodated within the wing structure, between the fuselage and engine nacelles, were a pair of engine cooling radiators, housed in the forward section of the wing profile. Bullet-proof fuel tanks, with capacity for 539 gallons, were also incorporated into the wing, their weight spread out across the entire span. Handley Page slots were incorporated into the leading edges of the wings outboard of the engines to cure an expected wing drop when the aircraft approached stalling speed.

The oval-section fuselage was also constructed from wood which offered the advantage of jig-building in two halves complete with seven bulkheads. The fuselage was built up from laminations of cedar ply, separated by a layer of balsa wood. At the point where the bulkheads were attached, the balsa core was replaced with a spruce ring. For local strengthening, where attachments were made to the skin, a bakelite plug was inserted into the balsa with a plywood flange glued to the inner surface to spread the load. The join line was along the vertical centre plane, the two halves being scarfed together with vee notches reinforced by ply inserts above and below and an additional overlapping ply strip on the inside of the joint. This simplified the installation of much of the controls, plumbing and equipment, which could be done before the two halves were joined. The underside of the fuselage was later cut out to accommodate the wing, which was attached via four massive pick-up points with additional bolts passing

Two views of the prototype Mosquito as it is assembled in its hangar at Salisbury Hall, sometime in October 1940.
(both © BAE SYSTEMS)

through the bottom flanges of the inner ribs. The lower portion of the fuselage was then replaced after assembly, the whole structure covered with Madapolam, doped, then painted.

The crew were accommodated side-by-side in a forward compartment, with the pilot sitting on the left. The cockpit canopy was a welded tubular steel structure, incorporating an emergency exit in the roof, covered entirely - apart from the windscreen - with Perspex. The flying controls were orthodox in operation, the control column and pendulum-type rudder pedals being connected to the flying surfaces by chains and cables.

The tail surfaces were conventional in design, but all fixed surfaces were wooden structures consisting of two box spars and stressed plywood skins, while the rudder and elevators were aluminium with fabric covering.

Both Rolls-Royce Merlin engines (together with their electric starters, booster coils and hydraulic pumps) were mounted in steel tube frames attached to the front spar and the fixed structure of the undercarriage. Within each engine nacelle was a self-sealing oil tank and automatic fire extinguishers. The landing gear consisted of two completely interchangeable main units, fitted with Dunlop pneumatic brakes, and a retractable tailwheel, all of which retracted rearwards under hydraulic power.

In the meantime Harry Povey, the De Havilland production wizard, had started to do the rounds of the local furniture firms, many of whose skilled men were put out of work by the war. Modern furniture would not suit the interior of Salisbury Hall, but a combination of some of the raw materials used in its manufacture, along with the craftsmanship and skills available from their workers, would be ideal to help build a Mosquito.

Handling wood in wartime may have been easy but obtaining the types required presented a problem. The Mosquito design devoured a forest of the finest balsa wood in Ecuador. When the first strips of this wood arrived on his desk, Rex King, at that time the Assistant Experimental Manager, stuck his thumb through it. 'What?..' he allegedly exploded '...this pappy wood? Don't be damned silly. It's not strong enough!'

The Mosquito contributed to a shortage not only of balsa but also of best-quality Canadian yellow birch and Sitka spruce used to create the laminate. During the war Douglas fir had to be substituted for these two woods as supplies ran down. English ash is rare even to this day as a result of this wartime demand.

Donald Gomme, whose G-Plan furniture factory was heavily involved with Mosquito-making, recalled: 'It will take fifty years to replace the best timber cut down during the war to build the Mosquito'.

Improvisation, according to timber available, dictated adjustments to the adhesives being used. Here Gomme, and others in the furniture industry with its specialist knowledge of the array of synthetic resins available, was of considerable value to the aircraft builders. Glue problems beset the Mosquito from its earliest moments at Salisbury Hall. The men working on the prototype were confronted by problems created from the traditional adhesives used in aircraft manufacture. The casein glue used, made by dissolving casein, a natural protein obtained from milk, in an aqueous alkaline solvent was troublesome, for it was apt to set too fast. Later the synthetic resins suggested by Donald Gomme helped to keep

The Administrative Block at Hatfield - now covered with camouflage paint, with barbed wire and air raid shelters out front.
(© BAE SYSTEMS)

Mosquitos together as solidly as the hardy furniture his factory was also producing for the barrack blocks of Britain.

Despite a myriad of problems to be overcome, the Mosquito was nearing completion. Throughout the summer of 1940 the 'cottage industry' had developed until nearly a hundred men and women were passing through the sandbagged entrance and crossing the moat to work every day. In spite of the increase of numbers of those in the know, careful security measures were observed. Even the local doctor, arriving to examine a case of suspected appendicitis, was led blindfold to his patient.

Contract No 69990 was issued on 1 March 1940 for fifty bomber-reconnaissance machines, including the prototype, even though much of the detail work had still to be completed. As the design was being worked upon and the mock-up was taking shape, thoughts again turned towards the long-range fighter - the need for which had become very apparent during the battle for France. Following the evacuation of Dunkirk, however, priorities had changed and home defence became of more immediate concern. Lord Beaverbrook, who had been appointed Minister of Aircraft Production in the new Churchill government, told Sir Wilfrid Freeman three times to stop the DH.98 project, on the grounds that anything that could not be used against the enemy by early 1941 was completely of no use - but on each occasion Beaverbrook failed to put out a firm written instruction to cease work, and therefore no such order was ever received at Hatfield.

Following the fall of Paris to the Germans, a plan previously agreed between Beaverbrook and the Air Staff came into effect. Aircraft production in Britain now concentrated on just five front-line types: Supermarine Spitfire, Hawker Hurricane, Vickers Wellington, Armstrong Whitworth Whitley and Bristol Blenheim. Apart from pure theoretical work, all energies in research and development had to be channelled in this direction. Any surplus capacity could be applied towards second-priority types such as the Handley Page Halifax and Short Stirling, but since the Mosquito would not be in action for at least eighteen months all work on it had to be stopped.

De Havilland could not make progress on the design now, for they could no longer purchase materials. They pleaded with Lord Beaverbrook to reinstate the aircraft, even as second priority; Cyril Long, the company's Chief Development and Purchasing Engineer, showed him the material schedule to demonstrate that their demands on the metal industry would be very light, with the amount of machining minimized. Even the normal oleo-pneumatic undercarriage leg was abandoned, and an earlier simple interchangeable rubber-in-compression type developed for the firm's pre- war series of light airliners was reverted to. Reinstatement would be considered, it was said, if the initial order of fifty Mosquitos could be delivered in 1941. But for the fact that at least a year earlier the decision had been made to build out of wood, the Mosquito could never have been revived after the fall of Dunkirk.

During July, Leslie Murray, General Manager at De Havilland, wrote to Beaverbrook, promising him the fifty Mosquitoes in 1941. Patrick Murray, assistant to Beaverbrook, replied the next day agreeing to reinstatement of the project as second-priority, provided that it did not interfere with more important work such as fitting bomb racks to DH.82 Tiger Moths - such was the air of desperation in the country under threat of invasion. On top of this welcome news, a letter was received later in the month which give permission to proceed with the fighter prototype, and Contract No 135522 confirmed this in November.

Close to Destruction

Great secrecy had been applied to all aspects of Mosquito design and production, and it seemed that the Germans were completely unaware of the new airborne threat that was to be unleashed upon them - or were they?

On 3 October 1940 weather conditions were poor when a Junkers Ju.88 belonging to KG 77 set off from its base at Laon in occupied France. The aircraft started its descent over Hertford, initially flying over Radlett three miles away, before returning at low altitude. For many years afterwards it was thought that the crew's target was a biscuit factory in Reading, but visibility was so bad with a low damp fog everywhere that the Germans failed to find their objective, eventually arriving over the Hatfield factory at around 11.30 am. Subsequent research indicates, however, that Hatfield, and the embryonic Mosquito production facility, had been the main target all along. At a height of about 100 ft with flaps and undercarriage down, the Ju.88 was close to stalling speed but the pilot made two runs over this 'target of opportunity', aligning his machine with Hatfield's power house chimney. The stick of four bombs dropped flat on to the wet grass, bouncing into the building known as the '94 shop' (so called because up to the outbreak of war it had been used for production of the DH.94 Moth Minor). The adjacent Student's Technical School was also put out of action.

Many of the staff had taken to the air raid shelters when the aircraft was first spotted, but the bombs collapsed one shelter and blew many other members of staff down the steps by the force of the explosions. The bombs destroyed 80 per cent of Mosquito machined parts and assembled materials, killed 21 people and wounded 70. More by luck than judgment, the Mosquito main assemblies had been missed. During the attack the Ju 88 was hit below its crew cabin by gunfire from an armoured truck carrying a single Browning machine-gun, stationed at Hatfield in the event of just such an attack. The raider swung away to the east, eventually crashing into a field five miles away at East End Green Farm near Hertfordsbury; the crew escaped, only to be captured a few hours later by farm workers. It is known that the pilot, Oberleutnant Fiebig, could speak fluent English, but rumours surfaced that he was a former de Havilland apprentice and a member of a party of foreign students who had learned to fly at Hatfield, disappearing when war was declared. If this were true, then Hatfield must have been the primary target, but fortunately for De Havilland the pilot had been confused by its appearance due to the use of camouflage.

Ironically this air raid brought about a premature end to another wooden aircraft that could well have been a stable-mate for the Mosquito. The De Havilland Technical School had been partly occupied by Airspeed Aircraft's design team since that company's take-over by De Havilland in early 1940. One design that was well advanced was the AS.48, a Napier Sabre-engined fighter of remarkably elegant lines. Airspeed had prepared provisional drawings in 1939 and, after the takeover by De Havilland, had given valuable support for the concept of a wooden fighter to support the Mosquito. It had been proposed that Airspeed's AS. 48 project team, under Hessel Tiltman, one of the founders of Airspeed, would move into Salisbury Hall along with the Mosquito project team. Tiltman's photo-lofting technique, developed to lay down the lines of the aircraft components direct from drawing to material in a very accurate manner, was to be used in the construction of both the DH.98 and AS.48 in the '94 Shop' at Hatfield in preparation for the move.

On the morning of the air-raid Tiltman was in his office at Hatfield, preparing for the drive to Portsmouth; he was taking with him a large roll of duplicate drawings of the fighter as a security measure in case Hatfield was destroyed by enemy action. Suddenly the Tannoy loudspeakers blared out its warning of the raid but it was too late because almost simultaneously the bombs dropped on the airfield, setting fire to the '94 Shop' and creating havoc. Both sets of drawings,

Damage to the '94 Shop' was extensive following the German air raid on 3 October 1940.
(© BAE SYSTEMS)

the only ones in existence, were destroyed, together with all the calculations and the mock-up. It was the coup de grace for the fighter, for the project would have to be completely restarted. The Hawker Typhoon, together with the Tempest, was well advanced on the drawing board, so the need for further lighter designs was now not so important.

First Flight

When the prototype Mosquito, carrying the Class B marks E0234, was completed at Salisbury Hall the one-piece wing, complete with installed engines, was removed from the fuselage and taken by road under tarpaulins to Hatfield on 3 November, where it was placed in a small, blast-proof building for reassembly. The machine was painted yellow overall to give both British pilots and anti-aircraft gunners a chance to recognize its unfamiliar shape as a friendly aircraft. The irony of this was that when the aircraft was rolled out for fuel flow checks, hydraulic tests and engine runs during mid-November the bright yellow surfaces had to be covered up again in order to keep the new shape secret from the eyes of German bomber

Above: The prototype is brought to Hatfield on 3 November 1940. As can be seen, moving the single-piece wing complete with a pair of Rolls-Royce Merlins attached was not a simple task.

Right: The prototype E0234 sits outside the old Tiger Moth paint shop at Hatfield after re-assembly. The aircraft is under wraps to prevent the machine being spotted by any prowling German aircraft.
(both © BAE SYSTEMS)

pilots snooping around Hatfield on daylight raids.

Taxi trials began during the afternoon of 24 November. The next day Geoffrey de Havilland Jnr, the company's test pilot since 1 October 1937, made a short hop. Sir Geoffrey de Havilland takes up the story in his biography *Sky Fever:*

My son Geoffrey, who had flown as a baby in his mother's arms in my first aircraft, was to be the pilot. He had followed the construction of the 'plane right from the beginning and was to be responsible for all the subsequent testing.

The Aerodynamics Department had worked out the performance of take-off run, rate of climb, high speed and stall speed, as had been done on all previous 'planes in the past years. This data of performance was seldom more than 2 per cent or 3 per cent at variance from the measured figures during actual test flying. Geoffrey therefore knew what to expect even on the first flight. The Rolls-Royce Merlin engines were given the usual thorough test run, and Geoffrey climbed into the pilot's seat; John Walker, the chief of the Engine Installation Department, took the seat at his side and slightly to the rear.

Above: Shrouded in tarpaulins to prevent enemy observation of its bright yellow shape, E0234 is prepared for flight. Note lack of undercarriage doors .

Left: 19 November 1940. E0234 being prepared for engine runs and fuel flow tests. Hereward de Havilland, Captain Geoffrey de Havilland's brother discusses the forthcoming trials with Company Chairman Alan Butler.
(both © BAE SYSTEMS)

Many taxiing runs were made to test ground control, landing gear and tail skid, the length and speed of each run being increased until take-off seemed very near. Then Geoffrey taxied back to the main group who were eagerly waiting for news. He said all was well and that he would take her into the air.

The great moment had come after only eleven months from the start of the design of the fastest aeroplane we had ever built—a speed record in itself. The tense excitement of the many watchers showed itself in various ways. We all tried to look and act normally, but I kept walking back to my car to open and shut the door quite without reason, while others walked off a short way and returned more quickly. It was a great relief when I heard the engines opened up fully with the 'plane held back by the wheel brakes. The engine roar continued as the brakes were suddenly released. The Mosquito gathered speed rapidly, the power to weight ratio being very high, and it lifted easily and was truly airborne on its first flight. As it continued its steady course, the pent-up feelings of awful anxiety gave way to relief and great hopes for the future.

If a new 'plane is up for about fifteen minutes on a first flight, the watchers can feel fairly certain that nothing much is wrong with the controls or trim. Geoffrey was up for nearly thirty minutes and then reappeared, circled and came in to make a perfect landing. When he climbed out we all surrounded him to ask 'how it went'. His brief verbal report was that only minor work and adjustments were required.

Above: The prototype is wheeled outside.

Right: Ready to go! The dark appearance of the yellow paint scheme is through the photographer inadvertently using orthographic film.
(both © BAE SYSTEMS)

Top: the prototype in the flight test shed at Hatfield.

Above: Geoffrey de Havilland and John Walker get airborne in E0234 for the first time.

Left: Captain Geoffrey de Havilland with his son Geoffrey Jnr after the first flight of the Mosquito.

(all © BAE SYSTEMS)

For the record, At 1545 hrs, just four days short of eleven months after the start of detailed design work - and a feat that has never been fully appreciated - Geoffrey de Havilland took off from Hatfield for a 30-minute flight with John Walker, the engine installation designer and also a qualified pilot, in the right-hand seat. The undercarriage was successfully retracted and a speed of 220 mph was achieved; the Handley Page slots, locked for this first flight, were found to be completely unnecessary since no wing-drop was found near the stalling speed in any configuration.

Wool tufts applied to W4050 at Hatfield. This view shows particularly well the 'short' engine nacelles.

Slipstream rectifiers and wool-tufts on W4050 on 10 January 1941.
(both © BAE SYSTEMS)

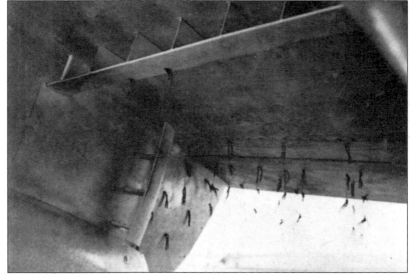

Company flight testing

Manufacturer's testing began with two test flights on 29 November. The performance astounded everyone: here at last was something that could not fail to attract official interest. By this time the Class B marks were no longer required; in their place the official RAF serial of W4050 was carried. Control and manoeuvrability were good, even in gusty conditions. On the ninth flight retraction of the tailwheel took place.

Pat Fillingham was a test pilot on Mosquitos with De Havilland: *Let me set the scene - Hatfield in 1940 was a grass field. There were no runways, no radio, no Met-we just landed into wind. There was a controller who sat in a small hut with a Verey pistol and an Aldis lamp - red and green to give landing clearance. We had just four Test Pilots at Hatfield - the Chief. Geoffrey de Havilland Jnr, George Gibbins, John de Havilland (Sir Geoffrey's youngest son), and myself.*

After a few flights it became obvious that the aircraft was extremely manoeuvrable. Geoffrey de H did some spectacular demonstrations for the Ministry and the Air Force. One big feature was the vapour trails formed at the wingtips under high 'G' which, when the aircraft passed you by, you could hear the crackle of the air as it closed up. This phenomenon soon became known as 'Audible Vortices'.

On one of these flights Ronald Bishop, our Chief Designer went aloft. At the end of this flight the undercarriage would not come down, so Bish - as he was known to us - had to use the emergency system. This involved pumping on an emergency pump and after some 300 pumps the undercarriage was still not down and they ran out of hydraulic fluid. Luckily the last 200 pumps were on air and the gear was locked down. That night there were some changes in the design office!.

The first problem to arise was buffet on the tailplane. It was caused by a bad airflow from the engine nacelles. Wool tufts were stuck on with 'Bostik' to show the flow pattern. Now I see in my log-book for December 9th 1940 that I "flew Hurricane P3090 - observing the airflow tufts on the Mosquito at various speeds". So that was 2 weeks' after the first flight. - this problem was finally cured by

Two pictures of E0234 undergoing fuel flow and engine runs in mid-November 1940, prior to the first flight. The aircraft is still missing the undercarriage fairings.
(both © BAE SYSTEMS)

E0234 out on the grass at Hatfield for engine runs and fuel consumption tests before its first flight.
(© BAE SYSTEMS)

extending the engine nacelles. However, because of this the flaps had to be split.

These extensions to the engine nacelles is well known, but it did not take the form that might have been expected - they were not re-built to the new, longer shape, but were literally 'extended' with additional material to create the new shape. Indeed, on the prototype, the form of the original nacelle shapes are still there to this day!

There was still plenty of criticism, even after the bomber had flown. On 2 December 1940. Sir Archibald Sinclair, Secretary of State for Air wrote to Lord Beaverbrook, saying that: *'War experience tends to show that this bomber would be useless for the purposes for which it was designed. On the other hand I am inclined to think that it may be useful for Photo Recce and target towing if the equipment can be installed'.*

He went on to suggest that it might be possible to use the aircraft for short-range bombing in suitable weather conditions, but suggested that no more orders be placed until satisfactory prototype trials were complete, when a further fifty might be ordered if the type was acceptable for target towing.

On 11 December, during the 30th flight, the starboard cowling blistered, forcing the machine to return on one engine. This was one of the few snags that was to plague the Mosquito for months to come; eventually the problem was traced to overheating exhaust manifolds which required forward-facing intakes for a supply of cooling air.

Geoffrey Roald de Havilland Jr., OBE (1910 - 27 September 1946)
(© BAE SYSTEMS)

On 29 December the DH.98 was displayed at Langley for the benefit of Lord Beaverbrook and other Ministers. Also present, at the invitation of De Havilland, was the Honourable Clarence 'C D' Howe, Minister of Munitions and Supply in the Canadian Government; hopes were high that the Mosquito could also be built in Canada with its plentiful timber supplies. The next day the Ministry of Aircraft Production overseer at Hatfield, Group Captain Forrow, told the company that another 150 airframes were to be ordered, so additional materials, space and sub-contractors were sought with great urgency in view of further extensive orders.

On 11 January the Ministry requested that a true reconnaissance prototype be built within the 50 contracted thus far, with the remaining 47 aircraft (a fighter prototype was subsequently requested too) from Contract 69990 to be finished

as 28 fighters and 19 bomber-reconnaissance machines. There were still no orders for pure bombers although it was expected that a bomber variant would figure in the next batch of 150 to be built.

W4050 taxies out for another test flight - the one piece flaps on each side and the short nacelles that indicated the prototypes can be clearly seen. *(© BAE SYSTEMS)*

Development flying continued, with all three planned roles in mind. W4050 reached an altitude of 22,000 ft on 17 January 1941, where it was expected to attain its maximum performance, but due to incorrectly adjusted engines, performance actually peaked at only 19,000 ft. Later, following adjustments, a top speed of 388 mph was recorded. Flutter of the tailplane became evident above 240 mph indicated airspeed, caused by disturbed airflow streaming back from the trailing edges of the nacelles.

Slipstream rectifiers were fitted under the stub-wings in an attempt to cure this, but they had no effect. During early February the aircraft flew with the engine nacelles lengthened and intakes modified, which helped ameliorate the tailplane flutter; the nacelles were lengthened again, but this created the need for further modifications to the flaps, torque tubes and levers. Directional and lateral stability was good, although with the centre of gravity towards the aftmost position the machine became unstable, but modifications were already in hand to cure this. All the controls were found to be satisfactory. A slight vibration of the cockpit instruments was noticed, which was cured by removing three inches from each propeller tip. The tailwheel castoring was not yet right and required still more work - a problem which was soon to cause trouble.

William Maxwell 'Max' Aitken, 1st Baron Beaverbrook, Bt, PC, (25 May 1879 - 9 June 1964)

By now the aircraft had flown 35 hours on manufacturer's trials. Before W4050 was despatched to the Aeroplane and Armament Experimental Establishment (A & AEE) at Boscombe Down for official trials on 19 February, the upper surfaces were camouflaged dark green and brown, but the aircraft retained the yellow undersurfaces to aid recognition from the ground.

Service Testing

When W4050 arrived at Boscombe Down it was met with a complete lack of urgency that surprised everyone, especially Richard Clarkson who was eager to prove both the De Havilland case and his own performance estimates. When flight trials began there was suddenly great surprise in official circles at the machine's capabilities, so much so that its speed was double-checked. After confirmation of the results, a stream of visitors rapidly arrived from

Another view of the prototype getting airborne, but by now the machine carries its RAF serial of W4050. The short nacelles and single-piece flaps are notable. *(© BAE SYSTEMS)*

London, including officers who previously had shown no confidence or interest in the unarmed bomber concept.

Then disaster struck. W4050 was taxiing across the muddy airfield during the evening of 24 February for the start of its 57th flight when the tailwheel castoring problem suddenly surfaced again, causing the tailwheel to jam and resulting in a fracture of the rear fuselage.

Pat Fillingham again: *The aircraft went to Boscombe Down to be checked. The pilots were very impressed and the top speed turned out to be I think, 10 mph above the Spitfire. Boscombe was a very rough and hilly field with no runways in those days, and unfortunately the tailwheel caught in a rut and cracked the fuselage above the rear door. Hatfield quickly came up with a repair scheme and a strake appeared on the starboard fuselage above the rear door. Every Mosquito built carries this strake and it is hardly noticeable.*

Geoffrey de Havilland, Richard Clarkson and Charles Walker arranged to meet W.S. Farren, Director of Technical Development at Boscombe Down, fully expecting that the fractured fuselage and tailwheel problem would kill off the Mosquito. When they arrived at Boscombe, all that Farren wanted to talk about was the aircraft's sparkling performance. The best rate of climb recorded was 2,880 feet per minute at 11,400 feet altitude and the A & AEE recorded a top speed of 388 mph at 22,000 feet. It was this latter figure that was to amaze everyone, despite the fact that during flight 48 on 16 January 1941 with Geoffrey de Havilland Jnr flying and his father in the observers seat they had been able to fly away from a Spitfire '...*in a fairly convincing manner*'.

The damaged fuselage was replaced by one being prepared elsewhere for the PR prototype and despatched to Boscombe Down by Fred Plumb, the Experimental Shop Manager on 7 March, together with a small working party to install it - a task which took only a few days. After repairs, W4050 was returned to Hatfield from Boscombe Down for minor adjustments on 15 March, returning to Boscombe on the 19th, only to be forced to return to Hatfield five days later with engine starter trouble.

The initial handling report (No AAEE767) issued by Boscombe Down on 5 March recorded that the pilots found the machine 'pleasant to fly' a comment which all subsequent service pilots would endorse, although the Mosquito became

General Henry Harley 'Hap' Arnold (June 25, 1886 – January 15, 1950) left, with Wilfrid Freeman are seen aboard HMS *Prince of Wales* in August 1942. Both men knew the potential of the Mosquito design - even if others could not or would not see it.

well known for its swing on take-off if not carefully monitored. The report went on to state:

'Aileron control is light and effective. Take- offs and landings are straightforward. The aircraft stalls at 105 mph ISA with flaps up, 90 mph with flaps down, and was flown up to 320 mph ISA. Estimated service ceiling was 33,900 ft, the greatest height reached was 29,700 ft... If attention had not been drawn to the buffeting by the firm's pilot, it is unlikely that adverse criticism would have been made. The heating is good, the seating a little cramped... found that the peep-hole of armoured glass fitted into the armour plate behind the observer is an excellent feature... as no auto-pilot is fitted the aircraft would need an improvement in stability for long endurance flights. The undercarriage is pleasant to travel on, the brakes efficient and the aircraft handled well when taxied.

'It accelerates rapidly when the undercarriage is retracted and a high rate of climb experienced. The aeroplane handles well at all speeds. As the aircraft is fitted with test instrumentation suspended from the dashboard on the right-hand side, no entry can be made to the nose in flight. The pilot's view is good all round, apart from downwards, this being restricted by the wing and engine nacelles. 'Blisters' are incorporated into the canopy to improve the view astern.'

At Hatfield the Boscombe Down report was considered a *'most favourable and heartening document';* it demonstrated that although there were the inevitable teething problems associated with any new product, in the main the company had achieved all its aims.

As already mentioned, problems with the airflow around the rear of the engine nacelles led to tailplane buffet; this resulted in a further series of modifications with the shape evolving into a much longer nacelle which protruded rearwards from the trailing edge of the wing. This, in turn, caused problems with the flaps and the flap-operating mechanism; so, to allow the flight-testing to continue with the modified nacelles, the flaps were locked in the 'up' position. On production

aircraft the flaps were to be manufactured in two pieces, allowing operation on either side of each nacelle.

W4050 was tested in such a configuration at A & AEE and a report issued on 19 April 1941 concluded that the aircraft was difficult to trim accurately with the flaps locked up. Differences were noted since the earlier tests, many originating from the fitment of the new fuselage. Better tailwheel castoring was noted, and the raising of the cockpit trim-wheel, placing it within easy reach of smaller pilots, was praised. Minor faults were also discovered relating to the fit of some of the Perspex panels in the canopy, a problem that could easily be put right with better quality control during production.

Pat Fillingham: *In the early summer of 1941, both John de H and I went solo on the Mosquito. I well remember my flight - there were no pilots' notes, I was given 5 minutes instruction in the cockpit, told "...to put the tail trim one division forward and land at 120 mph. Watch the swing and don't go too far away!". I enjoyed that flight, made an approach over the factory and landed safely.*

The Mosquito undercarriage was very good - rubber in compression. I was taught in the Technical School that you cannot compress rubber - only distort it - so it was always 'rubber in distortion' for me.

Electrics were mistrusted by all pilots at that date - they were always a problem. Indeed, the early Mosquito only had one generator - on the port side, I think, so if you lost that engine you had to rely on the battery and its amps for all the electrical services. The early Mosquitoes went to the Services with only one generator, but the RAF soon stipulated two.

On 20 April Lord Beaverbrook brought John G Winant, the US Ambassador, who had taken over from the pro-appeasement, Nazi-loving Joseph E Kennedy Snr, and General Henry 'Hap' Arnold, head of the United States Army Air Corps, together with other high-ranking officers, to see W4050 perform. The show consisted of upward rolls from ground level with one propeller feathered; a circle within the airfield, causing audible vortices at the wing-tips in the tight turns; and flying level at over 400 mph. The display was all the more spectacular for it followed a somewhat sedentary flypast of American lend-lease aircraft all of which appeared pedestrian by comparison! Six days later General Arnold set off for America with a full set of manufacturer's drawings in his luggage. As a result of a report submitted by General Arnold, five American aviation companies - Beech, Curtiss-Wright, Fairchild, Fleetwings and Hughes - were asked to evaluate the data brought over from De Havilland. The report issued by Beech Aircraft summed up their views:

'It appears as though this airplane has sacrificed serviceability, structural strength, ease of construction and flying characteristics in an attempt to use construction material which is not suitable for the manufacture of efficient airplanes.'

First of the Fighters

The fighter prototype, the Mosquito Mk.II, conforming to Specification F.21/40, was ordered in July 1940 and was allocated the serial W4052. The aircraft was to be armed with four nose-mounted Browning .303in machine-guns fired by a press-switch on the control column, and four 20mm Hispano cannon installed under the cockpit floor, these being fired by a trigger. A camera gun installed in the solid nose was automatically operated when either type of gun was fired; it could also be operated independently by a push switch next to the gun-firing switch on top of the control column. All the armament was fired electro-pneumatically, taking air from a Heywood compressor fitted in the port engine nacelle; this compressor also operated the wheel brakes and radiator cooling flaps. The Mosquito fighter also differed in that it had a flat bullet-proof windscreen, instead of the pointed screen of other variants. The crew entered the fighter through a door on the starboard side below the wing instead of a trapdoor in the floor, as this area was now occupied by 20mm cannon. A telescopic ladder was carried to give access to the cabin and the wing spars were strengthened to take the higher loads imposed by fighter manoeuvring.

Doubts had been expressed by the Air Ministry's gun specialists as to the ability of the Mosquito's structure to stand up to the recoil and return loads of the four cannon operating simultaneously, each one firing ten shells per second. In order to test this, Hydran Products of Staines built gun-butts in fields between Langley and Staines, where a representative fuselage from Salisbury Hall was installed. The experiment began with single shots being fired, gradually building up to longer and

W4052, the first Mosquito fighter in flight. The aircraft is fitted with Airborne Interception (AI) radar, notable by the arrowhead transmitter aerial in the nose and the 'broomstick-like' receiving aerials protruding through the wingtips.
(© BAE SYSTEMS)

longer bursts. A close inspection was kept on the mountings and adjacent glued structure, but the only stoppages experienced during these tests involved ammunition feed malfunctions. Later instrumentation tests on the Hispano gun mountings demonstrated that the timber structure absorbed the shock-loads very well, whereas breakages of metal mounts were common until new buffering methods were discovered. This fitment of cannon to the belly of the Mosquito was taken to the extreme with the fitment of the 57mm cannon fitted with the Molins automatic feed mechanism Test film taken showing a Mosquito dug into trenches well over half the wheel diameter deep and then the gun fires automatically one 6 pound round every one and a half seconds is amazing to behold The barrel recoiled

over 18 inches with every shot!

The prototype fighter was rolled out from Salisbury Hall during the evening of 15 May. To save a wasted month spent in dismantling and reassembling the aircraft to transport it by road, Geoffrey de Havilland Jnr with Fred Plumb as passenger flew the aircraft out to Hatfield from an adjoining 450-yard-long sloping field.

Legend has it that the idea came about 'in the pub' when Fred Plumb jokingly said to Geoffrey de Havilland *'why don't you fly her out of the field at the back?'* The next morning Geoffrey de Havilland was at Salisbury Hall, pacing out the field with Farmer Dixon at his side. Edward Bishop in his book *The*

The .303in Browning machine-gun installation in the nose in both 'real' and sketch form.

The ammunition tanks were installed above the guns with curved chutes to deliver the linked ammunition to the machine gun breeches in a continuous stream. The spent cartridge cases and links then fell away via chutes and were collected in a space underneath the guns to be retrieved by ground crew on completion of the mission. They were collected in this way, instead of being ejected into the airflow, to prevent them striking and damaging the aircraft's structure.

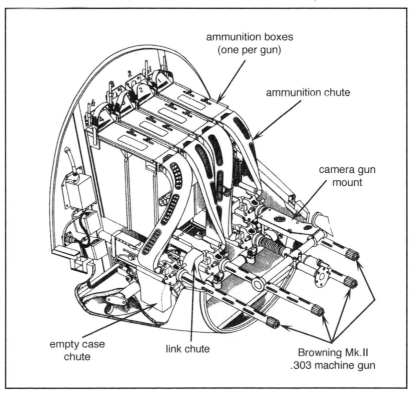

ammunition boxes
(one per gun)

ammunition chute

camera gun
mount

empty case
chute

link chute

Browning Mk.II
.303 machine gun

Wooden Wonder tells the tale beautifully: '*That hedge will have to go; so will one of the trees' he muttered. But the pilot had not reckoned on the feelings of Farmer Dixon in the matter. The farmer of this land, a dour Scot, was at the flyer's side. It's impossible' he said. 'You canna do it. First, because I want to sow. Second, you canna muck about with the hedges and trees. And that's final.'*

Farmer and airman looked hard at one another. Each had his own sense of war responsibility. 'It will save a lot of time if I can fly the boiler out of here,' de Havilland said, looking at the hedge. Farmer Dixon pleaded, 'But that hedge is a fine old hawthorn. Dig it up and it will never grow again. Besides, it's been there a very long time.'

A compromise was reached. The trees would remain but the farmer agreed to lose a section of the hedge, enough to allow the Mosquito through at take-off. 'But mind you get your boiler ready in time. I've got my field to sow.'

The take-off was not much above marginal, but they managed it and just five days later the cannon were being test-fired at the Hatfield stop-butts; the belt feeds for these cannon had previously been considered unsatisfactory, but British Small Arms (BSA) managed to obtain - just before the fall of France - a French-designed feed called the Chatellerault, which they copied. This became the standard feed for all future installations. However, there were problems.

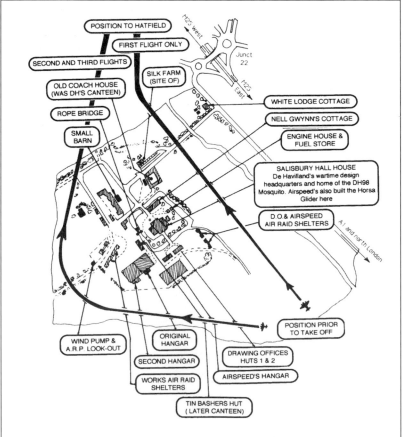

A sketch map showing the area, and direction of the Mosquito fighter prototype flight from Salisbury Hall. It is based on a drawing by Alan H. Copas.

The first version of the segmented Youngman frill airbrake as fitted to W4052 when the aircraft was at Salisbury Hall. The brake lay flush with the fuselage during normal flight, but could be extended into the airflow via a series of push-rods to create drag and so slow the aircraft down.

The first fighter was W4052, shown here with a further version of the Youngman frill air-brake, extended in the open position. Note the large 'P' in a circle painted yellow on the rear fuselage, denoting that the aircraft was a prototype. By this time the air-brake had been modified with a cut-out in the top section, possibly to improve the airflow over the fin and rudder when the brake was deployed.
(© BAE SYSTEMS)

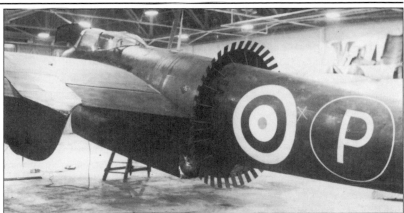

Molins Machine Co. Ltd were not only involved in automatic feeds for large calibre weapons, they were also involved with the Hispano 20mm cannon – a story behind which lies a tale of cloak-and-dagger adventure.

A study of the company archives reveals that the cannon feed was being made in a factory in Southern France at the start of the war in great secrecy; the design was still being perfected in 1940 when the German blitzkrieg hit France and it looked probable that Britain would lose the race to capture this 'secret weapon'. The plans were brought out at the last moment by way of St. Nazaire. But then nobody could put the belt feed into effect and produce a gun that could sustain a consistent 600 rounds per minute rate of fire; so the problem was handed to Molins, where a combination of concentrated effort and flair soon solved it. The French design was much improved and throughout the war the feed was largely produced by Molins at a well-guarded satellite factory on Dartford Heath in the outskirts of London.

From the company records it is clear that Desmond Molins took a personal interest in the problem from the start and put the whole resources of the Deptford works at the Ministry's disposal to develop the feed and ammunition for the Hispano gun. The attitude and abilities of Molins when compared to those of far bigger companies involved seemed to be very different. By the middle of 1941 the first Molins belt feeds were being delivered, and they proved so superior to other versions that other companies were told to base their production on Molins methods.– records show that The Austin Motor Company would take no advice from Molins or anyone else. They had some difficulty in getting their first belt feeds to work and they were inferior in workmanship to the Molins feeds and gave considerable trouble in service.

Molins discovered in development trials that it could improve the belt feed still further by fitting an extra sprocket to support the nose of the cartridge. 'Four belt feeds with this modification were made and air firing trials at Boscombe Down confirmed the Molins report. This modification was introduced at once, and so great was the improvement, it was then retrofitted to all belt feeds.

On 23 June W4052 was despatched to Boscombe Down where squadron pilots flew it and pronounced the aircraft's stability satisfactory for night flying. By 5 July, however, De Havillands, in agreement with Boscombe, thought that the longitudinal stability aspect when compared with the Beaufighter, was not good enough. This resulted in W4052 being experimentally fitted with two different-sized tailplanes of 88 and 98.5 sq ft area respectively during early 1942 in an attempt to improve matters.

During the gun heating part of the trials, thermometers were situated directly in the breech blocks of the cannon, the first time that this procedure had been used at A & AEE. These demonstrated, to everyone's surprise, that the cannon retained the heat generated by firing for a much longer period than expected. Hot air for gun heating

20mm Hispano cannon installation in the belly. Each cannon was fired by an electrical trigger on the end of the breech. The supporting structure, easily able to absorb the recoil, can be clearly seen.

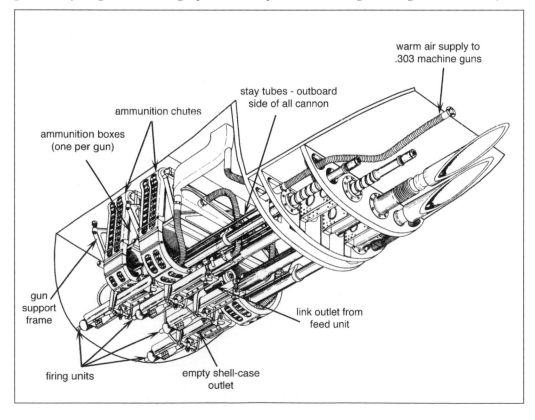

warm air supply to
.303 machine guns

stay tubes - outboard
side of all cannon

ammunition chutes

ammunition boxes
(one per gun)

gun
support
frame

link outlet from
feed unit

firing units

empty shell-case
outlet

had been taken from a special 5 inch x 9 inch x 12 inch section of the starboard radiator, travelling through a bifurcated duct before passing to the 20 mm and 0.303 in guns; and in the face of this evidence it appeared that the amount of heat being transmitted would need to be carefully controlled. Further tests, intended to establish this amount, were inconclusive due to a fault in the fuel system which restricted the aircraft's altitude and therefore the outside air temperature at which the system could be tested.

Studies of turret-equipped variants continued with some urgency. The Spitfire and Hurricane were adequate day fighters, but improvisations such as the Blenheim necessitated a follow-up design. The Mosquito showed great promise in this role, with fixed guns or a dorsal turret, and a version equipped with a Bristol turret carrying two or four cannon was deemed acceptable for its weight. The turret-fighter's top speed when equipped with Merlin XXIs was thought to be 12 mph slower than the fixed-gun version and an endurance of 4.6 hours gave a 1,380 miles range, compared with 5 hours and 1,570 miles range. The speed difference was most important, for if the turret was not faired, the condition would be 10 mph worse. Despite objections, De Havilland were told during mid-April to finish two of the fighters with four-gun Bristol turrets; they immediately earmarked two airframes for this task, of which W4073 became the first production fighter.

The first turret fighter, fitted with a dummy Bristol type B.XI two-gun dorsal turret immediately behind the cockpit, flew out of the improvised Salisbury Hall strip on 14 September, promptly shedding part of its mock-up turret on the way to Hatfield. The second machine left Salisbury Hall on 5 December, also fitted with a mock-up turret, but this was soon removed and faired over at Boscombe. The tests merely proved the considerable drag penalty of fitting the Mosquito with a turret. When this drawback was contrasted with the proven effectiveness of the fixed guns, it meant that the idea was not worth proceeding with.

It was already known that there existed a requirement for a defender/intruder night fighter and when Specification F.18/40 was issued in October 1940 the DH.98, with its speed and range, was considered the best candidate. While at Boscombe, the flame-damping qualities of the Mosquito exhaust system were tested, demonstrating that if the aircraft was to be used for night fighter work, improvements would have to be made to the existing twin ejector exhaust by fitting fishtails at the rear, along with further shrouding of the external duct.

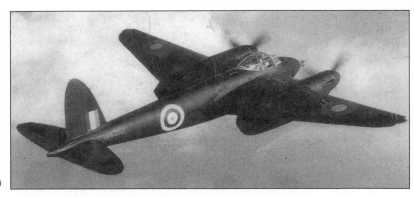

W4052, the fighter prototype is seen in flight. (© *BAE SYSTEMS*)

W4050 now painted with
camouflage and R-R
Merlin 61 engines.
(© BAE SYSTEMS)

By the end of July the official tests at Boscombe were finished, and W4052 was returned to Hatfield for fitment of the secret Airborne interception (AI) radar, a device distinguishable by the 'arrowhead' transmitter aerial. The planned 'saxophone' shroud exhaust was still not fitted, for it was burning out on the test-beds at Rolls-Royce, Hucknall.

In mid-September Frank Hearle received confirmation of the orders for fighters, together with a request that 20 have dual control. A large-quantity Mosquito production schedule was planned in both England and Canada, thus justifying the diverse development programme. A series of modifications was already being incorporated into the design: metal-skinned ailerons replaced fabric; and bomber-type hydraulic lines were replaced by reconnaissance type.

There was another problem to be overcome - deceleration! The high speed of the Mosquito allowed it to intercept enemy aircraft easily, but when the pilot was in range he needed to slow down rapidly — which was unusually difficult because of the Mosquito's fine aerodynamic shape - so as to match the enemy's speed and to give him time to aim. The first attempt to solve this was done by using the Youngman frill air-brake, a bellows-operated, segmented air-brake which encircled the rear fuselage immediately aft of the wing; it had previously been tried with some success on Spitfires. Between January and August 1942 it was tried on W4052 in many forms, with and without gaps and with differing chords. Although the time taken to slow from 250 to 150 mph had been reduced by one third using the air-brake, considerable buffeting was experienced due to the disturbed airflow travelling over the elevators and rudder, and this was accompanied by a slight change of trim. This buffeting, and the time reduction from 45 seconds to 30 seconds, was not considered sufficient to warrant operational use of the air-brake; instead, when compared, the same effect was

A view of W4051 in flight.
(© BAE SYSTEMS)

gained by lowering the undercarriage. This was adopted as standard practice, and the air-brake idea was dropped.

Photo-Reconnaissance

The last of the three prototypes to fly was W4051, the Photo-Reconnaissance Mk.I. Since the original fuselage had been sent to replace the damaged W4050 during February, this one had been replaced by a production fuselage which later allowed the aircraft to fly on operations. The assembly was completed by 24 May and the aircraft made its maiden flight on 10 June 1941. Two days later the Commanding Officer of the Photographic Reconnaissance Unit (PRU) at RAF Benson. Wing Commander Geoffrey Tuttle, eagerly went over to Hatfield to test the aircraft.

W4051 was handed over to the A & AEE at Boscombe Down on 25 June. Three days later a minor accident occurred while it was being flown by a PRU pilot. On landing the tail bounced and after several such bounces the tail wheel retracted and the machine came to rest with damage to the rear end of its fuselage and tail-cone. On examination it was discovered that the tail wheel lock had been completely inoperative but, luckily, the fuselage had not been cracked. The feet of the safety frame, provided to prevent damage in the event of a landing with the tail wheel retracted, had broken and caused all the load to go through the operating jack and into the anchorage, which eventually failed, allowing retraction to take place. In many respects this accident was a blessing in disguise for, by occurring early in the test programme, it revealed several minor design faults in the tail wheel down lock, warning light and operating jack anchorage that could be solved before the aircraft entered squadron service.

A further PR type, W4054, joined the development programme, only to be plagued by a series of engine cut-outs around 30,000ft. Throughout the summer of 1941 the two machines were used to check camera installations, complete climb trials, fuel consumption and radiator tests.

All three prototypes were used extensively in development programmes, with

W4051, the prototype photographic reconnaissance aircraft undergoing engine runs at Hatfield. Note the small exhaust shrouds and the small 'doughnut' tailwheel, which was later changed to the double-track type to cure tailwheel shimmy. The machine also appears to be fitted with Bendix B-3 drift meter - the long 'pipe' protruding through the lower fuselage.
(© BAE SYSTEMS).

W4051. The fuselage originally intended for this aircraft was used to replace W4050's which had been fractured at Boscombe Down, and so W4051 received a production fuselage instead.
(© BAE SYSTEMS)

the overall intention of maintaining the speed and/or increasing the armament. Different exhaust stacks and shrouds, linked with cowling modifications, were tested, as were under-wing bomb racks and tanks, balloon cutters, nose searchlights, undercarriage doors, propeller governors, radios, 40mm cannon, negative-G carburettors, lamp-black or 'Night' matt finishes, different tailplane sizes, a larger rudder trim-tab to improve single-engine control, ultra-violet lighting for the instruments in the cockpit, a sandwich windscreen, Hamilton propellers and convex trailing-edge ailerons - the list was endless. Many of these tests were simply 'fine tuning' of the design, but they were useful. The more cumbersome shrouded exhaust system fitted to bomber- reconnaissance W4072 was found to make this aircraft only 2 mph slower than the neater standard PR or bomber exhaust. Removing these shrouds to expose the bare exhaust stacks lost another 7 mph, but helped engine exhaust cooling. The matt 'lamp-black' finish tested on W4078 and W4082 disturbed the airflow so much that dc Havilland claimed that it cost 26 mph, increasing drag by 26 per cent. Fitting doped fabric patches over the cannon slots gained 4 mph, but the bomb carriers, complete with bombs, cost 10 mph. Any inaccuracy in engine air intakes meant that full throttle performance was lost. At this time a 'basic wing' was developed, strengthened for far heavier loads than had at first been envisaged and applicable for all variants of the Mosquito.

Thus were born the main types of Mosquito. From this point on development of the aircraft was mainly a case of rapidly modifying an existing type, or part of a type, to suit the ever- changing military requirement. Through this process the Mosquito became ever faster, heavier and more difficult to intercept. It now only remained to resolve where the Mosquitos were going to be manufactured.

CONSTRUCTION AND BUILD

The structure of the Mosquito design comprised a balsa-and-plywood sandwich monocoque, introduced by the company before the war, with a smooth surface and part stressed-skin construction. De Havilland, who were already highly experienced in wooden aircraft construction, were convinced that its method was the answer to doing things in a hurry, and anyway, wood was cheap, plentiful and easy to work. They reasoned that by employing skilled woodworkers, it avoided putting additional demands upon metal supplies and metal workers so desparately needed elsewhere with the war effort. Jigs and fixtures, along with a certain amount of tooling could also be manufactured out of wood.

Monocoque, from Greek for single (mono) and French for shell (coque), is a construction technique that supports structural load by using an object's external skin as opposed to using an internal frame or truss that is then covered with a non-load-bearing skin. When loads are properly distributed in a monocoque structure, the principle is similar to that of an eggshell. Although it is thin, it is adequate for normal stresses; however, it does require reinforcement where stress concentrations occur, as De Havilland discovered during the early days of testing the DH.91 Albatross airliner. This was resolved by having a separate thin internal skin, held away from the outer skin by stiffening strips.

The Mosquito fuselage monocoque was built up - from the inside-out - as a pair of half-shells using, in this case, mahogany forms. These seen here were in the E Gomme factory at High Wycombe who before and after the war built G-Plan furniture.
(© BAE SYSTEMS)

Stage one of making a half-shell. Bulkheads and other parts of the internal structure are located in slots within the form. They show up as light lines against the mahogany of the form in this picture.
(© BAE SYSTEMS)

The vertically-split fuselage that was adopted considerably simplified assembly operations in later production stages, when services, wiring and equipment were installed in what would have otherwise been very tight spaces.

Each fuselage half-shell was first built horizontally, with the vertical joint line downward. A male mould was used, initially made of mahogany but later from concrete and shaped to the interior form of the fuselage. This way neither heat or a pressure-chamber was required to obtain the required curvature.

The double skins were of thin birch ply, and the stiffening of the fuselage was achieved by the use of laminated spruce around the bulkheads, the remaining gap being filled with cemented balsa strips. The resulting thickness was of the order of only half an inch, a truly eggshell analogy that created a structure that was amazingly light. The stiffening construction was produced integrally with the skin, the first operation being the location of six of the seven structural members in the mould, retained by stops and held in place by the skin. For the bomb-aimer's floor-bearers in the nose - which also doubled up as the 'floor' to the .303 machine gun bay and 'roof' to the 20mm cannon bay on the fighter variant - were also located in slots in the mould.

This shows the fitting of the inner fuselage birch-ply skin and the between-skin structural re-inforcements.
(© BAE SYSTEMS)

Once all the between-the-skins reinforcements were in place, the balsa 'core' which formed the sandwich was placed over the inner birch plywood skin.
(© BAE SYSTEMS)

The bomb doors and fuselage lower side panels were an integral part of the half-fuselage at the initial build stage, but were subsequently cut out and received further manufacturing as separate units as the build progressed. Internal stiffening members and the main attachments for the wing were moulded into the half-shell assembly. The inner plywood skin was next applied over the structural members, the skin over the rear portion being applied in relatively large panels. Longitudinal joints were made on spruce stringers of the between-skin stiffening structure.

Broad, flexible spring-steel bands cramped the skin down over the mould, pressure being applied over the whole surface of the skin until the glue cured. Between the skins, a stiffening structure of laminated spruce, in strips, was screwed through the inner skin to the bulkheads. Areas where apertures were subsequently cut out were filled with balsa and cemented in position, filling the entire space between the inner and outer skins to stabilise them, the thickness being about 3/8in. The outer skins, also of three-ply birch, were similar. Once removed from the moulds, the shells were transferred to and initially held in a vertical cradle, holes being drilled in the fuselage skin from the inside, through a stop-template, so as not to break through the outer surface.

Next, the bomb doors and side panels were cut out and sent elsewhere for completion and jig-fitting with metal parts, such as bomb-door hinges. In the half-shells, some of the interior equipment was installed, including the floors. Then the fitment of armour plating and electrical metal bonding could begin.

A completed half-shell covered with broad spring-steel strapping clamps holding the outer skin tightly in position against the form to allow the glue to cure.
(© BAE SYSTEMS)

The characteristic operation of lifting the 'carapace half-shell' - as De Havilland called it - off of the form. According to the information board on the end, this was for a Mk.XVI and the date was 9 October 1943. (© *BAE SYSTEMS*)

The rear floor, rudder and elevator-operating linkage, electrical wiring and the oxygen and hydraulic systems were installed next. The control-cable runs were on the port side of the fuselage, and much of the hydraulic plumbing ran down the starboard side. Whichever variant was being constructed, the control column was mounted in the port shell and connected with the rudder and elevator linkage before the half-shell joining stage.

All of this allowed around 60% of the installation work to be completed in the half-shell during stages of maximum accessibility with relative ease; this created a huge saving in time. Both half- sections were supported in a divided cradle which could be drawn apart, the nose section being supported from beneath.

Due to the wing aperture in the fuselage, a temporary strut had to be inserted to prevent damage or distortion during assembly. The mating junction between the skins of the two half-shells was of V-section.

Equipment installation continued after joining the shells. This included the instrument panels, more plumbing and wiring runs. Bulkhead No 7 carried the rear fin and tailplane attachment fittings, and No 6 carried the front fin attachments, Hand fitting of the two halves was necessary to achieve the tolerance of only 0.015 inch permitted on the centreline, a very close allowance on a wood assembly.

The cockpit canopy was then lowered into place and bolted to the fuselage, followed by the fitting of instrument panels and radio equipment, and completion of hydraulic and electrical circuits in the nose section.

The Mosquito's two-spar, stressed-skin wing was made in one piece. Its birch ply upper double skins were reinforced by closely- spaced span wise square-section stringers, glued between them. The outboard lower-surface wing panels were of single-surface birch ply, the stringers being glued with the skin as a single unit. The fuel tanks were housed between the spars. Both main spars had laminated spruce booms and plywood webs, and were more than fifty feet long. Their handling alone presented problems.

Above: A half-shell in its vertical jig - some of the equipment, including the instrument panel has been fitted.

Right: The half-shell fitting out line at Hatfield, was alongside the DH.89 Dominie fuselage assembly line. *(both © BAE SYSTEMS)*

The top boom was made up of three 1.45 inch laminations, a larger number 0.4 inch thick being used for the lower boom. Casein cement on the booms and under the web, screwed down, provided pressure for bonding the joint. It was necessary to accelerate setting the cement. The setting of synthetic adhesives can be accelerated by raising their temperature, and electrical heating was needed, a difficult problem because direct heat on the cement line was not possible. The Northmet Car Company provided a solution, using sectional heating-panels on the top of the spar web, with thermostatic control. The spars were jig-drilled for all the metal fittings, including undercarriage and aileron hinge brackets. Producing such large components in wood to a tolerance of plus or minus forty one-thousands of an inch over such a length, was a considerable achievement.

The inner surface of the top skin was coated with casein glue, as a form of waterproofing the plywood. After doping and painting, the skins were ready for assembly with the wing, the front and rear spars being located first. In the case of the front spar, the engine bearer fittings were used. For the rear spar, the undercarriage radius-rod brackets were used.

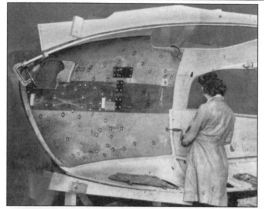

More work is done on the half-shells.

Above left: A woman using a hand-brace drill to put holes in the nose area. The strengthened areas with holes already drilled are clearly visible

Above right: Into these holes go ferrules, and this picture shows some of the fittings in place.

Left: This view shows just how easy it was for workers to get to all sections of the fuselage to install items of equipment. The item in the centre is the jig used to ensure alignment for wing attachment pick-ups when the two halves are brought together.
(all © BAE SYSTEMS)

With the spars located, the inter-spar ribs were fitted, sixteen a side. These were heavy three-ply webs, with upper booms of spruce laminations and lower booms of Douglas fir. Ribs 2 to 6 were of box construction, while rib 7 outwards were of half-box type with the web attached only on the inboard side, ribs 3 and 4 - the engine ribs - along with their fittings formed part of the undercarriage structure. The bottom-surface skin was fitted, extending from rib 6 to the tip on each side. The centre portion of each wing carried the engine nacelle and undercarriage.

The complete span wing was then removed from the jig, being picked up by an overhead crane and lowered on to cradles for fitting the leading-edge and flap and aileron shrouds. Apart from the undercarriage bays, the whole interior of the wing inboard of the No 6 ribs contained fuel tanks. Although stressed, the bottom surface over this portion was necessarily detachable for tank installation and removal for repair. The leading edges were then fitted, as were the aileron hinge brackets and flap hinge mountings. Flaps and ailerons were mounted to ensure proper operation and shroud clearances.

Engine and radiator fairings were fitted to the top wing surface, then aileron and flap-control cables were assembled. Doping and madapolam covering came next. The installation of electrical and hydraulic services was then completed, and the engine support struts assembled and tanks installed. The detachable wingtips completed the outboard ends, and the metal strip for the Perspex navigation lamp fairing was attached.

The fin and rudder were set slightly forward of the tailplane, both fixed surfaces having an almost identical form of construction closely following that of the mainplane. Because the elevator horn balances overlapped the tips of the tailplane, proper clearance was needed. The centre hinge and the elevator trimmer were followed by the outer hinge brackets. Covering, doping and painting completed the assembly. Fin assembly was the same as that of the tailplane, being completed in one fixture. The slotted flaps, in inboard and outboard sections each side of the engine nacelle fairing, comprised a single unit, connected by a torque tube.

When the initial fitting out of equipment was done, the two fuselage half-shells were brought together and cemented, being held in place with straps until the glue cured. *(both © BAE SYSTEMS)*

When the fuselage halves were brought together, more detailed fitting out of wiring, hydraulic piping and other systems could be done before the wing was fitted to it.

Below: The join down the middle of the half shells was finally covered with a re-inforcing strip of plywood.

Bottom: The levelling and drilling jigs in position for drilling No.6 bulkhead for the fin front pick-ups.
(all© BAE SYSTEMS)

The main undercarriage legs used rubber blocks for shock absorption and proved to be not only very simple in principal but very satisfactory in operation.

For final assembly the aircraft travelled down a track, laid at a low working level, that supported the aircraft through its assembly. The wing was mounted on cradles outboard of the engine nacelles. With the wing set and levelled in position, the fuselage was lowered on to it and bolted up, and the fuselage side panels below the wings assembled. Next, the complete tail unit was assembled on bulkhead 7, followed by the tailwheel. The leading-edge radiators were then installed. Assembly of the inboard fuel and oil tanks followed, then the installation of radio equipment, and the bomb racks were fitted in the bomb bay. The bomb-bay doors were then hung in position.

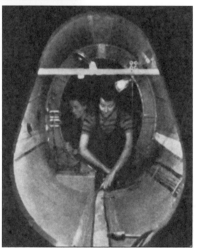

The engines, with all accessories fitted, were aligned and mounted, followed by the connection of the engine controls to the cockpit. The engine nacelle fairings were assembled and undercarriage wheel doors hung. Electrical connections and systems testing and an undercarriage actuation test followed the fitting of the wheels and axles. Pits sunk in the shop floor allowed the wheels to be operated without lifting the aircraft at the end of the line.

Flap operation was tested, and a general inspection was made of the hydraulic, pneumatic and electrical services. The overhead conveyor was arranged for mounting the DH Hydromatic propellers. Finally, tests were made of the bomb gear, followed by other works and Aeronautical Inspection Directorate inspections. The machine was then jacked up, the coolant system tested, and

The assembly fixture for the structure of the replaceable wing-tip.

The main features for rear spar assembly. For applying the skin to the forward face of the spar, the inverted fixture in the foreground is used. *(both © BAE SYSTEMS)*

the aircraft lowered on to its undercarriage and wheeled to the paint shop for final checks, engine runs and test flights.

The build - United Kingdom

In 1940, when the design was no more than an interesting development project, De Havilland had been told to keep all specialized tooling for the DH.98 prototype to the minimum. Even if the aircraft were proceeded with, many changes would be needed and possibly several variants produced. Despite this handicap, the company found itself making the rash promise to deliver 50 examples by December 1941, in order to keep the project alive. They actually managed to complete 20 Mosquitos in 1941 and the remainder of the first order by mid-March 1942, just two and a half months beyond the target set before the Battle of Britain. The first 20 aircraft consisted of the bomber and photographic reconnaissance prototypes, nine short-nacelle PR.Mk.Is, eight B.Mk.IVs (bomber-reconnaissance aircraft) and the first production F.Mk.II fighter.

The immediate problem was the division between bombers and fighters in the initial order, the 'basic' wing not yet having been developed. The bomber wings were too far advanced to be converted to fighter type, and there were 45 completed bomber/reconnaissance fuselages, 28 of which had to have their noses removed to be replaced by fighter types. This form of rapid conversion immediately demonstrated the benefits of working with wood.

On 30 December 1940 came the first large quantity order. Contract No 555 for 150 aircraft of undetermined variants ordered 'at once'. More sophisticated tooling and additional capacity were therefore sought - a move reinforced by an official hint of 'further extensive orders'. During April 1941 the Air Ministry's Contracts

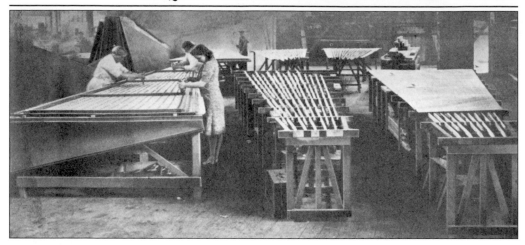

Department at Harrogate wrote to De Havilland to say that a further 50 fighters would be ordered in addition to the 28 on Contract No 69990, and that the 150 airframes on Contract No 555 were all to be fighters. There were also the nineteen PR machines on Contract 69990 and the three main prototypes - 250 aircraft in all - but still no bombers beyond the bomber- reconnaissance version and its prototype. A further 50 fighters were later to be added to Contract No 555 increasing the total to 300.

Above: Skin panels are drilled through wooden templates on the left; in the centre stringers are located in the slots on the assembly jig and on the right the skin is applied over a similar set.

With such large orders placed, it became much easier for de Havilland's to plan their sub-contracting and order long lead-time items in advance of the production lines. These orders also helped to finalize the details of the Second Aircraft Group, a completely duplicated shadow organization that had been in preparation since mid-1940, when the company had been approached to produce Armstrong Whitworth Albemarles, a requirement later switched to Vickers Wellington bombers. De Havilland had to find an airfield, design and build a factory, requisition dispersal premises and

The complete drilling jig for the rear spar.
(both © BAE SYSTEMS)

recruit staff for a completely separate organization that was planned to have an eventual production rate of 300 machines per month.

The airfield decided upon was Leavesden, close by and to the west of Hatfield, with building work starting in August 1940. Two dispersal sites had already opened up, the Alliance Factory on Western Avenue, Acton, where more than 170 people were at work and the Aldenham bus depot, where the first ten men had moved in. By May 1941 the Second Aircraft Group was working hard on Oxford parts. Mosquito fuselages at Aldenham and Mosquito wings at Acton. It now became clear that the Group could be built up into a separate Mosquito organization, devoted to one type, possibly fighters. Sub-contracting was progressing well, with Dancer & Hearne Ltd and E. Gomme Ltd - both furniture makers in High Wycombe - producing spars, wings, jigs and other components, while Van den Plas of Hendon were covering wings. Pollards were making wing noses, Bell Punch produced control columns. Lostock, doing detailed machining, and coachbuilders H J Mulliner & Co. of Chiswick were producing detail work. The DH.94 shop at Hatfield was bombed by the Germans in October 1940 but had been partially

Two views of the Mosquito wing being constructed. In the upper view the wing is 'standing' on the front spar, with the upper wing 'skin' fixed into place.

The photograph right, shows after the wings were removed from the assembly jig they were inverted and sat on trestles for further work. The spaces for the fuel tanks and area for undercarriage retraction is clearly visible.
(© BAE SYSTEMS).

A Mosquito fuselage comes together. The temporary bracing in the 'hole' where the wing will eventually go can be clearly seen, along with the temporary bracing frame.

rebuilt and was used as a secondary Mosquito production line until it became needed for the Mosquito Repair Organization. The wartime repair and servicing system set up by the Air Ministry ensured that the parent manufacturing firm was largely responsible for the servicing and overhaul of its products; the outcome of this was the Mosquito Repair Organization established at Hatfield. It evolved, with additional industrial and RAF capacity, into an organization operating nationwide, repairing and returning to service over 2,000 Mosquitos.

Problems had been encountered with defective plywood, adhesives and the new metal aileron, but these were soon overcome. Interchangeability standards,

Doping a completed wing. All the lamps in the Dope Shop were shielded by glass to protect from dope fumes. The wings were transported vertically from the Assembly Shop on two-wheeled bogies. *(both © BAE SYSTEMS)*

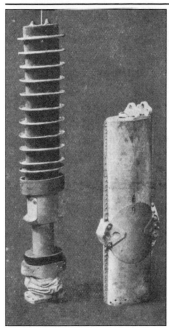

The components of the simple compression-rubber undercarriage leg, along with the external casing. (© *BAE SYSTEMS*)

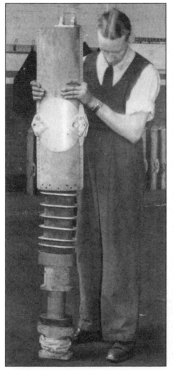

fixed with the Airworthiness Inspection Directorate, were applicable from the seventh PR machine. Much of the sub-contract process involved work being done by people and companies not normally connected with the aircraft industry, and resulted in a geographically dispersed production programme. These sub-contractors ranged from patriotic housewives and garden shed groups to coachbuilders and furniture makers, all drawing supplies from and returning completed items to Hatfield. The standards set for workshop wood-working techniques at De Havilland were such that it was normal to work to plus or minus one-hundredth of an inch (0.010in). The Mosquito had been designed from the outset to utilize ordinary resources of manufacture away from the aircraft industry, apart from engines and other specialized components. But all the additional people employed needed education in the aircraft manufacturing process, to appreciate each other's skills and how they could be applied, and then disciplined to the methods of production, precision tolerances and strict inspection methods involved in aircraft manufacture.

During the early days of Mosquito production jokes abounded about the new wooden aeroplane. One critic called it a 'flying tea chest', while other references were made to the cabinet-maker builders, calling it 'Flying Furniture'. The Americans, not to be left out, later nicknamed it 'The hollowed out log'. Possibly the best known comment at the time was that if a Mosquito ever fell apart in the air, all that would fall down would be thousands of matchsticks and copies of the *Daily Mirror!*

Francis T. Hearle of De Havillands took stock of the planning and realized just how difficult it was going to be, with no firm idea as to the requirements a year or so ahead. There were still no orders for the pure bomber version but, he thought, there must come a time in the future when it would be needed. He had been told that the Mosquito fighter was to have dual control, to provide the RAF with a Mosquito trainer, so the first ten of an order already built were converted to dual control and the remainder of the fifty were delivered as such. Orders kept increasing, up to 500 machines now. At last, in mid-July, a first mention of the bomber variant was made in the order schedule. It was now requested that the last ten PR machines in Contract No 69990 be converted into unarmed bombers, together with the last 50 of the 200 machines in Contract No 555, but it was also stated that it was hoped these would have some form of fixed forward armament.

The company and all its staff were stretched to the limit throughout the summer and autumn of 1941. Orders were coming in and contract requirements changed almost daily; the entire Hatfield staff were working an average 53-hour week, with a further two-hour increase planned. Company executives were working a 12-hour day and often longer, taking a half-day off only when imperative. Transport of goods and lack of housing for staff were creating bottlenecks. The war was changing on all geographical fronts, as well as in the Mosquito

Two views of assembling the flaps.

The first stage involved building the inboard and outboard nose sections up on the torque tube.

The nose sections were then assembled to the ribs and trailing edge. *(both © BAE SYSTEMS)*

production lines and test-shops, leading to a situation where no stability in either orders or design could be seen in the near future.

A letter from the Air Ministry on 28 January 1942 increased the orders again, confirming the requirement as 928 from Hatfield and 450 from the Leavesden-based Second Aircraft Group; there was also a 400-strong batch of Mosquitos planned to be built by De Havilland Canada. These were all of undefined marks but they gave a total of 1,778 machines. It was expected that by April 1943 there would be enough Merlin 61s to allow this target to be met and, by the end of the year, to change the fighter and fighter-bomber lines over to production of the NF.Mk.X and FB.Mk.XI. At Leavesden the Airborne Interception (AI) Mk.VIII radar was coming on stream, and strenuous efforts were being made to introduce this at the same time as the Merlin 61.

Throughout 1942 the Ministry of Aircraft Production kept advising the company of changes to their requirement programme, causing many headaches.

Wings ready for delivery
- 24 Mosquito wings,
complete with flaps and
wearing full RAF
camouflage await
transportation to the
final assembly shop.
(© BAE SYSTEMS)

Not all the changes were made to improve the aircraft, or to arm the neediest squadrons - many were made purely to assist production. This continual switching of the production programme required organizational leadership of a very special order. De Havillands sought and obtained on loan the services of Trevor C L Westbrook, a superb production engineer and trouble-shooter from the Air Ministry. He joined the Mosquito production effort on 4 August, working to co-ordinate the efforts of Hatfield, Leavesden and the sub-contractors. At that time it would have been easy for Westbrook to make a stand and refuse to keep switching the production programme. This would have resulted in more aircraft produced, but many of them would have been much less effective.

Standard Motors were brought into the programme with plans that they should build 500 aircraft, concentrating on the FB.Mk.VI variant. Talks were also held with the Director General of Aircraft Production with a view to bringing Airspeed into the Mosquito production plan, but a decision on this was deferred as Hatfield were experiencing enough problems introducing the type to Standard Motors. The first aircraft off the Standard Motors production line at Ansty was HP848, on 4 May 1943. On the same day a contract was placed with Percival Aircraft

Some of the Mosquito
builders.
(© BAE SYSTEMS)

The framework of a tailplane in the assembly fixture where the rear spar, leading edge and interspar ribs are brought together to make a complete structure.

for 250 B.Mk.IXs. Standard Motors completed this first order by the end of 1944, but a follow-on order for a further 300 kept the production line in business for the remainder of the war. The last aircraft off the Standard production line was TE932, completed on 21 December 1945; it was the 1,066th Standard-built machine. Many of these late production aircraft never saw RAF service, and were delivered directly to 10 Maintenance Unit for storage instead. A number were sold to the Royal New Zealand Air Force, others went to the Fleet Air Arm, but the majority of the survivors were sold to International Alloys during 1951 as scrap.

There was a tragic accident at Hatfield on the afternoon of 23 August 1943 when two Mosquitos, HX849 and HX850, collided in cloudy weather during test

Mosquito assembly tracks - in this case Second Aircraft Group At Leavesden Note the lines of Rolls Royce Merlins awaiting installation. *(both © BAE SYSTEMS)*

Before the wings were brought to final mating with the fuselage, the coolant piping, electrical wiring, control runs, hydraulic piping, and main undercarriage mounting points were installed.

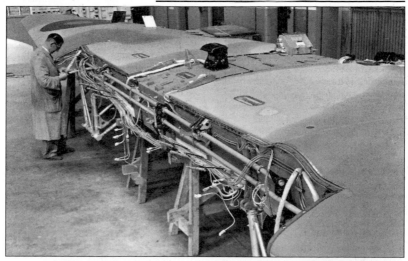

Final assembly started with the wing joining the fuselage, followed by the start of assembly of the tail surfaces and the engine mounts.
(both © BAE SYSTEMS).

flying between Salisbury Hall and Hatfield. All four men in the machines were killed. The blow to the company was particularly severe, for one of the pilots was John de Havilland, the founder's third son, along with George Gibbins, and observers G J Carter, Flight-shed Superintendent, and J H F Scrope, an aerodynamicist.

Production Testing

Test pilot Pat Fillingham: *So when production started we produced a flight-test schedule. It was a long roll of paper fitted to your knee-pad with all the gen being written on it. I'll quickly run through a typical first flight.*

After take-off, you took all the figures on the climb went up to 15,000 ft. Check the supercharger change over into high gear - up to 30,000ft to check pressure venting. Drop down to rated altitude and did some level speeds, then down to 15,000 to do the stalls. The stall was absolutely first class. It was caused of course

by the radiators being inboard of the engines and next to the fuselage and it gave you a perfect wing-root stall. There was never any trouble with the stall.

A few aerobatics were done to test the ailerons, a dive to the VNE to check the stick forces and the tailplane incidence and then in to land. This took about 50 minutes to an hour. Then we did a second flight of about 20 minutes to check snags. And a third flight of 10 minutes and the aircraft was off test. Sometimes we had an aeroplane with no snags at all and this was called 'A Lulu' - one with a lot of snags was called 'A Rogue'.

We attached great importance to good ailerons. You could shim them up or down; gear the tabs; put on droop, take it off and, in desperation, you could change the complete aileron, much to the disgust of the Works Manager. However, you had to watch for over-balance at low speeds.

Now, as far as I know there was no spinning done on Mosquitoes and in the early days very little was known about compressibility. Geoffrey de Havilland did go to the States to discuss the subject in late 1942 with senior American pilots. That was production testing and at one stage, I think we did 33 aeroplanes per week.

As we had no radio and no Met, the weather was a huge problem. The chief trouble was fog, for there was no smokeless fuel during the War, and on one bad February we had over 100 aeroplanes on the field awaiting test. We would fly to

The 1000th airframe which left the works of Wrighton Aircraft Ltd of Walthamstowe, East London on 8 July 1944.
(© BAE SYSTEMS)

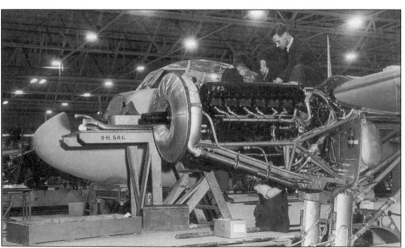

A Rolls Royce Merlin gets installed into a Mosquito on the Second Aircraft Group (SAG) production line at Leavesden.
(© BAE SYSTEMS)

Standard Motor's production line at Ansty near Coventry. Standard's built1066 aircraft - all FB.VIs. *(© BAE SYSTEMS)*

the northwest when clear of the Chilterns, climb up and return on the reciprocal for the let-down and use the railway lines to get you back to Hatfield. This was known as 'Bradshawing' after the well known railway timetable of that era.

I recall a very long flight over cloud with a new observer - it was his first flight. We went up to 30.000ft and did several level checks and were up a long time. When we came down, we broke cloud at about 1,000 ft but it was very misty so we flew along low to see what we could pick-up. The first thing we saw was three giraffes in a field. I turned to the observer and said, "Strong tail wind, we must be over Africa". He paled. We were of course over the zoo at Whipsnade - it was just a short trip back to Hatfield.

Mosquito production did not always entail the use of large factories. Mrs B A Hale formed a 'cottage industry' group with her neighbours to make Mosquito parts in a hut in the garden of her Welwyn home - it was a novel kind of 'dispersal of industry' to which many others took part. *(© BAE SYSTEMS).*

Mosquito FB.Mk.VI production continued steadily into 1946, when production switched to De Havilland's Chester plant. The NF.Mk.30, not having a pressure cabin, was an easy follow-on from the NF.Mk.XIX, and the installation of a pair of high-altitude Merlin 76s was accomplished fairly easily. The change-over to pressure cabin aircraft was undertaken easily by the factories, allowing PR.34s to appear in early 1945 The B.35, which followed a short while later, was considered a vital item of equipment for the RAF during the rearmament plans in the immediate post-war years. However, a halt to production was called before the new Chester factory could be brought up to full production, with the last machine, an NF.Mk.38, VX916, completed there on 15 November 1950. By then the worldwide production figure was 7,781 Mosquitos of all variants.

Mosquito B.35s in the fitting out hangar at Airspeeds during late 1947. *(© BAE SYSTEMS)*

The build - Canada
Even before the Second World War had started, Hatfield were thinking of building operational aircraft in Canada. With the evacuation of Dunkirk and the threatened invasion of Britain, it was expected that if the Germans did invade, the main De Havilland factory would be moved across the Atlantic to its subsidiary at Downsview, near Toronto. The British Government would order Canadian-built machines, and possibly the Royal Canadian Air Force too. De Havilland Canada's Downsview site was at this time finishing off a contract for 404 DH.82 Tiger Moths and was taking on orders for even more, along with the production of Avro Ansons. However, these plans could be adjusted, and space made for building Mosquitos.

During July 1941 Phillip Garrett, head of De Havilland Canada, cabled Hatfield to state that Downsview, given the support of sub-contractors, could produce 40 aircraft a month. The plans were approved and a target was laid down for two aircraft by September 1942 and 50 a month by 1943. The Ministry of Aircraft Production placed an order for 400, with parts despatched from Britain to get the Canadian production line going. W D 'Doug' Hunter, Senior Designer at Hatfield, and Harry Povey, Chief Production Engineer, went over to Toronto. Hunter, who was to remain in Canada as Director of Engineering for many years thereafter, took charge of design, adapting the production methods to utilize local materials and equipment wherever possible, while at the same time maintaining interchangeability. Povey was to organize the production programme.

Production problems occurred with jigs and sample parts from England

A Canadian-built fuselage shell is moved around the factory, with a number of half-shells in the background wrapped in straps while the glue dries. This photograph shows the temporary support rods in the gap where the mainplane locates, keeping the structure in alignment.
(National Aviation Museum of Canada)

awaiting shipping space, but that was not all. The Battle of the Atlantic was at its height and on the first shipment some 2 per cent of key Mosquito drawings were lost; and important assemblies never arrived, sunk by marauding U-boat packs running loose in the mid-Atlantic where no air cover could be given to convoys. Later incidents led to the loss of vital hydraulic assemblies and drawings covering changes in variants. By the time the fuselage jigs arrived from Britain, DH. Canada had built their own, so the British jigs were marked for onward shipment to Australia. A drop hammer and stretcher press were located and brought into new buildings at Downsview. Infra-red drying was developed to speed up the glue bonding process. As production increased, and to combat the U-boat threat, suppliers were found in North America for almost all the proprietary equipment fitted to the design. General Motors in Oshawa started making fuselages, as did De Havilland in one of their dispersal sites in Dupont Street; wings were built by Massey Harris, tailplanes were coming from Boeing Vancouver, and flaps from Canadian Power Boat.

Confusion and conflicts existed in requirements on this side of the Atlantic too; factories were asked to build bombers and then the Canadian Government asked for fighters. As a result, Hatfield asked the Ministry of Aircraft Production to switch only the last 100 of the contract into Mk.VI fighters and then sent over the Mk.VI drawings. A later Canadian contract was issued to cover fighter-bombers.

In May it was announced that Downsview was to receive a contract for 1,100 machines, the marks to be decided at a later date. These were to be financed by the USA under Lease-Lend, making a total of 1,500 Mosquitos on order at the Canadian plant.

Engine supplies for the Canadian Mosquitos were to come from Packard's, a company that before the war made luxury cars and aero-engines. In many respects this company was the American equivalent of Rolls-Royce, following a broadly similar product range with a reputation for high quality. Packard began building Rolls-Royce Merlins under licence; their early engines were Merlin 28s similar in design to the Merlin XX but with a two-piece cylinder block designed in the USA.

Twenty Mosquito B.XX bombers undergoing final assembly at De Havilland Canada's Downsview factory. *(National Aviation Museum of Canada)*

The later Merlin 38s were the equivalent of the British Merlin 22s using a Rolls-Royce designed two-piece block, as did all later engines. Technically the major difference between the British and American engines was the supercharger drive, the Packard using epicyclic gearing instead of the Farman drive. Other differences involved the fitment of Bendix carburettors and American magnetos. The Packard-built Merlins were manufactured to a very high standard and, when fitted to American aircraft, adopted the designation of V-1650 with 'slash' numbers to denote the mark number. Operating experience in the field proved that technical problems were not dissimilar from those encountered with British engines, and there was little to choose between engine sources.

In July the first Canadian bomber fuselage was mated with the wing. Based on the B.V, it was to be powered by Packard-built Merlin 31s and was provisionally allocated the designation B.Mk.VII; later, in order to give a clearer designation of manufacturer, this was changed to B.Mk.XX. Hatfield had a sample B.Mk.IV,DK287, ready to be shipped out by 13 September, but the usefulness of this machine to the Canadians was offset somewhat when, due to delays in shipping, salt corrosion left the aircraft in a damaged state when it was unloaded at Halifax.

On 23 September Geoffrey de Havilland Jnr left Poole for Baltimore, arriving at Toronto on the 27th. The flight of the first Canadian Mosquito B.Mk.VII, KB300, occurred on 24 September in the hands of Downsview's Chief Test Pilot, Ralph Spradbrow, accompanied by Pepe Burrell, the Prototype Flight-shed Engineer from Hatfield, as observer. This flight was not without mishap, for near failure of a hydraulic pump almost forced a belly landing. Geoffrey de Havilland flew it on the 29th, demonstrating the aircraft to senior officials a couple of days later. He later flew the machine on a series of demonstration flights around North America, including one at the United States Army Air Force's main test centre at Wright Field, near Dayton, Ohio. This raised again the question of US production, but by now the Australian production plans were well advanced, and a further spread of effort would not have yielded any great advantage.

Towards the end of January 1943 the Ministry of Aircraft Production agreed to send over a sample Mosquito T.Mk.III trainer, together with drawings and parts, so that the Canadians would be able to build their own dual-control aircraft. This machine could then be used for the dual purpose of training RAF Ferry Command crews to bring the Canadian-built Mosquitos over to Europe and converting Royal Canadian Air Force crews to the type.

A further five T.Mk.IIIs were sent out from England in late February, and another five in April, with the hope that supply of these aircraft would relieve Downsview of the dual-control conversion, for they were already facing more than enough work with the change-over to fighter-bomber FB.Mk.XXIs and the change to two-stage Merlins. The first 50 bombers were to be retained in Canada for Operational Training Units of the RCAF.

By the end of 1942 four Canadian-built examples were airborne. A year after the first flight the total was up to 67, with 92 by the end of 1943, but the slow start had been expected. All but two of these, which were completed as fighter-bombers, were B.Mk.XX bombers powered by Packard Merlin 33s. The two pre-production FB.Mk.XXIs were the Canadian equivalent of the British FB.Mk.VI, but powered by Merlin 33s. Production accelerated and the 271st machine, KB370, the first of the B.Mk.XXVs, was accepted on 7 July 1944. By the time the next pair of fighter-bombers was built, they were powered by Merlin 225s, and so designated FB.Mk.26.

The first two Mosquito B.Mk.XXs had been flown across the Atlantic in August 1943 - KB162 *'New Glasgow'*, crewed by American civilians, and KB328 *'Acton'*, flown by Flying Officers J.G. Uren and R.C. Bevington. Both these machines, and subsequent aircraft making the Atlantic crossing, used giant 200 gallon fuel tanks, designed by W.J. Jakimiuk and installed in the bomb bays, to

Two views of the roll out and first engine runs of the first Canadian Mosquito, KB300, a B.VII at Downsview. *(National Aviation Museum of Canada).*

achieve the desired range. The two aircraft arrived at Hatfield via Prestwick on 12 August, having staged through Greenland and Iceland to check the suitability of the airfields en route. Staff at Hatfield, Boscombe Down and the Air Ministry all viewed them with critical eyes, but later announced that they were well satisfied with the Canadian machines. However, there were problems. The Air Ministry would not accept the solid windscreens fitted to the Mk.XXs, so Triplex Glass hastily made up sandwich screens.

Much consideration had been given to the location of a reception base for the Canadian-built machines. 13 Maintenance Unit at RAF Henlow, near Bedford, was eventually chosen for its proximity to Hatfield and the Huntingdon area, where several Canadian squadrons expected to be using the aircraft were based. Non-common spares between British and Canadian aircraft were held at Henlow to assist with maintenance.

Shortly after the Canadian-built aircraft had been introduced into service they began to acquire a bad reputation on the airfields of Britain and the Far East. Assorted problems started to occur and were all traced to variations in fuselage dimensions. The half-shell fuselages were built up by wrapping sandwiches of plywood and balsa around a wooden pattern and held down by metal straps while the glue dried. It was desirable to heat the glue to achieve a good bond, but the high humidity levels found in Toronto's lakeside area and moisture in the glue caused the 40ft-long wooden mould to vary. It was Harry Povey's novel suggestion to use concrete fuselage jigs, made to an accuracy of 1/10th inch from a plaster female mould taken from the master wooden mould at Hatfield. This greatly increased the speed, accuracy and stability of jig manufacture.

An unidentified Canadian-built Mosquito comes together on the Downsview production line . *(National Aviation Museum of Canada)*

The production of Canadian dual-control trainers surfaced again in mid-1943 when a shortage of radio equipment and cannon occurred in Canada. Unarmed fighter-bombers could be put to good use as trainers when finished, rather than lie around uncompleted. Downsview completed this task with the aid of conversion sets sent over from Hatfield, re-engineering the FB.Mk.XXVI into the T.Mk.XXII with Merlin 31s or 33s and the T.Mk.XXVII when fitted with Merlin 225s.

Discussions took place in November 1943 between Downsview and the USAAF Headquarters at Wright Field, Dayton, Ohio the surviving correspondence of which provides a rare insight into the complexity of the finish applied to the aircraft for delivery to the USA - the occasion was the change-over from green/brown camouflage to a two-tone blue scheme.

Doping Process Schedule

Finishing of DH.98 Mosquito fuselage

A - Exterior of shells - After removal of Jig and prior to Boxing

1   *Protect all ply edges with plywood sealer, Berry Brothers Aircraft Sealer No.14113. 3 coasts (mask edges which require glueing).*
2. *Stop all holes with plastic wood; use Plastic Wood solvent if the plastic wood becomes too hard for working.*
3. *Sand all over with #2/0 sandpaper.*
4. *Brush or spray one coat, red brown dope 83A reduce 15% to 25%.*
5. *Fill with #5 stopper and sand with #2/0 sandpaper.*
6. *Repeat operation #5 until a smooth finish is obtained.*
    It is not possible to state a definite number of coats but the average is 2 to 3.
7. *The number of coats depends to a great extent upon the person spraying the dope.*

Interior of the Shells

1. *Spray one light coat of grey primer DTD.63A and use thinner spec IGP-31 if necessary.*
2. *Give a light sand with #2/0 sandpaper on any rough parts.*
3   *Refer to drawing Z.98533 and spray one coat of aluminium cellulose DTD.399 to the areas shown on the drawing.*
4. *Spray one coat of grey-green cellulose, DTD.308 all over.*

B - After Boxing

Exterior after boxing.

1. *Fill holes in jointing strips with Plastic Wood.*
2. *Sand with #2/0 sandpaper.*
3. *Apply same instructions as in Operation 5 of the exterior, treatment of the shell before boxing.*
4. *Bring all painting up to the same finish as in operation 6 of the exterior treatment of shells.*
5. *Madapolam cloth is now doped on using red brown dope, spec. 83A.*
6. *All serrated tapes and patches are now applied with red brown dope. IGP-31.*
7. *Brush one coat of red brown dope 83A over all.*
8. *Spray one coat of grey filler DTD.63A using thinner IGP-31 if necessary.*

9. Sand with #240 wet sandpaper.
10. Spray two coats of aluminium cellulose DTD.63A.
11. Sand with #280 paper and Varsol (or level with levelling solution).

Interior after boxing
1. Jointing strips and ply gussets are to be finished as per instructions above in
    the interior of the shells before boxing.

Finishing of DH.98 after final assembly - exterior
1. Spray two coats of sea-grey medium cellulose on lower portions.
2. Mask fuselage at 83 degrees tangent. Spray top surfaces with 2 coats of
    Ocean-Grey and two coats of Olive-Grey. For camouflaging scheme refer to
    Drg. No. Z.98714 issue 7.
3. Stencil to Drg. No.98733 issue 7C2

Canadian production of the two-stage supercharger version had been scheduled
for deliveries to start in mid-1944, but it was realized that with demands for both
low- and high-altitude flying, the Packard Merlin 69 would not be suitable. Production
was therefore to continue using the Packard Merlin 225 in the fighter-bombers until
the new 14 SM two-stage engine could be produced by Packard. At the same time
the engine company was asked to produce the equivalent of the Merlin 76 to give
the Canadian Mosquito bombers satisfactory high-altitude performance.

Pat Fillingham also tested Mosquitos in Canada: *I was lucky to be sent to
Canada to set up the Production there at the de Havilland Plant at Toronto. To
my horror I was sent up to Liverpool and put on a ship to cross the North Atlantic
in the depths of winter. I well remember its name, it was the 'Empress of Japan'
- not a good omen! It was full of Air Force personnel and four of us civilians. We
were not allowed to undress at night and wore life-jackets all day. There was
also a rota for U-Boat spotting - I for one saw at least 50 imaginary periscopes!
We went flat out across the Atlantic, zig-zagging all the way and arrived safely
at Halifax, Nova-Scotia. I have never been on a boat since!*

*The Canadian aeroplanes were very good. We had some minor troubles with
the fuel injection system on the Packard-built Merlins, which had a tendency to
ice up. Whilst in Canada, I took a Mosquito to Colorado Springs for the
Americans to check. The English accent caused some amusement to them, and
why do we call the gear 'the chassis?' - all the Mosquitoes used this extraordinary
word, and why Punka Louvre for the air vent? Perhaps we had some retired*

Six brand-new
camouflaged FB.26s on
the flightline at
Downsview with KA283
in the foreground.
*(National Aviation
Museum of Canada)*

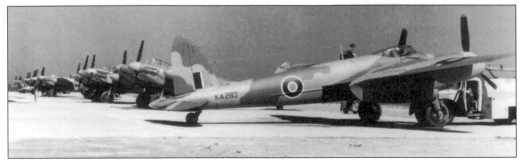

Indian Colonel in the Drawing Office! One morning I went into the Hangar and under each wingtip was a pile of sawdust with a placard saying. Termites at work'. But the performance of the aeroplane was no laughing matter, they were most impressed.

Delivery of Mosquitos to the USAAF is described elsewhere, but as flights across the Atlantic increased a number of speed records were set. In May 1944 Wing Commander John Wooldridge, DSO, DFC, DFM, flew in a bomber from Labrador to Prestwick coast-to-coast in 5 hours 39.5 minutes (or 6 hours 46 minutes runway-to-runway). By April 1945 this time had been regularly reduced to five and a half hours, an average ground speed of 390 mph.

RAF and RCAF personnel expressed satisfaction with the aircraft, but for some time 8 Group of RAF Bomber Command had been requesting that their Canadian aircraft be fitted with a 4,000 lb capacity bomb bay and the new type of target indicators. However, the installation of pathfinder equipment in 8 Group's aircraft had forced the centre of gravity position aft, thereby creating a condition that would only be made worse if an enlarged bomb bay were fitted. The only safe way to achieve the conversion was to use two-stage engines. By chance, some 800 Packard Merlin 68s were located in a Maintenance Unit store, originally intended for installation in Spitfires, but with modifications they could be fitted into Mk.XXV bombers if the direction of cooling was reversed. Marshalls of Cambridge were to undertake the conversions, but difficulties were expected with supplies of radiator cowlings and other items. As the spares situation was difficult enough with the Canadian aircraft, things could only get worse.

Flight trials of the Marshalls conversion began in January 1945, using the aircraft's existing single-stage radiators, oil coolers and cabin heaters. After tests, recorded coolant temperatures were pronounced satisfactory. Consideration was also given to converting the aircraft before they left Canada for the United Kingdom, but again, this would create delays. The changing war situation cast doubt on the value of the programme, so it was eventually decided not to proceed with the engine changes, but to modify a few machines with 4,000 lb bomb doors to allow the accommodation of two 1,000 lb target indicators or two Type 7 mines.

With the end of the war Canadian production ceased in October 1945, having accounted for one-seventh of the total with 1,034 machines built. Some 420 Canadian-built machines were taken on charge by the RCAF, together with 24 British-built trainers. Forty B.Mk.VII and B.Mk.XX bombers went to the USAAF with the remainder of the production run, including 210 of the 444 RCAF aircraft originally assigned to the RAF overseas.

The build - Australia

Any form of aircraft production in Australia was beset with the problems of importing equipment, engines, proprietary components and initially, in many cases, raw materials. De Havilland Australia had been formed in 1927, the company being headed since the early 1930s by Allan Murray Jones. In November 1940 he submitted a report to the Australian authorities weighing the possibilities of building an operational aircraft locally.

During 1941 the Packard Merlin project made it possible for engine supplies to be made available from America, thereby allowing the possibility of building the Mosquito to move one step nearer. At the time Hatfield was under great pressure and could not really assist. They suggested that Jones contact De Havilland Canada for supplies, even drawings. In January 1942 a number of staff from De Havilland's in Australia visited De Havilland Canada, where they obtained promises that Downsview would supply some jigs, materials and samples. By February the project was almost a certainty, with engine supplies arranged with Packard's. In early March the Australian Government instructed de Havilland Australia to build Mosquito fighter-bombers for the Royal Australian Air Force, the parent company being asked to provide a sample machine. D.H. Australia was not able to finance the purchase of supplies from Hatfield over a long period, so Contract No 2419 was arranged between the Ministry of Aircraft Production and drawn on Hatfield with reimbursement from the Australian Government.

M.M. Waghorn, one of Hatfield's young engineers, was seconded to Australia, taking out data during June. John Mills, Senior Engineer of the Australian company, had been over in Britain to study the task of supplies, leaving England for home in May, but not before he had sent ahead many thousands of Mk.VI drawings, schedules, notes, photographs and 30 lb weight of 35mm film in a Consolidated Liberator belonging to the Atlantic Ferry Organization. De Havilland's in Sydney received the drawings in July, allowing them to start work on much of the detailed engineering and to arrange for sub-contracting; the latter was to prove much more difficult because Australia had few engineering resources available compared with what could be found in Canada. The first Australian Mosquito, using much of the imported equipment, was expected to fly during August 1943. Following the convention already established with the Canadian production line, a separate 'mark block' of numbers was designated, with all Australian-produced Mosquitos allocated marks in the 'Mk.40' range.

Hatfield was by now in a position to help out so a Mosquito F.Mk.II, DD664, was packed at Sealand in June and shipped out. It flew for the first time at Bankstown on 17 December 1942 with Bruce Rose at the controls, carrying the RAAF serial A52-1001. The company then installed a pair of Packard Merlin 31s, flying the aircraft on 23 March before delivering it to Mascot for assessment.

Drawings had been requested for the dual-control version but it was hoped that these aircraft could be supplied direct from England; eight T.Mk.IIIs were duly promised in order to relieve the Australians of this task. The Australian Air Board planned to have the two-stage Merlin 69 engine fitted by the end of the year, so Hatfield agreed to supply the Mk.X drawings as they became available, with Frank Wormald of Rolls-Royce going out from England to assist with the engine installation. By the end of April a new assembly hangar and flight shed had been completed at Bankstown, just in time for the Packard Merlins to be removed from A52-1001 and installed in the first Australian-built FB.Mk.40 (A52-1), which was first flown on 23 July by Wing Commander Gibson Lee. Sadly this Australian prototype did not survive for long; it was destroyed when an oxygen bottle exploded during refilling at RAAF Laverton on 14 June 1944.

The first dual-control trainers from England began to arrive in Sydney without

Australian FB.Mk.40 A52-1 was built at Bankstown NSW for the Royal Australian Air Force. It is seen here posing for the camera with one Merlin stopped.

(© BAE SYSTEMS)

engines during the last few months of 1943; seven had been assembled by November but it took more work than expected to install the Packard Merlin 31s. Britain was reluctant to supply any more trainers, so the RAAF requested further dual-control conversion parts; finally the RAAF received fourteen RAF T.Mk.IIIs, serialled A52-1002 to A52-1015. The RAAF planned to take four versions of the basic FB.Mk.VI fighter-bomber, night fighter, long-range fighter and reconnaissance. Interest was also expressed in the Mk.XVIII version with the 57mm Molins gun, 40mm cannon and rocket projectile armament.

Shortages delayed the second aircraft, the main problem being a lack of skilled labour which persisted for many months. The first delivery to the RAAF occurred on 4 March 1944, but soon a cementing fault was discovered that could have led to fatal accidents. After the first few sets of wings had been built at Bankstown, the wing assembly work was contracted to the Pagewood factory of General Motors Holden, the Australian car builders. They experienced difficulties in manufacture, so production was halted pending the results of non-destructive testing. This problem became confused with the failure of the wing on A52-12 during pre-acceptance tests, which resulted in a fatal accident. Investigation revealed that the failure was caused by wing flutter at high speed and high G. The method of fixing the detachable plastic wing-tip and the gluing process for this item were therefore modified.

It was discovered at Holdens that the fitting of a blind joint between the top of the spar and a member that formed the edge of the top skin could be done incorrectly, leaving a gap instead of a solid bond. By the time the Director of Aeronautical Inspection called for modifications to cure this fault, 49 wings had been built, with the 50th in the jig. Twenty-two aircraft were almost complete and this hold-up caused disastrous effects on deliveries.

Another accident occurred for no apparent reason, this time to A52-18; it forced the reopening of investigations into flutter, torsional stiffness, plastic wing-tip attachment, aileron balance and cementing. Detailed examination of the wreckage revealed that in this case the gluing was satisfactory, and no clear-cut cause was found, but again production had been set back.

Pat Fillingham was also involved in Australian Production test-flying: *I was sent on to Sydney Australia to start production there. Six of us went in the bomb-*

A52-41, a FB.MK.40 of
the Royal Australian Air
Force.
(© *BAE SYSTEMS*)

*bay of a Liberator, each had a seat and a light. We went via San Francisco,
Hawaii, Canton Island and on to Brisbane. I spent most of my time expecting
the bomb doors to open! When in Sydney I tried to pluck up courage to fly under
the Sydney Harbour Bridge, but I never made it.*

Conversion to photographic reconnaissance was made to A52-2, which first
flew on 26 May 1944, followed by type trials. The armament had been replaced
by the usual complement of three vertical and two oblique cameras. Internal
fuel capacity had been increased to 636 gallon and 100 gallon drop tanks were
fitted, giving a range of around 3,000 miles, but only six PR machines were
produced. The FB.Mk.42, powered by Merlin 69s, was not proceeded with;
instead the PR.Mk.41 conversion with Merlin 69s was produced. The conversion
entailed extra radio equipment, long-range oil tanks, additional oxygen and
enlarged radiators. A further development conversion of the FB.Mk.40 was the
T.Mk.43 dual-control trainer which had dual elevator trim tab controls and was
powered by Packard-built Merlin 33s.

By the time of the Japanese surrender in August 1945, 108 Mosquitos had been
built in Australia, the final total being 212. Almost all of the basic aircraft was being
made locally. All castings and forgings were being made in the country, as were
all sheet metal and fabrications, cowlings and control system parts. Later, radiators
and oil coolers were produced as well, giving Australia almost complete
production control.

In all over ten years from the first flight, 7,781 Mosquitos were built, the last being
completed on November 15, 1950.

PHOTO-RECONNAISSANCE

During the late 1930s the RAF regarded the installation of cameras in any aircraft as merely a useful item of equipment. Before the start of World War Two Britain - unlike Germany - had no really effective reconnaissance aircraft, but with the war clouds gathering over Europe in 1938, a British civilian aerial photographic unit was formed at Heston Airport, to the west of London, under the control of Fredrick Winterbotham and Sidney Cotton, an Australian pilot who had served in World War One. Operating under the guise of a businessman dealing in colour film. Cotton flew his two Lockheed 12A airliners - which were officially registered to the airline British Airways - to many industrial and capital cities in Europe while three cameras, either F24s or 35mm Leica equipment hidden in the belly of the aircraft, recorded details of airfields, factories and ground defences far below.

Less than an hour after the declaration of war a Bristol Blenheim from RAF Wyton, near Huntingdon, took off for the first official photographic reconnaissance sortie to photograph the German fleet at anchor in the port of Wilhelmshaven, in preparation for an attack. This flight was to prove that the Blenheim was unsuitable for photographic reconnaissance work or unarmed daylight attacks, being vulnerable to both anti-aircraft guns and enemy fighters. It was also discovered that unless the Blenheim was flown at dangerously low altitudes, its cameras froze up, causing the lens to frost over and the photographic film to crack with the intense cold.

Cotton's Air Force

Sidney Cotton had been given a free hand in the recruitment of personnel, so he went into the civilian fields of industry and commerce to obtain administrative and technical staff. He realized that aerial photography in itself provided only the means of extracting intelligence - interpretation of the data obtained was another matter. At that time there were very few photographic interpreters in the RAF, so in an attempt to overcome the problem. Cotton formed another 'unofficial' association, this time with the Aircraft Operating Company, a survey organization based at Wembley, Middlesex, which had considerable experience in photographic interpretation for oil companies operating in the Middle East.

Cotton's unofficial but nevertheless highly effective work soon began to attract the attention of the Air Staff, so much so that he and his staff were conscripted into the RAF during September 1939. Once 'inside' they were formed into a tight, highly secret organization that was administered by 11 Group, Fighter Command; it was called 2 Camouflage Unit in an attempt to disguise its real work. The use of small, fast, unarmed high-flying aircraft had always been Cotton's main aim, so he fought with the hard-pressed Fighter Command for a pair of Supermarine Spitfires - and won. With the guns in the wing replaced by a camera and all superfluous equipment removed. Flight Lieutenant Maurice Longbottom took one of the freshly painted light blue aircraft on a historic sortie to photograph the Franco-German border from an altitude of 33,000 ft. The colour scheme had been arrived

at through a series of studies done by Cotton, who had discovered that this light
blue, later to be adopted as standard PRU blue, was the most effective camouflage
for high-altitude reconnaissance aircraft. In many ways Cotton's unorthodox
approach proved to be an advantage, for it provided great flexibility within the unit
and the attached photo-interpretation section. This was highly satisfactory for a
man of such temperament, but it led to many objections from senior RAF officers
whom he had bypassed at various levels to reach higher authority directly.

From January to June 1940 Cotton's personal star was very much in the
ascendant as he undertook much important work, with results from the Heston
unit coming to the attention of the Army and Navy. In mid-June he was in France,
arranging for the evacuation of the unit's aircraft, men and equipment. Cotton
returned to England on the 18th, to find a letter waiting from the Air Council
stating that the unit had been officially constituted into the RAF under the control
of Coastal Command and giving orders for him to hand over command to Wing
Commander Geoffrey W. Tuttle, a regular Air Force officer. The official feathers
that Cotton had ruffled during the unit's formation had finally extracted their
revenge. Cotton certainly deserved better treatment than this - and the OBE he
was later awarded - for it was he who had sown the seeds for effective photo-
reconnaissance and photo- intelligence in the future. Many of the pilots recruited
by Cotton went on to command PR squadrons overseas, and his enthusiasm for
the task in hand persisted long after his removal.

Photographic Development Unit

Tuttle split the unit into four detached Flights to give better coverage of enemy-
occupied territory, with aircraft operating from Heston, Benson, Wick and St. Eval.
The organization had named itself the Photographic Development Unit (later
retitled the Photographic Reconnaissance Unit) during the previous January and
was soon well established. News of the Mosquito bomber-reconnaissance aircraft
reached Tuttle's ears, so he arranged to visit Hatfield on 12 June 1941 to try out
W4051, the prototype PR Mosquito. Here was the answer to problems that had
dogged the PDU since its formation.

In some respects the Spitfires were preferred, as their single engines tended
to create less interest from the defenders in enemy territory than those of a twin-
engined machine. Spitfires were also useful for closer range targets such as the
Ruhr in Germany, but on longer distance photographic-reconnaissance flights,
operating out as far as the north Norwegian coast at Trondheim, Spitfires could

W4051 is prepared for a
test-flight at Hatfield.
With its proven speed at
altitude performance, it
is not surprising that the
PR Mosquito was given
priority.
(© BAE SYSTEMS)

only make it if they refuelled in the Shetlands. The Mosquito offered extra range, twin-engined security, and radio and navigational assistance via the extra crew member; furthermore, the navigator's excellent view improved the accuracy on missions and because the aircraft could bear a greater load, two more cameras could be carried in the belly.

Operations Commence

The unit now had its headquarters at RAF Benson in Oxfordshire and received its first Mosquito, W4051, on 13 July 1941 from Boscombe Down. The aircraft was coded LY:U and named *'Benedictine'* after the drink, a practice that continued on all the unit's aircraft. A second Mosquito, W4054, arrived on 22 July, followed by W4055 on 7 August. The flying personnel took to them well, but not so the squadron's engineering staff. The younger generation of ground crews had been educated to think that wooden construction was a retrograde step in aeronautical development, but this soon changed after a few months experience when it was realized, and proved in combat, that the extra bulk of timber could both absorb more damage and make the repair work easier.

Much time was taken up during the early days in testing the camera installations. The steel mounts were changed to wood to damp out vibration, and heater controls were fitted for the cameras. Good results were obtained from practice flights but in mid-September, when operations were imminent, the engines' oil tanks began to swell mysteriously, causing a fouling of the undercarriage mechanism. The tank shop at Hatfield worked around the clock to manufacture two modified tanks, which were flown to Benson on the evening of 14 September for overnight fitment to W4055. All the next day the aircraft was thrown around the sky and thumped down hard on each landing, but the modifications seemed to have cured the trouble, and the ground crews prepared the machine for its first operational sortie.

A pair of cameras are loaded into the rear equipment bay of this PR Mosquito ready for the next mission.
(Simon Peters Collection)

PR.Mk.IV DZ383 was a conversion from a B.Mk.IV. It served with 540 Sqn at Benson until being scrapped post-war.
(© BAE SYSTEMS)

At 1130hrs on 17 September 1941 Sqn Ldr Clarke took off from Benson in W4055 on a 5¼-hour sortie to photograph Brest and the Spanish frontier area. Although the flight itself passed off successfully, an electrical fault prevented the cameras from working. Three days later, on the 20th, Flt Lt Taylor with Sergeant Horsfall as navigator, took the same aircraft on a fully successful 4-hour photographic sortie to the Heligoland-Sylt area.

Nine Mosquito PR.Mk.Is were built; all were powered by Rolls-Royce Merlin 21s and had short nacelles. The machines were very adaptable, they normally carried some 700 gallons of fuel and oil, and their cameras were installed as three verticals and one oblique. Two Mosquitos, W4060 and W4061, were modified into long-range aircraft with an increased operational weight of 19,300 lb. Two others, W4062 and W4063, were similarly modified and also tropicalized. In fact, the adaptability of the Mosquito concept was amply illustrated when the PRU found itself in desperate need of more aircraft; their shortfall was met by diverting two B.Mk.IV bombers (DZ412 and DZ711) and four F.Mk.II fighters (W4089, DD615, DD620 and DD659) to the PRU where the unit's personnel installed cameras.

The Williamson F.52 camera as developed by the RAE Farnborough.
(RAE)

The ability of the Mosquito to reconnoitre large areas of enemy-held territory was ably demonstrated by the PR.IVs when a 7.5 hour sortie was flown from Benson to Spezia, Lyons and Marseilles. The adapted fighters lacked the extra fuel tanks and their range was therefore limited. Pilots eased the problem by adopting a fuel management technique to conserve usage and therefore increase range. After take-off they would climb on a weak mixture with +4 lb boost, 2,650 rpm with the supercharger in MS (low) gear and an airspeed of 175 mph. After about 25 minutes they would level out, having reached around 25,000ft. The run over the target depended on the weather, but normal photographic runs were made at around 22,000 ft if the sky was clear. The return flight could be made at slightly lower levels with +4 lb boost and 2,000rpm, again to conserve fuel.

The new 36in F.52 camera developed by the Royal Aircraft Establishment at Farnborough and manufactured by Williamson's was just beginning to enter service in 1942, and with this new tool placed in the Mosquito it could be

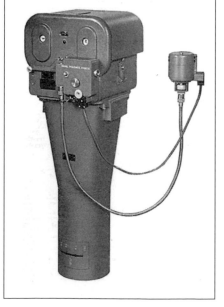

used to great effect. By using overlapping cameras, it gave lateral coverage of three miles from 35,000 ft on an 8.25 inch by 7 inch picture format. Normal operation was 1/300th of a second at f5.6, which gave a scale of about 1/8,000 from 24,000 ft. Such was the clarity and quality of prints obtained using the new camera that it was possible to distinguish the markings on aircraft carried by the German cruiser *Prinz Eugen* when photographed from 24,000 ft. The Mosquito now ranged over Europe far and wide, even making the first of many flights to Russia and back in a day.

During August a PRU detachment departed for north-east Russia. It sailed from the Clyde and arrived at Vaenga on the 23rd. Its mission was to obtain photographic coverage of the anchorage in which the battleship *Tirpitz* lay. Three Spitfires were used but Mosquito W4061 was flown over on 23 September and based at Vaenga until disbandment of the unit on 18 October, when it flew home. A further worthy demonstration of the Mosquito's contribution to the war effort was made by aircraft flying from Gibraltar over North Africa to aid the planning of the Allied landings for Operation 'Torch'. Such trips were not without risk, the aircraft receiving unwanted attention from Vichy French fighters.

So successful was the PRU that it was re- established into four squadrons. Its twelve Mosquitos were transferred to the newly formed 540 Squadron, made up from 'FT' and "L' Flights of 1 PRU, at Leuchars in Scotland.

8 OTU, operating as a photographic reconnaissance training unit, based at Fraserburgh, Scotland, received its first Mosquitos in December 1942. The unit had been formed on 18 May 1942, the same day as the airfield (built as a satellite for Peterhead and opened on 6 December 1941) was transferred to Coastal Command. 8 OTU was tasked with training crews for the specialist PR squadrons, but as no proper maintenance facilities were available, its aircraft spent much of the winter outside. Despite this the only problem in this rigorous climate was the Madapolam fabric peeling off the wing structure.

Before the end of 1942 two PR.IVs were fitted with multiple ejector exhausts in place of the flame-damping saxophone type. It was decided that the extra 10 mph obtained from the propulsion effect of these exhausts was worth the loss of flame suppression, and all future aircraft were to be similarly equipped.

PR.Mk.IX LR432 in flight. Some ninety PR.IXs were built, the first two production aircraft being delivered to 540 Sqn at Benson. (© *BAE SYSTEMS*)

High-Altitude and Night Photography

Many of the PR sorties naturally received attention from the Luftwaffe with Bf 109 and Fw 190 fighters attempting to intercept these aerial spies. Normal tactics in the event of interception, given that the PR machines were unarmed, were to resort to Geoffrey de Havilland's original concept - speed. Pilots increased their engine rpms to 3,000 in high boost which soon resulted in an indicated airspeed of over 400 mph, leaving the enemy fighters far behind. The Merlins were only supposed to be run at full combat power for less than five minutes, but crews regularly reported exceeding this for as much as 20 minutes at a time with little damage sustained.

One way of avoiding interception was to gain more height, and to this end the PR.Mk.VIII was built. Five of these machines were constructed as the forerunners of the higher flying PR.IXs; to increase their range they were fitted with 50 gallon drop-tanks. The aircraft were powered by Rolls-Royce Merlin 61 engines fitted with two-stage superchargers. The Mk.VIIIs came along at a time when German high-altitude fighters were starting to pose a problem and many of the current photo-reconnaissance aircraft were fast becoming unserviceable as a result of badly fitting bulkheads, water soakage and delays in modifying the elevator noses (all of which faults were eventually overcome).

The first PR. Mk.IX (LR405) came into service after delivery to 540 Sqn on 29 May 1943. It was fitted with Rolls-Royce Merlin 72 two-stage supercharged engines but had no pressure cabin, although a small blister was incorporated in the cabin roof, to improve the navigator's rear view, which became a standard feature in the Mk.IX variant.

As the PR.Mk.IX became available in useful numbers it was put to great use on night reconnaissance missions for tactical intelligence-gathering. One of the most valuable services it performed during the 1942-43 period was in photographing

The method of obtaining flash target photographs at night with a flash bomb exploding outside the aircraft camera's angle of view. The target indicator flash is released six seconds after the main stores release and has been set to explode at 5,500 feet above the target.

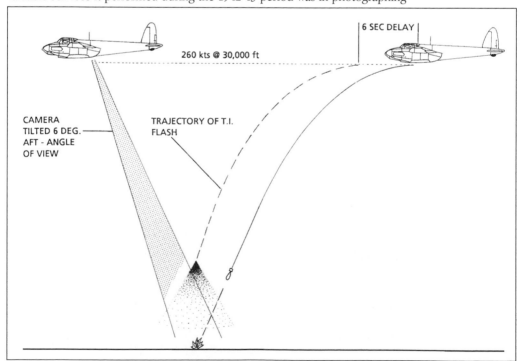

6 SEC DELAY

260 kts @ 30,000 ft

CAMERA TILTED 6 DEG. AFT - ANGLE OF VIEW

TRAJECTORY OF T.I. FLASH

...

DD744 was originally a NF.II but was converted to PR.Mk.II standard and served with 60 Sqn SAAF. *(© BAE SYSTEMS)*

research and development centres and launching sites of the German V-weapons. Reports from agents as well as eavesdropping into the German *'Enigma'* coded radio traffic led the RAF to send Mosquitos to an area near Peenemunde on the Baltic coast where it was thought that the Germans were developing a series of long-range bombardment weapons and small pilotless aircraft. Interpretation of all the data gained from agents, photographs and radio traffic, led to the discovery of the V-I 'Doodlebug' flying bomb and the V-2 rocket. As a result of this reconnaissance. Mosquitos and Spitfires photographed the whole of northern France and discovered a large number of other such sites.

This high-flying variant of the Mosquito proved itself to be fairly immune to enemy attack, mainly because it could not be easily detected. But, as the European winter came closer and the stratus layer fell to around 23,000 ft, the Mosquito started to leave condensation trails at lower and lower levels. The PR aircrews tried to alleviate this by flying at around 33,000 ft, so that any enemy aircraft climbing up after them would be as conspicuous as they were. Contrails also attracted light flak, which became increasingly effective as the war progressed but there was little defence against it other than good intelligence and flight planning to avoid known areas of enemy flak concentration.

During early 1943 two Mosquitos were used to further the art of night photography. They flew experimentally with the American M-46 photo-flash which, with its 600,000 candle-power and a peak of brilliance that lasted only 1/10th of a

Left: the American K-19B camera. The cameras shutter was triggered by a photocell which detected the flash bomb ignition and is seen here attached by the cable.

Right: a number of M-46 photoflash bombs in the bomb-bay of a 25th Bomb Group Mosquito. *(both USAAF)*

second, was three times more powerful than the existing British alternative and could be carried internally. Other problems existed on night missions; these were ones inherent with the use of long focal-length lenses, but they were solved by Spring 1943 and good quality night photographs were finally available.

The USAAF also made use of a number of the later, improved PR.Mk.XVIs for night photography. The aircraft were converted to American flight instrumentation and radio equipment, plus a camera and flash-bombs. This meant that the 58 gallon fuel tank had to be removed from the forward bomb bay and seven shackles installed to carry the photo-flashes. The K-19B night camera was carried forward of the photo-flashes and could be adjusted to provide a five degree tilt forward and ten degree tilt aft. The specification was later changed to include a pair of K-19Bs, one in the forward bomb bay and one in the rear fuselage. This version was known as the Model B. By using a technique developed by the RAF, photographs could be taken at 1/25th of a second with the lens aperture down to f6.3; this was possible thanks to a slit-type shutter which moved across the film at a speed synchronized with the forward speed of the aircraft. A short-range version was also planned capable of carrying up to fourteen photo-flashes with the 63 gallon rear bomb bay tank removed. It was intended that the USAAF would receive four short-range and eight long-range versions, with both types able to carry two 100 gallon external wing tanks if required. Only eleven such night PR.Mk.XVIs were delivered to the 654th Bombardment Squadron. They flew missions under the code-named *'Joker'*, normally at an altitude in excess of 20,000ft until the target area was reached when they descended to 15,000ft.

A remarkable Night Joker photograph of the canal towns of Nippes and Essen, Germany taken on the night of 4/5 October 1944 using M46 photoflash bombs of 700,000 candlepower. The system had been perfected in 1943 by the RAF, using a pair of Mosquito PR.Mk.IXs to test the American flash bombs, which were three times brighter than the British equivalents. *(USAAF)*

NS590'B' was a PR.Mk.XVI serving with the 25th Bomb Group, 8th Air Force and shows the newly applied stars and bars. However, the overall PR Blue paint scheme seems to have failed to totally cover the RAF roundels from it's previous owner!

NS519 also served with the 25th Bomb Group and is seen here at Watton with invasion stripes.
(both USAAF)

In December 1943 544 Sqn's Mk.IXs began to test the new *'Gee'* navigation system. These tests were unfortunately interrupted by a series of engine failures which grounded the squadron's aircraft. The fault was traced to a combination of both hoar-frost formation in the main filters and assorted pressure differences in the fuel system which prevented fuel reaching the carburettors. The fuel cooler was blanked off and both the main and long-range tanks were all linked together to create a balanced system; these series of modifications cured the faults. As events turned out, the groundings were not the disaster it first seemed, because the weather over Europe had deteriorated to a point where effective reconnaissance sorties were impossible.

NS569, a PR XVI with the 654th Bomb Squadron being flown by Lt. Robert A Tunnel (left) along with photographer Lt David J. McCarthy (right) was sent several hundred feet skywards when PBY4Y-1 'Anvil' mission drone being flown by Lt Joseph P Kennedy Jnr and 'Bud' Wiley exploded. The Mosquitos port engine was put out of commission and the aircraft peppered with flying fragments. They managed to make a landing at Halesworth just before the starboard engine quit. *(USAAF)*

Greater Height

In the never-ending effort for a greater ceiling, a Mosquito Mk.IX at Benson was experimentally fitted with Merlin 76/77 engines driving wider chord paddle-bladed propellers (four such conversions had been made by the end of February 1943, with another four to follow). When these machines were tested it was found that although the paddle-blades slowed the aircraft at lower levels, above 35,000ft the speed increased. Furthermore, the aircraft had a ceiling some 3,000ft higher than before, but a constant-speed unit (to prevent over-speeding) was required to cure engine surging.

Still greater height was obtained when a pressure cabin was developed and installed in a converted B.Mk.XVI, MM258, which became the prototype PR.Mk.XVI. The mark had entered production in November 1943 but offered no advantages in its initial form because of a lack of cabin heating. Such hurried deliveries during December were not popular with the aircrews who complained about the cold after around an hour's flying, at a time when operational flights usually lasted for three hours or more. Pilots also suffered severe physiological problems caused by extreme altitude, with several reporting that they could not remember where they had flown. The squadrons thought that the operational ceiling of the Mk.XVI was around 36,000ft, but before the type could be used on operations the cockpit canopy needed top and side rear blisters fitted to improve all-round vision. The serviceability of these early Mk.XVIs was seriously affected by internal misting and the formation of ice crystals on the windscreens and icing up of the non-sandwich windows. Urgent work was put in hand to cure this, for it occurred when operational pressure on the squadrons was at its highest, but a solution was not found and reported as cured until 18 May.

In all, 432 Mosquito PR.Mk.XVIs were built, and these aircraft carried the main photographic reconnaissance responsibility until the end of the war. Five machines, given the designation of PR.Mk.32, were modified with wing-tip extensions to increase the span to 58ft 10in and had Merlin 113 engines installed. Not all reconnaissance was done at high altitude; a Mosquito fitted with the K.19 camera and moving film used in conjunction with the Mk.II photo-flash, obtained the best results so far from a height of 3,000-5,000ft.

When the D-Day landings in France were expected, six B.Mk.VIs were converted into special camera aircraft by the Heston Aircraft Company to record the invasion on film. Upon arrival at Heston the aircraft were stripped of all their armament and extra oxygen was fitted in its place; space then had to be found in the nose for a cameraman to lie prone with a 35mm cine camera to record live-action footage of the invasion's progress. An extra glazed panel was installed in the lower front fuselage behind the transparent nose cone to improve the visibility for both camera and operator.

Weather Reporting Rights

Another form of reconnaissance of equal importance in taking the offensive to the heart of Germany was the making of regular meteorological flights over enemy-held territory. Knowledge of future adverse weather allowed raids to be better planned, thereby reducing losses and avoiding unnecessary sorties. The flights began with Supermarine Spitfires flown by 1407 Flight, under Coastal Command, in August 1941 and were code-named 'Tampa' operations. The aim of these was to provide information on which reliable forecasts of weather over enemy territory could be made and used to form the basis for planning and timing raids to the best effect. It was soon realized that with two crew the Mosquito would be far more suitable for these flights. So in April 1942 the first machine (DK285, fitted with external thermometers) was delivered; another (DK289) arrived soon after. The following

ML897 'D' a PR.Mk.IX which flew a total of 163 flights in advance of Bomber Command and USAAF flights over Germany with 1409 Bomber Command Meteorological Flight from RAF Wyton. *(via Martin Bowman)*

August the Flight was awarded squadron status as 521 Sqn and further PR.Mk.IVs were added to its strength to cope with the increased work load. As raids were normally undertaken by Bomber Command, in March 1943 they decided that meteorological flights were better operated by themselves too; the Mosquitos were therefore taken to 1409 Flight based at Oakington near Cambridge and placed under the command of 8 Group.

The expansion of RAF Bomber Command meant that more aircraft were needed and extra PR.Mk.IVs were transferred. The Flight received PR.Mk.XVI aircraft too and for the next three years the Mosquito flew ahead of every major Bomber Command attack, regularly setting out in weather so bad that flying seemed impossible. It was common for the meteorological Mosquitos to fly for long periods in the icing layer to check its extent and position, or to break out of low cloud only a few hundred feet above enemy territory to check the level of the cloud base. Close co-operation occurred between the Meteorological Flight and the photographic reconnaissance units in sharing details of flak evasion, contrails and the interception and evasion of high patrolling fighters.

LAC Bennett paints up ML897 'D's 141st completed mission log on the nose of the aircraft. Each mission is represented by a small lightning flash. *(via Martin Bowman)*

Very Long Range

The Mosquito PR.Mk.34 was to be a very-long- range, high-altitude aircraft intended for use with Air Command South-East Asia, where it was expected that there would be a requirement for such a machine in the forthcoming campaign against the Japanese. Powered by the handed Merlin 113 and 114 engines, the PR.Mk.34 had a range of over 3,500 miles, which was achieved by fitting an overload tank in the bomb bay and doubling the size of the wing tanks to increase the fuel load to 1,255 gallons. It was equipped with four F.52 vertical cameras and one F.24 oblique camera. The first production PR.Mk.34 flew on 4 December 1944 and some fifty examples were completed before the remainder of the contract was cancelled at the end of the war; the only machines to see active service belonged to 684 Sqn.

During the post-war period at least two Mk.34s were used for record-breaking flights across the Atlantic and down to South Africa. The Merlin 113 and 114 engines were found to be liable to supercharger surging problems under certain conditions at cruising rpm. There was no real solution to this, so a chart advising the pilot of what altitude/boost/speed combinations should be used to avoid this problem was listed in the pilot's notes. Pilots were also advised that: *'The aircraft is stable laterally and directionally, but is slightly unstable longitudinally. At full load, especially at high altitude, there is a tendency to build up excessive accelerations in bumpy conditions or in dives. Great care is necessary to avoid overstressing the structure in these conditions."*

Many of these post-war Mk.34s were modified by Marshalls of Cambridge into

Mk.34As. These received Merlin 114A engines, improved *'Gee'* navigation equipment and redesigned undercarriage retraction gear. On 1 September 1946 684 Sqn was re-numbered 81 Sqn and equipped with nine PR.Mk.34s. Their prime role was to conduct an aerial survey of western Thailand, Java, Malaya and adjacent areas; this was later extended to include Hong Kong, Borneo and much of the Far East.

Operation *'Firedog'*, the clearance of Communist terrorists in Malaya, which was to last for twelve years, started in July 1949 and the PR.Mk.34s belonging to 81 Sqn, commanded by Sqn Ldr P D Thompson, DFC, DFM, made daily reconnaissance flights over the jungle. For seven years these Mosquitos brought back vital intelligence on terrorist movements, often resulting in bombing raids on them. The Mosquito remained in front-line service with 81 Sqn in Malaya until 15 December 1955 when PR.Mk.34A RG314 made its last sortie.

Mediterranean Operations

The Air Ministry were very wary of releasing the Mosquito for prolonged overseas operations. They were aware that many of the airframes had been built using casein glue which was unable to resist for any amount of time the humid, tropical conditions found in many of the foreign theatres of operation. (It was not until 1944, following the break-up of a Mosquito wing in flight, that Hatfield ordered an immediate and complete change-over to a formaldehyde glue, resistant to these types of conditions.)

However, such was the need that the PR.Mk.Is from Benson continued to range far across Europe, usually reaching Malta after a 4.5 hour flight and photographing Italy on the way. A series of detachments to Malta was made throughout 1942, but these machines were all UK-based aircraft.

The battle for North Africa was now reaching its peak and 60 Sqn, South African Air Force, operating under RAF control, was tasked with the photographic reconnaissance of the Western Desert, using Martin Baltimores and Marylands, for the 8th Army Survey Directorate. To assist in his North African campaign, Field Marshal Montgomery demanded full photographic coverage of Rommels movements and troop positions. Since the German airfields were only a few miles from the targets, 60 Sqn suffered heavy losses, so when Monty asked what would be needed to ensure successful photographic coverage he was told in no uncertain terms 'Mosquitos'. Eventually two F.Mk.IIs were allocated to the squadron; the first of these, DD744, arrived on 15 February. These two aircraft had originally been intended for trials in the desert to see how they would stand up to the severe climatic conditions, but a local maintenance unit hastily converted them to the PR role by fitting a camera under the seat of each aircraft. The machines were soon flying four

Long range fuel tanks in the bomb-bay of the later PR variants gave fuel sufficient for nine hour sorties. One of the holes in the fuselage for a camera can be seen towards the top of the picture.
(© BAE SYSTEMS)

sorties a day without trouble. Deliveries of further Mosquitos were slow; nevertheless. 60 Sqn ranged deeply and successfully into enemy territory, relying on the aircraft's speed to avoid interception. But by March 1944 they had started to come in contact with German Messerschmitt Me 262 jet fighters, a problem which continued to occur for the rest of the European war.

Meanwhile, in Malta 683 Sqn had been formed in May 1943 to operate over Sicily and southern Italy. It was equipped with Mk.IIs and a few PR.Mk.IVs; then, in the summer of 1943 three PR.Mk.IXs were detached from 540 Sqn to the area to find out how the two-stage Merlins would behave in the climate.

Also active in this theatre was 680 Sqn which had been based in Tunisia since its formation from 2 Photographic Unit in February 1943. All these sometimes overlapping activities were given a degree of co-ordination later that month when the North African Central Intelligence Unit (CIU) was formed to oversee all photo-reconnaissance work, with 680 Sqn looking after the eastern Mediterranean and Greece with the exception of Corfu. During the early months of 1944 the squadron received one PR.Mk.IX and nine PR.Mk.VIs. By the end of December 1944 the squadron had increased in strength by one Mk.XVI, and had split the Mosquitos into two flights: 'A' Flight covering Breslau, Bratislava, Munich, Stuttgart and Vienna; and 'B' Flight which looked after Athens, Crete, Rhodes and the Dodecanese.

The activities of all the PR units operating in this theatre were combined during early 1944 into 336 PR Wing which incorporated Nos 680,682,683, and 60 (SAAF) Sqns; only 682 did not fly Mosquitos.

NS502 'M' - a PR XVI - served with 544 Squadron from 23 May 1944 , flying on many trips over Europe until it crashed on 21 February 1945. After repairs, it was transferred to the Royal Navy at Fleetlands. *(via Martin Bowman)*

Far East
Four PR.Mk.IIs were shipped to India in May 1943, two of which had been built using the new formaldehyde gluing technique, in the hope that this would form some protection against insect attack. Two of the machines were posted to 681 Sqn (ex 3 PRU) which operated out of Dum Dum airfield, Calcutta; from there the aircraft could range out over Japanese-occupied territory. It is interesting to note that in this area the aircraft operated under weather conditions where temperatures could be as high as 130° F, with a humidity of 88%; the rainfall at Dum Dum between April and August was recorded as over 53 inches!

PR.Mk.IXs were also released to the Far East; very long duration flights in

A PR.Mk.XVI Mosquito painted blue overall undergoes an engine change at Dum-Dum airfield in India. Note the cockpit and engine covers in place.
(© BAE SYSTEMS)

excess of eight and a half hours were made from Dum Dum which extended way out past Rangoon. In September 1943 five Mosquito Mk.IXs together with four North American B-25C Mitchells, became the embryonic 684 Sqn under the command of Sqn Ldr Basil S. Jones. It was controlled by 171 PR Wing, which itself merged with the USAAF 8th Photographic Reconnaissance Force (PRF). As the Allied offensive developed. 684 Sqn moved to China Bay in Ceylon via the Cocos Islands and Yelahanka in East Mysore before eventually arriving in Mingaladon. From then until the Japanese surrender this small South-East Asia Command PR force provided a complete photo-map of Burma, Malaya, Siam and many other territories, including the Japanese escape routes, thereby providing intelligence of supreme importance for the advancing Allied forces. Reports filtering back to Hatfield of this work brought the message home that there was a requirement for a very long-range variant (it eventually appeared in the shape of the PR.Mk.34).

Australasia
Beginning with A52-2, a number of Australian-built Mosquito FB.Mk.40s were modified at Bankstown into PR.Mk.40s by replacing the armament with the usual complement of five vertical and oblique cameras. The first PR.Mk.40 flew on 26 May 1944, demonstrating a range of about 3,000 miles. Its internal fuel capacity had been increased and provision made for fitting 100 gallon drop-tanks.

1 PRU of the RAAF was re-formed as 87 (Photographic Reconnaissance) Sqn; it was equipped with PR.Mk.40s, later boosted by a number of PR.Mk.XVIs which were supplied from the United Kingdom in March 1945. The modified Mk.40s were slower than the Mk.XVIs, but the latter used more fuel and were therefore restricted to short-range operations. The crews who made up this unit were drawn from those who had served overseas and completed operational tours, together with pilots who had either served with reconnaissance units or had high operational hours. Conversion flying was conducted at Williamtown, New South Wales, and the first operational sortie took off on 1 June 1944 from the Coomalie airstrip north of Darwin. It was intended that these aircraft would take over from American reconnaissance units which had been operating in north-west Australia with aircraft at the limit of their range. To ease the range problem it was planned

to use forward airstrips such as Broome in Western Australia; from there Japanese installations in east Java, some eight hours away in total, could be reached. The reconnaissance Mosquitos were subsequently used to great effect when the Japanese were being cleared from New Guinea in 1944.

A52-610 was formerly NS727 a PR XVI of 87 Sqn RAAF at Coomalee Creek (via Stuart Howe)

Many operational problems occurred when operating from primitive airstrips that had been built using crushed coral or sand; the resultant grit tended to find its way into the engine intakes, causing a build-up of silicon on the spark-plug points and leading to engine failure. The local Rolls-Royce and De Havilland agents modified the intake filters on site, thus reducing the instances of malfunction. The area was well known for its severe weather conditions, with tropical storms and cyclones; quite frequently visibility would rapidly be reduced to a few feet as rain fell in a torrential downpour. The leading edges of the fin, main and tailplanes had to be strengthened to survive the impact of these storms.

Above: A PR.Mk.XVI of 87 Squadron RAAF taxies out for take-off at Coomalie Creek, northern Australia in 1945.

Right: A52-6, a PR.Mk.40 also at Coomalie Creek. *(both via Stuart Howe)*

During March 1945 it was suspected that the Japanese light cruiser *Isuzu* along with three escorts was moving towards Toepang on Timor Island. The ships were successfully photographed despite unsuccessful attempts by Japanese '*Oscar*' fighters sent to intercept the Mosquitos.

The last 20 undelivered FB.Mk.40s, and eight others selected at random from machines in storage, were fitted with Packard Merlin 69 engines and the full PR.Mk.40 camera package for designation as the PR.Mk.41. Most were used by the RAAF to reconnoitre and photograph the west and north of the continent, and were later used for a large-scale post-war survey of Australia.

USAAF F-8

American interest in the Mosquito stemmed from Colonel Elliot Roosevelt, son of the US President, who commanded the USAAF photographic reconnaissance organization in North Africa. There he became impressed with the performance and capabilities of the Mosquitos used by the RAF in the theatre.

During February 1943 the Americans indicated an interest in obtaining Mosquitos, for they considered that the type was better for this work than the F-5 reconnaissance variant of the Lockheed Lightning, which lacked the range and ceiling and could not be modified to take the desired 36in focal length camera.

In 1943 the USAAF ordered 90 Mosquitos, each costing $110,000, from the Canadian production line, and gave them the designation F-8-DH. These were supposed to be modified to PR standard at Bell Aircraft's Niagara centre in New York State, although in the end only 40 aircraft, serialled 43-34924 to 43-34963, were transferred. The F-8 was a modification of the Canadian B.Mk.XX, powered by two Packard-built Merlin XXXIs or XXXIIs driving Hamilton Standard three-bladed propellers. It could carry two K-17 or K-22 12in cameras mounted in a split vertical arrangement in the forward bomb bay and front fuselage; the camera controls were mounted in the cockpit and accessible to both crew members; a duplicate set of controls was situated in the extreme nose. Sixteen of these machines, equivalent to the RAF B.Mk.IV, arrived in Britain for onward despatch to the 25th Bombardment Group (Reconnaissance), USAAF, at Watton during July 1944. These aircraft did not match up in any way to the PR.Mk.XVIs that were currently in use with the group. The F-8's performance was far from satisfactory above 25,000 ft and it needed

A rather scruffy-looking Mosquito B.Mk.20, 43-34943, with drop-tanks fitted under each wing, is towed into the hangar at Downsview. *(USAAF)*

USAAF F.8 Mosquitos undergo work at the Bell Niagara Modification Center. Closest to the camera is 43-34934. *(Bell Aircraft)*

extensive radio and navigational equipment changes to meet the Group's requirements.

The Americans experienced trouble with the rear camera mounts, as the Flight Operating instructions (Pilot's Notes), T.O. 0.1- 150JA-1, explained: *'The rear camera support is adjustable to provide for installation of various focal length cameras in standard mounts. However, due to moisture, the wood support for the channels may warp so that the channels do not retain their original alignment. This condition may prevent the use of camera mounts having their mounting studs rigidly attached to their mounts. However, the mounting points of the type A.8 mount are flexible enough to allow installation of this mount regardless of the alignment of the channels.'*

Inspection of the airframes also revealed that the standard of construction was generally inferior to that of the PR.Mk.XVI. Nevertheless there was pressure on the group to operate United States-funded aircraft and thus the option of converting these aircraft into 'chaff- dispensing machines was considered but, after some thought, rejected because of the type's poor upper altitude performance. The F-8s were stored at Watton for a few weeks before ten were transferred to the RAF and the remainder were returned to the USA.

USAAF Meteorological Duties

Incorrect forecasting of weather conditions over targets during the spring and summer of 1943 resulted in much manpower, time, fuel and equipment being lost by the USAAF 8th Air Force. This created great frustration among the crews, with bomb groups arriving over a cloud-covered target that had been predicted before take-off as being 'clear'. In turn, this caused problems with morale, so something had to be done. The idea of using fast 'scout' aircraft, flying ahead of the main bomber formations, to radio the weather conditions over the targets back to the bombing leaders was suggested, eventually resulting in a request for Mosquitos from General Eaker in September 1943. The Air Ministry agreed and by the end of

Pilots Flight Operating Instructions for the Army Model F-8 Airplane are now somewhat scarce on the ground, but this copy shows the Observers side panel, with camera controls and fold-down table. *(USAAF)*

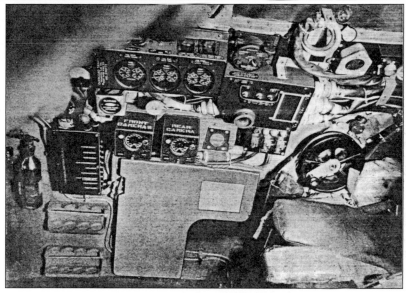

the month 30 FB.Mk.VIs (the only model readily available) were allocated to the 8th Air Force to establish a target weather reconnaissance unit at Mount Farm near Bedford. But after testing by American pilots, the type was considered to be inferior to the true PR variant and the modifications required to meet their demands would take too long to effect. The USAAF decided to wait until the PR machines would be available and on 1 December they were promised 20 PR.Mk.XVIs which would be delivered during February 1944. The use of the PR.Mk.XVI and the number of specialist conversions carried out to just this one particular mark by the Americans ably demonstrates just how versatile the Mosquito airframe was.

The US 8th Air Force also planned to establish its own meteorological flight, operating in a much more extensive manner than the simple 'scouting ahead of the main formation' weather-reconnaissance flights. The RAF was already supplying the Americans with comprehensive meteorological information, but the planning of high-level daylight operations required specialized information.

NS569, a PR.Mk.XVI at a rather damp Watton in late 1944. *(USAAF)*

The original caption states: *'That's T/Sgt Sherman H Housman of Paducah, Kentucky, seated on the wing of a twin-engined 8th Air Force Mosquito. The figures at which he is pointing signify that this aircraft, of which he is crew-chief, has completed 50 missions over Germany on weather and photographic reconnaissance flights without once having to turn back because of mechanical failure. This is the first American Mosquito to have accomplished such a feat'. (USAAF)*

The Americans were particularly interested in cloud level observation at night by the light of flares (so as to be better able to predict the next day's weather) and H2X radar-scope photography. The Americans found PR.Mk.XVIs with the pressure cabin to be much better than the B-17 Fortress, B-24 Liberator and P-38 Lightning they had previously used. The Mosquito was used to great advantage in situations where encounters with the enemy were likely and high speed was necessary.

The USAAF Mosquitos based in Britain were concentrated under the title of 'Light Weather' operations at Watton in Norfolk. Originally the Mosquito had operated under the control of the 802nd Reconnaissance Group; by 9 August 1944 the group had its full complement of aircraft, although the number of specialized conversions caused operational delays. The 802nd flew Mosquitos in two of its three squadrons: the 653rd, which used its Mk.XVIs for long-range weather flights over enemy territory; and the 654th, which used its Mk.XVIs for

Another specialist use the Americans put the Photo-Reconnaissance Mosquitoes to was filming operations. Here 1st Lt Dean H Scanner and St Augie Kurjack film a 2,600lb *'Batty'* glide bomb release from B-17G 42-400043 whilst flying aboard MM370. *(USAAF)*

Colonel Leon Gray, Commanding Officer of the 25th BG oversees work on his aircraft during morning engine check-out. *(USAAF)*

photo-reconnaissance work and later expanded to scout work, night photography and 'chaff dispersal. By early September the unit had lost sixteen aircraft as a result of enemy action or through crashes, and plans were put in hand to supply a further eight PR.Mk.XVIs per month during 1945. By March 1945 the situation was reversed with the attrition rate now so low that a request was made to suspend deliveries until July unless special requirements arose. That same year the new PR.Mk.34, meant to replace the PR.Mk.XVI, was inspected by USAAF officers but was found to be totally unacceptable without a large number of modifications.

American pilots found the Mosquito reliable and pleasant to fly - US ground crew were impressed by the type, too - but care had to be taken on take-off because of the swing produced by the powerful Merlins. The aircraft's speed allowed it to escape from hostile fighters, but many reports suggest that a far greater danger lay in its misidentification by USAAF bomber-escort P-51 Mustangs rather than the enemy! At least one Light Weather Mosquito was reported to have been shot down by a Mustang whose pilot mistook it for a Ju.88; as a result the entire tail area of all Light Weather aircraft were painted bright red as an identification aid.

The need for Light Weather Mosquitos led to the alteration of some 20 PR.Mk.XVs. The first (MM338) was modified with *'Gee'* equipment fitted in the nose and SCR-287 liaison radio, SCR-522 VHF and SCR-297N command radios which were installed in the forward bomb bay. An American RC-36 interphone system, turn and bank indicator, gyro fluxgate system and RC-24 radio altimeter were also installed. Eventually some 60 PR.Mk.XVIs were modified by the Americans and used by the 653rd Bomb Squadron (R)(L). These aircraft concentrated on strategic weather reconnaissance and operated under the code-name *'Blue Stocking'*. Their missions were flown at all hours of the day, in order to provide the weather forecasting service with detailed knowledge of conditions near or over enemy-held territory, with occasional sorties out into the Western Approaches to allow longer range forecasts to be made.

Radar Target Location Photography

The high performance and survival rate of the Mosquito led to its selection as the most suitable aircraft to obtain and permanently record radar screen images of target locations in Germany. In January 1944 arrangements were made with De Havilland's for two PR.Mk.XVIs from the American allocation to be specially modified to take a nose radar. The prototype, MM308/G, was flown to the 8th Air Force's radar centre at Alconbury where the APS-15 equipment was fitted in February 1944. However, only the pre-production scanner, which had been hand-built, could be fitted into the nose space and covered by a bulbous nose as production examples of the radar were too large. The only pre-production scanners in existence were fitted to the twelve B-17s at Alconbury and these smaller scanners had to be plundered in order to create the H2X Mosquito conversion. The radar scope, with a modified 16mm K-24 camera fitted directly to it, was successfully located behind the new scanner where the navigator could use it, and the flight instrument and radio installation modifications were copied from the Light Weather version. Unfortunately, after all this effort, the prototype crashed shortly after its first flight; it overshot the runway at Alconbury on 12 May (used in preference to the rough grass runways at Watton which were unsuitable for aircraft packed with sensitive electronic equipment). A problem with fuel fumes building up in the rear fuselage caused operations to be suspended for a while, with a threat of replacement by H2X-equipped P-38s, but the early problems were soon overcome and missions successfully resumed.

NS538, a H2X equipped Mosquito PR.Mk.XVI is seen at Watton. The aircraft was extensively used during radar-scope photograph sorties by the 654th BS during the summer of 1944. The bulbous solid nose was the distinctive feature, which covered the H2X scanner that moved through 180 degrees. *(USAAF)*

A typical H2X instrument package in a USAAF Mosquito XVI in the fuselage aft of the cockpit. *(USAAF)*

Secret Agents and Radar Counter-measures

As the ground war intensified in Europe during 1944, there was a need for a high- performance machine capable of receiving signals transmitted by agents in enemy-held territory. The Mosquito was again the obvious choice and two were made

available to the Office of Strategic Services (OSS), the American equivalent of the British Special Operations Executive (SOE). In March 1944 the OSS set up the Special Operations Group to fly missions as part of the patriot support operations, code-named *'Carpetbagger'*.

Five PR.Mk.XVIs were operated by the 654th Bombardment Squadron in a similar series of sorties code-named *'Red Stocking'* and *'Skyware'*. The Americans assigned the codename Red Stocking to the missions in an attempt to persuade German intelligence services that they were weather flights similar in concept to the more familiar *'Blue Stocking'* missions.

The aircraft, among them a night photographic aircraft and a former H2X machine, were painted with gloss black undersides and carried an extra crew member in the converted bomb bay, which was equipped with oxygen, recording equipment and an S-Phone, code-named *'Joan-Eleanor'*. Mysteries still surround this equipment, and the so-called 'code names' used. Some sources state it had been developed for the OSS by a young engineer from Ohio named Al Gross. Others state that Gross' actual contribution to the project was relatively minor and that the main developers were Dewitt R. Goddard and Lt. Cmdr. Stephen H. Simpson (Goddard's wife's name was Eleanor, and reportedly Joan was an acquaintance of Simpson).

There is also some controversy as to if the code *'Red Stocking'* was ever used - in the OSS records at the National Archives in Washington, DC. there appears to be no mention of *Red Stocking* in the documents covering these secret operations. Such operations are all titled *'Joan-Eleanor Project'*, or *'JE Project'*.

It seems that when the OSS operations began at Watton in September 1944, the group headquarters wished to receive credit for all the missions flown for the OSS. So for statistical purposes they labelled all missions flown for the OSS as *Red Stocking*. In the monthly reports sent to 325 Recon.Wing HQ the various types of mission flown were covered by various nomenclatures, and all OSS mission fell under the *Red Stocking* title.

An all-black painted PR.Mk.XVI Special Operations Mosquito seen at Denain/Prouvy, France sometime in the spring of 1945. *(USAAF)*

Whatever the facts, it was a short-range, two-way radio weighing only 4 lb; it transmitted on a high frequency and broadcast in a tight cone, therefore allowing the aircraft to pick up the transmissions from secret agents using the ground half - *'Eleanor'* of the set that featured a highly directional beam that pointed up, to a circling aircraft equipped with a complementary radio, *'Joan'*, and a wire

recorder to store the message. *Eleanor* and *Joan* communicated with each other around 1.15 meters (260 MHz).

Three machines were later transferred to the 492nd Bomb Group, during the spring of 1945. The unit was based at Harrington in Northamptonshire but also used Dijon in liberated France as a forward base for operations. A number of Douglas A-26 Invaders were used for dropping agents into Germany and Austria, with the Mosquitos later monitoring their signals.

The technique used was for the Mosquito to fly to a predetermined place at an appointed time and then tightly orbit at around 30,000ft. Hopefully the operator in the bomb bay would be able to converse directly with the agent on the ground with little fear of detection or interception of messages by the Germans. This proved to be much simpler than using codes and clearly more information could be passed in a 20-minute contact than by using other radio techniques. The main drawback of the scheme was that if the contact point had to be changed at a late stage for any reason, it was impossible quickly to arrange for the ground agents to move to a new location.

The first successful operational use of the system was made on 22 November 1944 by Stephen H. Simpson; he recorded transmissions from an agent codenamed 'Bobbie' while orbiting at 30,000 ft over occupied Holland.

One of the most daring was flown on 12/13 March 1945 when a Mosquito PR XVI was operated at 25,500 ft near Berlin to establish radio contact with agents who had earlier been dropped on 1/2 March from an A-26 Invader.

On 6 October 1944 the 8th Air Force Command decided to combine in a single Mosquito airframe the functions of weather scouting and 'chaff dispensing. *'Chaff'* was the American code-name for what the British called *'Window'* - strips of aluminium material acting as reflectors to the radar waves to produce a

Above: A S-Phone operator shows how contact was made with the orbiting aircraft.

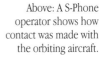

The SSTR-6 'Eleanor' radio equipment installed in a Mosquito aircraft. Some items visible in the picture: the SSTR-6 at lower-right, dynamotor at lower left, a wire recorder at upper centre, and the antenna rotating spindle in the centre of the shot.

PHOTOGRAPHIC RECONNAISSANCE DATA						
	PR.I	PR.VM	F-8	PR.IX	PR.XV1	PR.34
Span	54ft 2in	54ft 2in	54ft 2in	54ft 2in	54ft 2in	54ft 2in
Length	40ft 6in	40ft 9.5in	40ft 9.5in	40ft 6in	40ft 6in	40ft 6in
Height	12ft 6in	12ft 6in	12ft 6in	12ft 6in	12ft 6in	12ft 6in
Tareweight	12,824lb	14,800lb	13,400lb	14,569lb	14,635lb	14,180lb
All-upweight	19,670lb	21,395lb	21,000lb	22,000lb	22,350lb	22,100lb
Maximum speed	382mph	436mph	380mph	408mph	415mph	425mph
Cruising speed	255mph	258mph	265mph	250mph	250mph	300mph
Initial climb	2,850ft/min	2,500ft/min	2,325ft/min	2,850ft/min	2,900ft/min	2,000ft/min
Ceiling	35,000ft	38,000ft	30,000ft	38,000ft	38,500ft	43,000ft
Maximum range	2,180 miles	2,550 miles		2,450 miles	2,450 miles	3,340 miles
Engines: RR Merlin	Mk.21or23	Mk.21or23	Packard31	Mk.72&73	Mk.72&73	Mk.113&114

Performance charts for the main types of photo-reconnaissance variants, incorporating known data
Note. PR.VIII and American F-8 models were 3.5in longer.

'smokescreen' on the enemy radar. By removing the lower rear fuel tanks in the Mosquito PR.Mk.XVI it was possible to install two 8ft-long wooden magazines to dispense radar-jamming 'chaff' through metal chutes in the bomb bay doors. 1,400 to 1,800 bundles of 'chaff type CHA-28' could be carried and discharged through A-l automatic stripper heads at the rate of 200 units per minute (the total load being slightly under 600 lb) to create a screen for heavy bombers following behind. Twelve aircraft of the 653rd Bomb Squadron were sent to the Abbots Ripton Depot at Alconbury for modification during late October but, due to the shortage of the A-l dispensing heads and the fact that many of the fittings had to be prefabricated, the first aircraft was not delivered until December. A further four machines were then allocated to the project, code-named *'Graypea',* but by mid-February 1945 only five aircraft had been converted, a number which only rose to twelve by the end of the war. These machines were allocated to the 25th Bomb Group (Reconnaissance) - as the 802nd had been redesignated - but were available on an 'as required' basis to each Air Division headquarters. The aircraft also did some scouting work and night photography.

Conclusions
Thus the unarmed version of the Mosquito served in every theatre of Allied operations, playing a vital part in obtaining photographic and weather information that greatly aided planners making decisions and who then used this information to devastating effect. The Mosquito progressively flew higher and faster than almost all the opposition it encountered - the reconnaissance variants never 'met their match' until some of the German jet-powered reconnaissance aircraft appeared on the scene a number of years later. The Mosquito was blessed with an airframe that was so adaptable that it could be put to a considerable number of specialised uses, especially by the Americans. It utilized equipment that was, at the time, in the forefront of technology and which could never have originally been intended for the design. Nevertheless, no matter what the purpose of the mission, the Mosquito returned with information, justifying time and again the unarmed concept.

SQUADRONS THAT USED PR VARIANTS OF THE MOSQUITO

SQN	CODE	VARIANT	FROM	TO	REMARKS
4	NC	PR 16	1/44	4/44	Used by 'Q' Flight only. Based at Aston Down for PR duties over France. Later re-equipped with Mosquito bombers
13	-		PR 34	9/46	12/46 Unit renumbered from 680 Sqn. Based at Ein Shemer, Palestine. Re-equipped with Gloster Meteor PR.10
58	OT	PR 34 PR.35	10/46	1/53	Based at Benson. Used in photo-survey of Great Britain. Re-equipped with Canberra PR.3
81	-	PR.16 PR.34	1/46	12/55	Re-numbered from 684 Sqn at Seletar, Singapore. Served in Borneo in campaign against the Communist terrorists in Malaya. Operated last RAF Mosquito front- line flight. Re-equipped with Meteor PR.10
140	-	PR.9 PR.16	11/43	7/45	Initially based at Hartford Bridge. Moved to many bases, eventually moving to Belgium 9 44. Returned to UK 7/45 without aircraft. Disbanded at Fersfield 10 November 1945
169	VI	Mk.1	6/42	9/43	Based at Middle Wallop. Used a few Mk.1 aircraft in the tactical reconnaissance role for Army Co-operation Command. Disbanded 30 September 1943. Later re-formed with Mosquito fighters
192	DT	PR.4 PR.16	1/43	8/45	Initially based at Gransden Lodge as 1474 Flight. To Feltwell 4/43. Re-numbered 192 Sqn 11 June 1943. To Foulsham 11/43. Used on radar counter-measures work. Disbanded 22 August 1945 and became nucleus of the Central Signals Establishment
400	-		PR.16	12/43	8/45 Royal Canadian Air Force Sqn. Initially based at Kenley before moving in July 1944 through a number of bases on mainland Europe. Disbanded 7 August 1945
521	-	PR.4	8/42	3/43	Renumbered from 1401 Flight at Bircham Newton. Used for meteorological duties. Transferred to Oakington 3/43. Disbanded 31 March 1943
540	DH	PR.4 PR.8 PR.9 PR.16 PR.34	10/42 12/47	9/46 12/52	Formed from 'H' and 'L' Flights of 1 PRU. Initially based at Leuchars. To Benson 2/44. Used for PR work all over Europe as far as Austria and the Canary Islands. to France 3/45 for photographic survey duties. Disbanded at Benson 30 September 1946 Re-formed at Benson 1/12/47 until re-equipped with Canberra PR.3 from 12/52
543	-	PR.4	6/43	10/43	Formed from 1 PRU. Based at Benson. Aircraft used for PR training
544	-	PR.4 PR.9 PR.16 PR.32 PR.34	3/43	10/45	Based at Benson. Formed from the remainder of 1 PRU. Used for PR duties all over Europe. Flew courier service during Yalta conference. Disbanded at Benson 13 October 1945
680	-	PR.9 PR.34	2/44	9/46	Formed from 2 PRU. Initially based at Matariya. Moved to Italy. Did survey work in Iran, Iraq and Palestine. Re-numbered 13 Sqn
681	-	F.2 FB.6	9/43	11/43	Based at Dum Dum, India, after re-numbering from 2 PRU. Aircraft taken over and used to form 684 Sqn
683	-	PR.4	2/43	-	Formed in Malta by refilling 'B' Flight of 69 Sqn. Primarily a Spitfire unit, but operated at least two Mosquitoes in 3/43 and flew a number of sorties before aircraft transferred to other units
684	-	F.2 PR.4 PR.9 PR.34	9/43	1/46	Based at Dum Dum, India, when formed with aircraft from 681 Sqn. To Comilla 12/43, Dum Dum 1/44, Alipore 5/44, Saigon 10/45. Re-numbered 81 Sqn at Bangkok, Thailand, 1 September 1946

Note. This chart details only the main variants used. It does not include training variants supplied to many squadrons

FIGHTERS

During 1940 the Germans began to harass Allied shipping in the Bay of Biscay and off the west coast of Ireland using Focke-Wulf Fw 200 Condor long-range anti-shipping bombers (adapted from a pre-war airliner design), joining up with the U-boats in the attempt to cut the supply lines feeding Britain. The Condors became such a grave threat that Lord Woolton, the Minister of Food, pressed the Air Ministry for urgent help.

Plans for both long-range convoy-escort fighters and home-defence night fighters were summarized by August and in October Specification F. 18/40 was drawn up for a defending and intruding night fighter. It was clear that the Mosquito fighter, with its speed and range, fitted the requirements exactly.

Before the Mosquito fighter could enter squadron service with Fighter Command, a ground-controlled radar interception system linked to a usable airborne radar target location set was devised for use at night to intercept enemy raiders. This breakthrough enabled a successive series of Mosquito night fighter variants to take advantage of further rapid advances in electronic technology.

Efforts to refine the design brought forth other changes, some of which were intended to make use of the Mosquitos speed and range in order for the design to take up a more offensive role. This resulted in the fighter-bomber version. Several different variants of this sub-type were produced, combining in one airframe the tremendous firepower of the fighter with the destructive ability of the bomber, albeit at a lesser rate due to a reduced bomb load carried in a smaller bomb bay behind the cannon. The fighter-bomber Mosquitos were used during the latter stages of the war, when the Germans were beginning to go on the defensive, and took over some of the duties of the pure Mosquito fighters which had been at the forefront of the early Allied offensives. However, because use of the Mosquito fighter-bomber was spread across both Fighter, Coastal and Bomber Commands, certain aspects of their operations were orientated far more towards Bomber Command's operations and are therefore covered in the chapter on Mosquito bombers.

The classic Mosquito night-fighter - in this case a NF. Mk.II DD607, showing the early airborne interception 'arrowhead' transmitter aerials in the nose, just above the Browning .303 machine guns.

DD737, an NF.Mk.II in night-fighter finish of rough matt-black with the serial in dull red. Note the A.I. azimuth receiver aerials through the wingtips.

DZ238 'Babs II' of 23 Sqn is pictured about to depart. It was the squadron's last Mk.II and is in the modified day camouflage scheme with black undersides.
(both © BAE SYSTEMS)

Night Fighters

The honour of being the first squadron to receive fighter Mosquitos (and the first night fighter variant) went to 157 Sqn, which formed at Debden on 13 December 1941 under the command of Wing Commander Gordon Slade, who had flown the prototype during the official trials at Boscombe Down. The first machine, W4073, a dual-control Mk.II, was delivered to Castle Camps, Debden's satellite airfield, on 26 January 1942. The airfield, which subsequently became home to the entire squadron, had poor accommodation and workshops; it also lacked equipment and the bitterly cold winter weather made this south Cambridgeshire base a bleak place.

31 MU at St. Athan had received seventeen Mosquito Mk.IIs during the Christmas period which were to be fitted with the new Mk.IV Airborne Interception (AI) radar. This had been developed by the Air Ministry Research Establishment as the RAF's first mass-produced airborne radar. It had a distinctive 'broad arrow' transmitter aerial, mounted between the machine-guns in the Mosquito's nose, and wing-tip mounted receiver aerials. The complete installation comprised a R3066 or R3102A receiver; T3065 or T3065B transmitter; Type 3 control panel; Type 20 modulator; Type 20, 40 or 40A indicator unit; and Type R generator fitted to the port engine to supply additional power. The display of received signals was via two cathode ray tubes (CRTs) in the cockpit.

Experiments were conducted with the night fighter's colour schemes. Early F.IIs had a textured black finish applied to their skin, known as Specification RDM/2A. Similar in touch to velvet, it was designed to eliminate the reflections of searchlights, but it was found to be less effective than first thought and produced a serious

The AI Mk.IV indicator unit installed in a Mosquito. The two tiny CRTs are enclosed by the visor - each has its own brilliance and focusing controls.
(© BAE SYSTEMS)

W4052, the prototype Mosquito fighter seen at Panshanger after Geoffrey de Havilland made a forced landing there on 19 April 1942. The damage was soon repaired and the aircraft went to A&AEE.

The Mosquito carried and ever-increasing amount of electronic equipment - including *Gee* for navigation. All had to be 'found a home' and here the *Gee* indicator and associated RF equipment was mounted behind the pilot's seat in a Mk.II. *(both © BAE SYSTEMS)*

speed loss of up to 26 mph caused by aerodynamic drag. The A&AEE conducted their own tests and discovered only an 8 mph reduction. It was eventually decided that the discrepancy in recorded figures between W4082 and W4076, the two aircraft involved was caused by the differences in application. The RDM/2A paint finish was soon replaced by plain matt black paint, but this produced too strong a silhouette against clouds on moonlit nights. Further experimentation took place until it was discovered that this silhouette could be reduced by using a modified day camouflage scheme on upper surfaces with lighter shades on the undersides; a scheme approved by Fighter Command and used for the rest of the conflict.

Teething Troubles

Small modifications were soon introduced to cure the problems normally encountered during the rapid introduction of any new type of aircraft into operational use. A blind was fitted to shut out the glare of airfield floodlights and modified gun sight brackets were installed. Several lamps and switches were relocated in the cockpit following the first experiences of operational flying.

Night gun firing practice on the North Sea ranges demonstrated that the Browning .303 machine-guns installed in the nose needed flash eliminators to prevent the pilot from being blinded when they were fired. It seems that during the gunnery trials at Boscombe the guns had never been fired, hence the problem had gone undiscovered! Flt Lt Stoneman, 157 Sqn's Engineering Officer, devised a tubular venturi device to fit on the end of each gun-barrel which sucked the flame downwards on firing. There was much less of a problem with the 20mm cannon, largely because they were located under the aircraft's belly which shielded most of the flashes; however, it was noticed that when the cannon were fired in wet conditions there was some reflection from the propeller discs, but it was difficult to do anything about this.

Tailwheel shimmy also occurred in squadron use, just as it had during the official handling trials. The A & AEE had conducted an extensive series of tests on W4060, resulting in the discovery that tailwheel shimmy occurred through

use of rudder and brakes during the latter stages of the landing roll, or early stages of the take-off run; once shimmy had started it could not be eliminated. The standard ball-bearing thrust races in the tailwheel (which were designed to resist sideward loads) were replaced with a bakelite bearing which greatly reduced the problem. Several aircraft were similarly modified and rapidly placed into squadron use to check the modification results but the shimmy problem, although ameliorated, was never entirely cured until the fitment of a Marstrand double- track tyre.

By far the biggest problem was the continued unserviceability of the exhaust manifold with its flame-damping shroud. This had occurred across the entire Mosquito production range but was particularly noticeable on the night fighters, with the exhaust gases from the Merlins burning through the shroud and even the side of the engine cowling. Trouble was also encountered with the spiral slipstream flow around the engine nacelles, especially on the starboard side where it led the gases directly into the radiator and caused overheating. These problems gave maintenance people and the designers nightmares during this early period. Frank B. Halford, designer of the famous de Havilland Gipsy engine series and head of the De Havilland Engine Division, commented partly in jest and partly in exasperation: '...*the next time it would be better to design the aircraft around the exhaust system*'.

Two sets of cowlings were returned to Hatfield for investigation, but by mid-May 1942 more than half of 157 Sqn's aircraft had been grounded through this fault and a team of civilian workers were despatched from Martin Hearn's to assist with repairs. Eventually, following a series of repairs and modifications, the trouble was cured on around sixty aircraft.

Two close ups of the exhaust shrouds that caused so many problems. With an air intake at the front, the exhaust gasses exited under the wing. The outer shrouds contained cooling ducts for exhaust manifold flanges, spark-plugs and exhaust fish-tails. There was also an inner shroud that covered the fishtail exhausts to reduce as much glow as possible.

The picture on the right shows the fishtail exhausts with the outer shrouds removed. The small intake to the front and below the saxophones is an air intake to provide cooling to the spark-plugs. *(both © BAE SYSTEMS)*

Difficulties in solving the problems had been compounded by Rolls-Royce, who incorporated a change of material specification on the Merlin production lines by introducing a series of austenitic steel studs with special metallurgical properties. Used on the exhaust manifolds, it was thought that they would have better heat-resisting properties than the standard item, but shortly after their fitment a series of exhaust manifold stud fractures were reported. This failure allowed the exhaust stacks to come adrift, resulting in the exhaust flames playing on the engine and ignition harness with potentially deadly results. The problem had been made worse by the use of open-ended copper-covered asbestos exhaust gaskets which collapsed in use and thus slackened off the joint. It was obvious that the new stud material had not the strength or ductility required for the task. The solution was a lengthened stud with a waisted shank and reach nut, to be used with a totally enclosed copper-covered asbestos washer and solid copper gasket. Eventually, the shrouded exhausts, which were never popular with maintenance people, were only retained for night work to shield the visible flame, and oval exhaust stubs were fitted to machines operating on day raids.

Radar Innovation

At the outbreak of World War Two the RAF's night defences relied on squadrons equipped with day fighter types of aircraft. A breakthrough in night-fighting techniques was initiated by using the newly devised radar (then known by the code-name Radio Direction Finding or RDF) which meant that an aircraft could be accurately directed into the general area behind its target by a ground controller using Ground Controlled Interception (GCI) radar which established contact with the incoming aircraft. This ground-based radar provided 360 deg coverage over a range of about 50 miles and could be linked with others to create a defensive barrier. The ground controller worked directly from his radar screen or Plan Position Indicator (PPI) which gave him a plan view of the area swept by the radar. A trace revolved around the screen with each sweep showing the relative positions of both the night fighter and the target. All directional course information was passed directly to the pilot of the interceptor.

The GCI system was advanced for its day and proved to be a boon for pilots; however, the very nature of this form of interception highlighted another potentially deadly threat to the Mosquito. Many RAF aircrew expressed concern that the leading-edge radiators were vulnerable to damage under particular circumstances, especially during night interceptions. As already explained, the Mosquito pilot was vectored by radar on to the enemy aircraft before picking up and identifying it visually. This was particularly difficult with the Focke-Wulf Fw 190, for it presented a small silhouette when viewed from behind. Pilots found that because it was difficult to judge the range, they were regularly opening fire below 100 yards and sometimes as little as 50 yards from the target.

The initial burst would produce an area of debris from the enemy aircraft through which the Mosquito would have to fly; some of this debris would pierce the radiators. Protective grilles were fitted immediately in front of the radiators but they could not stop more than the lightest of pieces. Throughout the entire period of hostilities, this was a problem that was never fully solved and became something that the aircrew learned to live with.

Nevertheless, the GCI system laid the foundations for the entire network of radar-directed defence systems still in use, in upgraded forms, to the present day.

The first enemy aircraft to fall to the night fighters directed by GCI appears to have been a Dornier Do 217 which was attacked in the early hours of 30 May 1942 by Squadron Leader Ashfield of 157 Sqn flying W4099. He received radar vectors from the ground to direct him on to the target, then used his own radar to close in to around 250 yards, from where he opened fire. The enemy went into cloud, but Ashfield fired again, using all 450 rounds of cannon shells to no effect. He then closed again, this time to as close as 60 yards before firing on the Dornier with his machine-guns and watching it dive vertically into cloud to the south of Dover. At the time it was claimed only as a 'probable' but in the light of information now available it is almost certain that it was a 'kill'.

These early radar-equipped Mosquito night fighters proved to be effective machines, but there were still technical difficulties with the night fighter defence system because the equipment could not locate the position of enemy aircraft accurately enough. An attempt to solve the problem led to the development of an airborne searchlight - the Turbinlite' - by Wing Commander W. Helmore, which he arranged to be fitted in the nose of a modified Douglas Havoc Mk.II. The idea

The Ground Control Interception radar system. During the latter stages of the war GCI was introduced, rapidly, progressing to the Type 7 using a 10-metre by 10-metre plane reflector 6 rpm rotating aerial array, with a range of around 60 miles. This radar operated at a frequency of 200 Mhz, with a beam width of 15 deg, the receiver being housed in an underground shelter. Low-level coverage was poor until the introduction of CHEL - Chain Home Extra Low radar. The enemy aircraft at A remains undetected with this system, whereas the Mosquito B and the enemy C are located, with the IFF fitted to the Mosquito giving a distinctive 'blip' on the PPI screen.

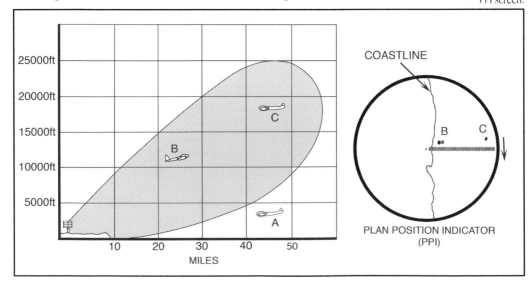

COASTLINE

PLAN POSITION INDICATOR
(PPI)

MILES

The cockpit of the fighter prototype. *(© BAE SYSTEMS)*

was that the Havoc would use GCI and its own AI radar to locate the enemy, then close in to a point where the target could be illuminated with the searchlight to allow the accompanying non- radar-equipped Hurricane fighters to attack.

The Havoc proved to be too slow for enemy interception and, having what was in effect a small formation of single-seat day fighters operating almost blindly around the target in the dark, it was considered too dangerous for the good that might be achieved. The speed and weapon-carrying ability of the Mosquito airframe offered an attractive alternative in order to do away with the Hurricane fighters flying in close proximity, so W4087, an unarmed Mk.II was modified by 1422 Flight at Heston with a 'Turbinlite' in the nose. After testing by 85, 151 and 532 Sqns, whose pilots, by all accounts, did not like the idea at all, the proposal of a four-cannon Turbinlite Mosquito was dropped, for in the meantime technological advances had been made in radar accuracy which rendered such airborne searchlights obsolete.

A rare - possibly the only photograph of the 'Turbinlite' Mosquito W4087 seen at Heston where it was converted. *(© BAE SYSTEMS)*

Perhaps the most famous of all the Mosquito exponents was John Cunningham: *'Operations on the Mosquito night-fighters started at the end of December 1941, when Wing Commander Gordon Slade was given command of 157 Sqn. Gordon Slade was a Boscombe Down pilot, mainly involved in flying the Mosquito prototype, and before taking Command of 157. He spent some time learning the trade of night-fighting by flying Beaufighters in my Squadron, 604, based at Middle Wallop, which was almost next door to Boscombe.*

It was in May 1941 that the first Mosquito fighter prototype was flown, and I was able to fly it at Hatfield at the beginning of July. I had already flown the prototype Mosquito W4050 in early February 1941, before it went to Boscombe Down, and it was clear to me that when the Mosquito was fitted with radar it would be a splendid replacement for the Beaufighter.

I continued with the Beaufighter in 604 Sqn until the end of July 1942, and after a six month break, I returned to operations as the C.O. of 85 Sqn in February 1943 at Hunsdon near Ware: the squadron was equipped with Mosquito II which used Mk.V radar very similar to the Mk.IV equipment fitted in the early Beaufighters. Both these types of radar used external aerials with an 'arrowhead' transmitter aerial on the nose and receiver aerials on the wings near to the wing tips.

In early 1943, Junkers 88s and Dornier 217s were the main targets, and being faster than the Heinkel III, the night-fighter had less time to make his interception and catch the bomber between the East Coast and London. We also needed longer radar range than we had with our Mk.V radar, and a much better Mosquito night-fighter - the Mk.XII was produced and re-equipped my squadron in March 1943.

Centimetric Radar

The AI Mk.IV mentioned earlier operated on a 1.5-metre waveband at a frequency of 190 - 195 MHz which, because of the non-directional nature of the set's transmission signal, produced very strong ground returns. The nature of the signal governed the maximum range, for the lower the altitude the greater the strength of ground returns,

DD744, a F.Mk.II undergoes servicing with the flaps down and cannon-bay doors open to allow access to the guns and ammunition tanks. The machine is also connected to a ground battery pack. *(© BAE SYSTEMS)*

The Type 73 Indicator Unit of the A.I. Mk.VIII radar installation, with the rubber visor in position. *(Simon Peters Collection)*

making it difficult to distinguish the target blip. A new radar was therefore developed which operated on a 10-centimetre waveband instead of the earlier metre band. This shorter wavelength meant that much smaller transmitting and receiving aerials could be used and, by use of electric switching, the same aerial array could be utilized. This compact arrangement allowed a reflector dish to be installed behind the aerial in order to direct and focus the transmitted signal into a narrow beam about 12 degrees wide; this, in turn, created a greatly increased maximum target acquisition range of up to 8 miles, with little of the identifiable ground clutter so noticeable in the Mk.IV. It was discovered that if the aerial and reflector were fixed to point directly ahead of the aircraft, the field of coverage was far too narrow; so the reflector dish oscillated and revolved at high speed to allow a scanned cone of 30 degrees in elevation and azimuth from the centre-line, thereby greatly improving the all-round capability. The Massachusetts Institute of Technology [MIT] in America designed a second system to complement the AI Mk.VIII. This was given the US designation SCR. 720, or RAF AI Mk.X.

When this centimetric radar equipment came into full-scale squadron use, it paved the way for a drastic modification of interception techniques. Instead of the ground controller attempting to get the attacking aircraft into a position behind the target, he was now able to direct the fighter into contact as soon as possible and allow the navigator in the intercepting aircraft to direct the turn on to the enemy aircraft himself. By handing responsibility for the final turn over to the crews themselves, a greater number of interceptions could be handled by the GCI crew, thus increasing the overall efficiency of the radar network. An added bonus of this form of interception was that, by allowing the crews to decide when to start the interception, valuable time, and therefore fuel, could be saved on an otherwise lengthy chase.

The innovative Radiation Laboratory at MIT continued to work hard on improving existing technology and came up with the AI Mk.XV (US AN/APS 4), a very compact scanner - just 14 inches in diameter - with a single CRT display using 'double dot' representation. It proved to be a reasonable low-level radar and could also be used as a navigation aid in a similar manner to an H2S set; its scanner system was fitted in a small torpedo-shaped housing known as the 'thimble' nose.

DZ659/G, a modified Mk.II with a pair of Merlin 21s and the A. I. Mk.X radar fitted in what became known as the 'Universal' nose. *(© BAE SYSTEMS)*

From the very early stages of the use of radar, a means of identifying 'friendly' traces on early warning and GCI equipment was needed. This led to the development of an equipment known as 'Identification Friend or Foe' (IFF). It took the form of a separate transmitter that could be triggered by searching radar beams to give a coded response; such IFF sets were fitted to all Allied aircraft. Problems related to either breakdown or misuse of IFF could and did develop; they taxed the RAF night fighters throughout much of their operational life and

The inside the 'Universal nose' radar dish. Below the access hatch is the camera gun fairing.
(© BAE SYSTEMS)

attacking Mosquitos often made a visual check to ensure that their victim was not friendly. Eventually an IFF infra-red (IR) system was introduced: an IR light-source was fitted to the tails of Allied aircraft and a cockpit-mounted sight was placed in the Mosquito which showed a green spot when a friendly source was viewed.

John Cunningham again: *The new radar was the Mk.VIII, it was housed in a shapely nose-cone and it was the first 10 centimetre wavelength radar, which did away with all external aerials and used a powerful transmitter with a parabolic reflector housed in the nose cone. It still had its four 20 millimetre cannons firing through your feet of course, but it dispensed with the four machine guns that used to be in the nose of the Mosquito II.*

It was in April 1943 that Focke-Wulf 190s were first used at night, mainly to attack London, and to counter these fast raids my Squadron was moved to West Malling near Maidstone. To our great joy and satisfaction we found that using max continuous power from the Merlin throughout the whole climb - from take-off to interception, and with skilful use of the radar by one's Radar Operator - it was just possible to intercept and close in, identify, and then shoot down a Focke-Wulf 190 carrying a bomb. It was really quite remarkable how the Merlin stood up to such harsh treatment.

By the next month, June 1943, the Messerschmitt 410 appeared over Britain, and with performance very similar to the Mosquito, called for all that the Mosquito could produce in performance to close in and destroy it. In October 1943 the Junkers 188 appeared in operation, and was one of the first German bombers to have a tail-warning radar that made the night-fighter's task more difficult. The German bomber force also began to use Window - that was the name given to metal strips that could be dropped in large quantities to confuse both the ground and airborne radar by illuminating the radar tube and obscuring the radar return from aircraft in the Window area.

By February 1944 my Squadron was re-equipped with the Mosquito XVII. It had a change of shape in the nose to house the much improved Mk.10 radar which, with a skilled radar Operator, could see through Window much better than the earlier Mk.VIII radar.

By April 1944 the bomber attacks against London ceased. But in June, the V-l appeared on the scene and the Mosquito played a major part at night in intercepting and shooting them down in the area between the Coastal Anti-Aircraft gun belt - where the guns had freedom to fire at anything - and the London Barrage Balloons.

Airborne Interception Radar Display'

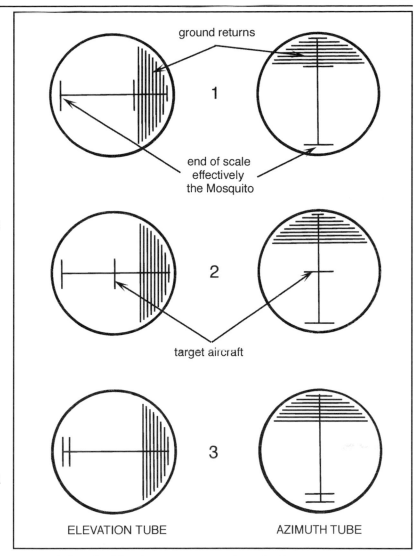

1. The target 'blip' image has emerged from the ground returns at extreme range. The blip on the azimuth tube shows that the target is directly ahead, while the elevation tube indicates that the target is above.

2. The range has decreased with the target directly ahead and above.

3. Target is now almost at minimum range, directly ahead and above. The range is now around 1,000ft and visual contact should be made.

ground returns

1

end of scale effectively the Mosquito

2

target aircraft

3

ELEVATION TUBE   AZIMUTH TUBE

Until the allied landings in Normandy took place in June 1944 radar-equipped night-fighters were not allowed to fly over occupied or enemy territory - to make sure that the radar we used did not fall into enemy hands. But, from June onwards, radar equipped night-fighters were allowed to fly into Germany and had very many successful sorties.

Assistance to Bomber Command

Following a request in 1942 by Sir Arthur Harris, Commander-in-Chief of Bomber Command, to Sir Sholto Douglas, Commander-in-Chief Fighter Command, a number of Mosquitos were used as night escorts to mix in with Bomber Command's bomber streams and engage the enemy night fighters, which were appearing in increasing numbers. *Intruder* Mosquitos were already active in the two-phase *'Flower'* sorties during which Mosquitos first attacked enemy airfields

This NF.Mk.II Mosquito, DZ726 and crew of Wing Commander F W Hillock (left) and Flt Lt P O'Neill Dunne had been on an Intruder flight over Appledorn, Holland on the night of 15 April 1944. They returned with three hundred feet of copper wire wrapped around its fuselage and tail after hitting some overhead cables. *(© BAE SYSTEMS)*

to keep their night fighters on the ground, after which long-range Mosquitos patrolled the enemy's airfields for targets of opportunity while the bombers were operating; but the fear of losing aircraft and their valuable, highly secret radar to the enemy meant that these machines were initially not equipped with radar. This lack of radar meant that crews were operating under a great handicap and reliance on visual identification resulted in a far lower success rate than might otherwise have been expected. (Mosquitos also flew escort duty with the USAAF. In the winter of 1944/45 seven Mosquito NF.XIIIs were assigned to the 425th Night Fighter Squadron based at Etain, France).

Eventually the Mosquitos were allowed to fly over enemy territory carrying radar, albeit in an obsolete form, and protection of the bomber streams passed to 100 Group.

Higher and Faster

Since 1941, when they had first appeared in the Middle East, German high-altitude reconnaissance aircraft had been expected over England. Finally, in mid-August 1942, Junkers Ju.86Ps began lone operations over the south of England. Interception was attempted using the pressure-cabin Spitfire VII fitted with extended wings, but time and time again this proved impossible with heights of 41,000ft often being maintained by the Germans.

Discussions took place at Hatfield on the subject of the modifications required to build an armed Mosquito that would be capable of meeting this intermittent, but serious, threat. Following a request from N E Rowe of the DTD, the De Havilland design staff set to work on converting MP469, the prototype pressure cabin bomber into a fighter. Experience in the use of such cabins was limited at that time but the experimental shop worked flat out on the project for a week. They made use of the nose and four machine-guns that had been cut from DD715 when that machine had been converted to centimetric airborne interception radar; they replaced the bomber's control wheel with a fighter-type stick; changed the front armour plate for a duralumin pressure bulkhead, and the pilot's rear armour for a plywood sheet, but retained the observer's armour as part of the structure.

Following poor results from tests, the four- bladed propellers were 'borrowed' from W4050 to improve high-altitude performance. The entire airframe was then stripped of all unnecessary equipment: bullet-proofing was removed from oil and fuel tanks; the outer and fuselage tanks were removed entirely, leaving just the stub-wing tanks with a capacity of 287 gallons; duplicate radio equipment and aerials were removed; junction boxes were simplified; the bomb door jacks and hydraulic system were replaced and lighter doors were fitted.

The most noticeable external differences were the small-diameter undercarriage wheels and the extended wing-tips which increased the span to 59ft. It was hoped that with these modifications the machine would be able to reach 43,000ft and therefore outclimb the Ju.86s.

The low-pressure cabin, which allowed a 2 lb/sq in differential pressure, was formed in the fuselage by a straight and continuous vertical bulkhead about a foot in front of the instrument panel, together with an aft bulkhead built up in three steps in such a way that all the radio equipment could be included in the cabin behind the occupants. The cabin was pressurized by a Marshall supercharger mounted on and driven by the port engine; this delivered air to the cabin when required, the pilot simply altering a three-position cock behind him to spill air outside the cabin or receive it either hot or cold. The pressurization system was also governed by three controls (two manual, one automatic) plus an emergency relief valve built into the starboard cabin wall. When the manual controls were set to either hot or cold with the relief valve closed, the pressure cabin was automatically controlled by a Westland valve. The valve was designed to allow a gradual build-up of pressure from 15,000 ft until a full differential pressure was reached at around 30,000 ft, after which the pressure was constant. A separate

MP469, the prototype NF.Mk.XV, photographed at Hatfield on 16 September 1942, following the rapid conversion from prototype high-altitude bomber to high-altitude fighter, complete with extended wings and four-bladed propellers. *(© BAE SYSTEMS)*

altimeter and pressure gauge indicated the pressure cabin 'height' with a red warning light set to indicate when the pressure fell below the normal level.

The front panels (pilot's direct vision panel, upper front panels and bulged side panels) of the canopy were made up of double layers of transparent material with silica gel reservoirs connected to the interspaces of these sandwiches to maintain dry air and prevent misting; the remainder of the canopy was single layer Perspex. Entry to and exit from the pressure cabin was via the normal hatch or overhead jettisonable hatch. In general, the installation of the pressure cabin required very few modifications to the normal Mosquito cockpit layout.

By 14 September 1942 all this work had been completed and the aircraft, now some 2,300 lb lighter than a standard Mk.II, was ready for flight. The next day John de Havilland took the machine up to 43,500 ft where it performed well. The aircraft took around 35 minutes to reach 42,000 ft using 105 gallons of fuel to do so; this left enough for about 2 hours' flying at 360 mph. The pressurization of 2 lb/sq in reduced the altitude effect by some 12,000 ft.

Fears were then expressed that the enemy might exploit the high-altitude tactics to stage special night operations in order to distort the defensive radar

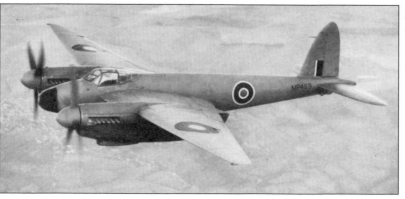

Above: MP469 undergoes engines runs. By now the aircraft had been fitted with the Mk.VIII A.I. radar in the nose, forcing the four .303 machine guns to be re-located into an external, underbelly pack.

Left: MP469 in flight after conversion to Mk.XV standard.
(© BAE SYSTEMS)

The long wingspan of the Mk.XV are clearly visible as MP469 banks away from the camera to also reveal the under-fuselage gun pack. This view also reveals that no underwing roundels were carried and that the underside of the tailplane had exhaust staining all over it! (© BAE SYSTEMS)

screen; thus MP469 went back into the workshops to be fitted with the AI Mk.VIII centimetric radar in a specially constructed nose radome. The machine-guns were relocated in a ventral belly pack which could accommodate 750 rounds per gun, although in normal combat only 500 rounds per gun were carried. Previously the aircraft had been flown as a single-seat fighter to reduce weight, but now, with the AI radar fitted, the observer's position was reinstated and two 24 gallon wing tanks were attached. During manufacturer's tests the aircraft still managed to reach 42,000ft, and was then climbing at an impressive 500ft/min. The aircraft now passed to A&AEE for radar trials at Desford and by late November it was decided to build a further four machines to this standard, to be designated NF.XV.

The A & AEE tested MP469 thoroughly during January 1943 and concluded that the aircraft could normally reach 43,000 ft, taking just under 33 minutes to do so, and could gain another 800 ft by carefully operating the radiator flaps. The pressure cabin was satisfactory and the extent of cabin misting was small. The aircraft's handling qualities were acceptable at all heights and speeds, but there was considerable tail buffet when approaching the stall. The machine was returned to Hatfield to take part in further research flying with the High Altitude Flight. During one of these flights the pilot reported that, when flown with a reduced fuel load, the aircraft was capable of reaching 45,000ft.

These new aircraft were eventually sent to Hunsdon for use by 85 Sqn, under the command of Wing Commander John Cunningham, where they were placed in 'C' Flight for operational trials. Most of the time they were fitted with only two machine-guns, which improved performance somewhat, but with the Germans experiencing trouble with the Ju 86P. John recalls: *'In March 1943 my Squadron received 5 Mosquito XV's which had increased wingspan, and an up-rated high altitude Merlin 77, which enabled them to be flown and use their radar at heights above 40,000 ft. The four cannon were dispensed with, the four machine guns moving to a pod under the fuselage and it had a bomber type windscreen, all with the object of making it a much lighter and more powerful Mosquito. It really did have a remarkable climb and ceiling. Their expected target was the Junkers 86P high altitude reconnaissance aircraft - which had been flown over England without being intercepted in daylight in the Autumn 1942, but it never materialized at night so this very remarkable Mosquito was never put to good use'.*

Combat experience revealed other shortcomings in the Mosquito family: it needed a better rate of climb; greater speed at a height of 20,000ft; and a reduction of windscreen ice build-up. Improvements were already in hand for later marks, either on the drawing boards or production lines, but as an interim measure steps were taken to improve the performance of the existing aircraft. Their Merlin 23s had their cowlings thoroughly cleaned, oil leaks were sealed and carburettor air intake ducts were examined for correct fitment. Despite these and other measures, the improvements were not sufficient and technicians began to work on creating new ways to boost speed. The solution was shortly to present itself courtesy of the Luftwaffe!

During 1943 Britain experienced a new threat, the 'tip and run raider'. RAF fighter pilots discovered that when they closed in for the kill the German raider began to pull away from them. German aero-engine designers were finding extra power from somewhere, but it was not until detailed inspection was made of a captured enemy aircraft that the secret was revealed - the Germans were injecting nitrous oxide gas directly into the engine.

Two Mosquitos were sent to the RAE at Farnborough for the installation of nitrous oxide gas injection equipment. The aircraft were then to be used on trials by 85 Sqn and the Fighter Interception Unit. By the end of 1943 the first machine had made test flights during which a speed increase of 47 mph at 28,000ft was reported, with enough gas carried in pressure bottles for six minutes' use. Such was the urgency of this work that instructions from Cabinet level dictated that no aircraft undergoing such conversion was to be grounded for more than a day. The order was given for fifty Mk.XIIIs to be equipped with the nitrous oxide equipment by Heston Aircraft Co. for operational use by 96 and 410 (RCAF) Sqns. A Fairchild Argus communications aircraft was put at the disposal of the works superintendent to ferry him and essential equipment from Heston to the airfields so that he could resolve problems on the spot. The immediate task, and problem, was to provide nitrous oxide gas from three bottles, of the same size and weight as commercial welding cylinders, directly into the carburettors of the Merlin engines. The bottles were installed in the fuselage and the relevant pipework ran out to each engine with extra controls fitted in the cockpit. The engines were not designed to stand up to the sort of punishment the gas injection was expected to inflict, but such was the desperation to catch the raiders that the 'punch' given by 'overspeeding' was considered worth the risk. Rolls-Royce's technical experts were therefore somewhat surprised when, after stripping the engines after 200 hours' running time, they found them in excellent condition. The conversion of the 50 aircraft was completed in just 20 days and their first 'kill' occurred on 2/3 January 1944 when HK374 'VY:L' of 85 Sqn, flown by John Cunningham, caught and destroyed a Messerschmitt Me 410 near Le Bourget. The frantic work to increase the Mosquito's speed was completed just in time, for the German 'tip and run' raids climaxed in late January 1944 with 'The Little Blitz', a series

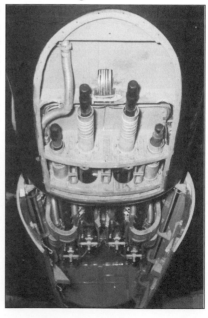

A close up of the four 20 mm Hispano cannon fitted to a Mk.XIII night fighter.
(© BAE SYSTEMS)

The AI indicator unit for the AI Mk.X radar as mounted in a Mosquito Mk.30. showing the two scopes. The small CRT below is for either *Monica VIII* or *Perfectos II*. The circular mounting top left is for an infra-red telescope.

of heavy raids on London.

Let John Cunningham explain what happened during the final stages of a night-time interception: *'Once radar contact had been made - ideally at some two to three miles range, one's own radar operator would aim to turn one on to a heading that would bring you on to the target's heading and usually slightly below its height. Your operator would call out the range, and you would adjust your speed so that you would close to a range of about 1,000ft. behind your target at the same speed, and about 100-200ft. below it. From that point you might, on a dark night, see a flicker of exhaust flames, for the minimum range that your radar could work to was about 6-800ft.*

Having seen the exhausts or an outline of some aircraft, you closed in very slowly right beneath your target so that you could identify what it was. Having satisfied yourself that it was not one of our aircraft you then had to very gradually move back and up to a point immediately behind and about the same level and then, as the target gradually sank down into your gunsight, you fired. We never used tracer in our ammunition because if you did not hit it immediately, you did not advertise your presence and alarm your target.

I clearly remember firing once and seeing no hits - every one in two or three rounds we fired was an explosive shell, which would show if you hit your target and my target or its gunner did not react, and I had to sink down below it and close in further to see it again clearly, and then come up slowly again, and closer, and on the second firing I demolished it!

Being close behind your target when you hit it, you were liable to fly through bits left in the air - and the only weakness of the Mosquito was that it had its radiators in the leading edge between the engines and the fuselage, and it only needed a piece of perspex or light structure to penetrate it and you lost your coolant, then had to feather your propeller.

Another hazard which shows what happened to one of my Squadron's Mosquitos when it was close in and covered in burning fuel from its target. You will see the cockpit canopy was completely blackened with soot, and all the fuselage madapolam and wing surface were burnt, and the fabric on the rudder was completely burnt away. Yet this aircraft flew back and landed safely at West Malling.

Finally, there was the hazard of fire from the rear gunner of the target aircraft, and I would not be here today but for the effectiveness of the bullet-proof windscreen deflecting two very well aimed shots, from a Junkers 188 that I had just identified from beneath, and just as I was slowly going up to get in position to shoot his gunners saw me and fired on me from above. As my view was spoilt and I had a face showered with small sharp granules from

The results of getting too close to one's opponent!

This Mosquito night-fighter appears to be distinctly 'toasted' after destroying an enemy aircraft. Unfortunately all markings and the aircraft's serial number appear to have been burnt off!

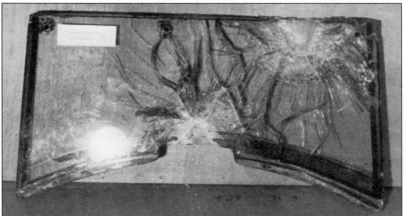

The bullet-proof windscreen taken from John Cunningham's fighter Mosquito after it had been stuck by shells from a German night-fighter. John Cunningham escaped with splinters of glass in his face.
(both © BAE SYSTEMS)

Group Captain John Cunningham CBE, DSO & two Bars, DFC & Bar, (27 July 1917 – 21 July 2002)
(all © BAE SYSTEMS)

the broken screen, I had to break off the engagement and return to West Malling.

Day Fighter Conversions

Day fighter escort patrols, code-named 'Instep', were flown by Mosquitos from Coastal Command in 1942, the aircraft taking over the role from the slower Bristol Beaufighters. The patrols were partly defensive, as the aircraft were intended to protect shipping in the area, but they were beginning to adopt a more offensive posture by attacking enemy fighters protecting U-boats which had to pass through the area on the way to the occupied French west coast ports. With the introduction of Mosquito fighter-bombers. Coastal Command went completely on the offensive, attacking U-boats and enemy shipping, as will be related later.

In December 1942 Air Marshal Leigh-Mallory decided that Fighter Command's Mosquitos were also to adopt a more offensive stance with the formation of an independent tactical force of Mosquito fighter- intruders. These would concentrate on offensive roles and be held at readiness under the code-name of '*Intruder*' patrols. A number of aircraft from 25, 85, 151, 157 and 264 Sqns had their radar sets removed in order to prevent capture by the enemy and *'Gee'* (equipment to ensure accurate navigation) installed in its place. To give the aircraft a greater punch the ammunition carried for the 20mm cannon was increased from 175 to 225 rounds per gun.

A complementary form of Mosquito operation were *'Ranger'* flights in which aircrew were allowed to make freelance deep penetration raids into a specified area. The aim of these *'Ranger'* missions was to force the enemy to maintain a fighter force at a high state of readiness, to deploy it and hopefully suffer destruction, to disrupt his training schedules and to attack his transport. *'Day Ranger'* flights were only made during daylight hours when there was good cloud cover from well out to sea into the target area, but *'Night Ranger'* flights could be undertaken in any weather, although only against ground targets on moonlit nights. *'Ranger'* aircraft were as often as not out of contact with home base, whereas on *'Intruder'* patrols they were not.

During late December 1943 it was decided that, in order to increase the amount of aircraft available for *'Ranger'* operations, some of the night fighter Mosquitos in Fighter Command were to be equipped with long-range tanks, thus permitting them to make daylight cloud cover patrols.

Tactical requirements were changing with the Allies now prepared to take on the role of attacker, so the stage was set for many of these fighter-orientated operations to become even more offensive by exchanging their Mosquito fighters for fighter-bombers.

Malta and the Middle East

After five months of successful intruder operations in Europe, a number of Mosquito NF.IIs were despatched to Malta and the Middle East in December 1942 where they served initially with 23 Sqn. The Mosquitos in Malta were charged to harass the enemy at night by operating *'Ranger'* and *'Intruder'* flights over Sicily, where the long, open roads full of enemy troops offered tempting targets for ground-strafing Mosquitos. Torpedo-bombers were already operating out of Malta and, with the British Army preparing to attack Tripoli, the easiest way of affording

DD673 YP:F of 23 Sqn is seen after crashing into a steamroller at Manston. *(Simon Peters Collection)*

fighter protection was by pre-emptive strikes on the enemy's air bases.

Night sorties were also flown against the open roads of North Africa, filled with German motor-transport, which offered fine targets for ground-strafing Mosquitos. It became common practice for pilots to let off a few rounds of tracer in the direction of a convoy, then watch the German gunners return their fire, thus revealing their positions. The attack would then be made where the transport column was unprotected. The final ground-level escape often caused the German gunners to hit their own trucks in an effort to get the marauding Mosquito in their sights.

Difficulties encountered during ground-strafing led 23 Sqn to borrow an idea from 151 Sqn which they modified to suit local conditions. A Barr and Stroud GM.2 day reflector sight had its glass screen removed so that the reflection shone directly on to the windscreen; this left the entire windscreen clear apart from the red target image floating in front of the pilot, who was now able to judge his distance from the ground and sight on the target at the same time. This was, in effect, an early version of the head-up display. The idea had first been tried by 609 Sqn flying Typhoons from Mansion and led by Roland Beamont, but was frowned upon by Air Ministry experts who regarded the optical qualities of the windscreens as a poor reflecting medium. Problems were encountered with a troublesome 'double image' occurring on the glass when the graticule was turned up to full brilliance, but since the modified sight was used mostly at night, or during very poor daylight conditions, full brilliance was rarely if ever used.

With many of the operations taking the form of low-level attacks, Mosquitos were frequently returning with battle-damage from flak and small arms rifle fire directed at them by members of the Italian Home Guard. Difficulties in getting spares to Malta meant that repairs to the wooden structure were of a make-do nature, using wood from cigar boxes, bits of already damaged bomb doors or old tea chests. Even the local coffin-maker's talents were called upon, and he got some very strange looks from the squadron's pilots when he was seen working on the aircraft. Such improvisation showed, once again, the benefits of timber construction. By February the spares had still not arrived from Britain, but the mechanics still managed to keep all the aircraft in the air. Many ground-strafing trips along the coastline of the Italian mainland were flown at this time and the

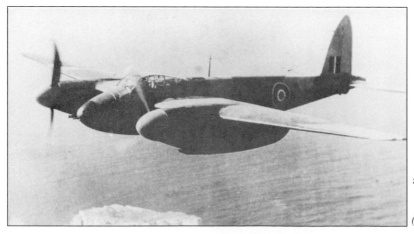

The first Mosquito to arrive in Malta was DZ230 - a Mk.II intruder belonging to 23 Sqn. *(Simon Peters Collection)*

squadron took great delight in attacking any train they could find. Since much of the Italian railway system was electrified and received its power from overhead wires the enemy could not mount any sizeable flak guns on the trains; this was an unexpected advantage for the pilots and made any attacks that bit easier. During one such incident a pilot managed to create a short circuit that melted the rails beneath the train!

Mosquitos constantly patrolled the Italian airfields, and to great effect. When the battle for North Africa reached its peak, the stranglehold held by the Mosquito on the Axis bases was so great that all enemy night movements were reduced to the minimum. The speed of the Mosquito allowed Tripoli - by now in Allied hands - to notify Air Headquarters of an outgoing enemy raid and the AHQ would direct the speedy Mosquitos to the bases from which the enemy had set out, keep them closed and await their return in order to ambush them. If the Mosquito intruder did not get the enemy machine while it was in circuit, there was a good chance of catching it while it landed on its own runway.

The Malta units were further strengthened by a detachment from 256 Sqn equipped with NF.Mk.XIIs - an interim conversion of the NF.Mk.II with an AI Mk.VIII installed in the nose in place of the Browning machine- guns. The remainder of the squadron flew out to Malta during October and a month later re-equipment with more sophisticated NF.Mk.XIIIs began, allowing the squadron to take on the commitment of the defence of Malta by day and night.

After the fighting in the Mediterranean basin peaked, the Allied High Command's focus of attention shifted towards the forthcoming invasion of Western Europe. However, the Malta-based Mosquitos played their part attacking the south of France - 'the soft underbelly of Europe'.

HK128 of 256 Sqn at Luqa in 1944. A detachment of six Mosquitos from 256 arrived in Malta on 2 July 1943, to be joined by the rest of the squadron in October. (Simon Peters Collection)

Flying Bomb Interdiction

At 4.28am on 13 June 1944 a new menace revealed itself when the first of the German Fieseler Fi.103 flying bombs fell on Swanscombe in Kent. When tested over the ranges at Peenemunde, this weapon was designated FZG.76 (*Fernziegerat,* or long-range target apparatus 76); it later became known to the Germans as *Vergeltungswaffe 1* (reprisal weapon 1, or simply V-l). The Home Defence forces reacted to the threat by installing anti- aircraft guns to the south

of London and barrage balloons to provide close-in protection. Outer defence was the responsibility of fighters including four Mosquito squadrons - 96, 219, 409, and 418 - which were tasked with the destruction of flying bombs. The Mosquito fighters, usually NF.Mk.XIXs, formed 'Anti- Diver' patrols, extending to a line over the French coast.

The speedy Mosquitos had no great difficulty in catching the V-ls when they were at about 2,500ft and travelling at about 350 mph. The Mosquitos had Merlin 25 engines with their flame dampers removed so they 'breathed' better and their superchargers were adjusted to give +24 lb boost with 150-octane fuel. Localized strengthening was carried out around the nose area to withstand the effects of cannon fire at such high speeds. The normal aim was to catch the bomb in the 30 miles between France and the UK ground defences; the tactic used was to patrol at around 8,000ft - if the weather was clear - in an attempt to spot launches and to have a 5,000 to 6,000ft height advantage over the V-l. The pilot of the Mosquito could then use the dive to increase his speed and intercept his target.

That was the theory, judging the course and distance of these small flying machines was another matter. If the V-l was spotted early enough, it was possible to fly just in front of the flying bomb and use the turbulence of the Mosquito's slipstream to force the V-1s gyroscopes to topple and lose control of the machine. Various ranging devices were tried, with little effect, so it fell to the Bomber Support Development Unit to come to the rescue of Fighter Command by installing the 'Monica IIIe' tail-warning radar in the forward position to provide accurate ranging.

This may well have been a posed picture, but it demonstrates the excellent access afforded to the armourers to arm, or work on the cannon.(Simon Peters Collection)

Several problems faced the pilot of a fighter attempting to intercept a flying bomb. First, he had to get on a course behind the V-l and then close in for the attack. Secondly, he had to make contact well before his own ground defence guns opened up with proximity-fuse shellfire which did not distinguish between his aircraft and the flying bomb; finally, when he got within range there was always the difficulty of being too close to the bomb when his shells hit. Several aircraft returned to their bases with the paint scorched and fabric torn off the control surfaces, caused by flying through an exploding V-l. These difficulties notwithstanding, of a total of 7,547

MM652, a NF. Mk.XIX (Simon Peters Collection)

flying bombs ramp-launched against Britain, 1,866 were brought down by fighters. At the peak of these attacks more than 600 were shot down in two months - a large number of which can be credited to the Mosquito.

Bomber Support and Electronic Warfare

As mentioned earlier. Mosquitos without radar were introduced as fighter escorts for Bomber Command sorties in 1942, but it was not until June 1943 that approval was given for such sorties to be flown over enemy territory with radar-equipped fighters. Given the relative slowness of the Beaufighter, the Mosquito NF.Mk.XVI was proposed as the ideal aircraft for the purpose.

Eventually, on 23 November 1943, 100 Group, under the command of Air Commodore E. B. Addison, was formed in Bomber Command to control the operation of radio counter-measures from both the air and ground, and to organize night fighter protection for the bomber streams; it was also known as Bomber Support or Special Duties Group.

The pioneering operations of the group resulted in an escalation of 'attack and counter- attack' equipment, developed to meet a particular threat from the opposing side.

In this branch of service the superbly performing Mosquito came into direct contact with the experimental, highly secret world of high-technology electronic equipment - the realm of 'boffins' and 'black boxes'. The bewildering array of devices staggered the aircrews, but from this crude beginning there evolved the whole range of passive and active electronic counter-measures that are available to the world's armed forces today. In many respects, 100 Group was self-contained for it was equipped with its own support training facilities - in the form of 1692 Bomber Support Training Unit, which taught aircrews the specialist techniques involved in their sort of operation - and its own Electronic Development Unit, which worked closely with the scientists to facilitate the rapid development of new equipment from experimental to operational use.

The *'Serrate II'* black boxes mounted in the nose of a Mosquito Mk.II. This picture shows also the Type 19 transmission aerial for the AI IV radar and the lack of machine guns in *'Serrate'* equipped aircraft.
(Simon Peters Collection)

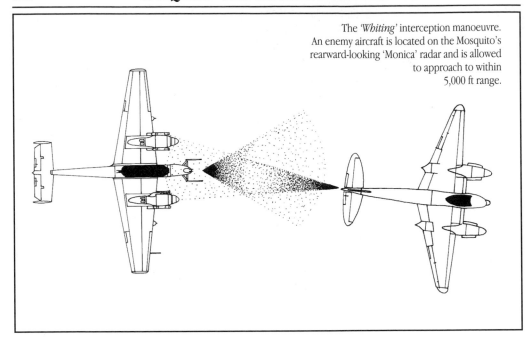

The *'Whiting'* interception manoeuvre. An enemy aircraft is located on the Mosquito's rearward-looking 'Monica' radar and is allowed to approach to within 5,000 ft range.

When the enemy has reached this point, the Mosquito pilot makes a rapid swing around through 360 degrees in an attempt to close with the radar contact from astern.

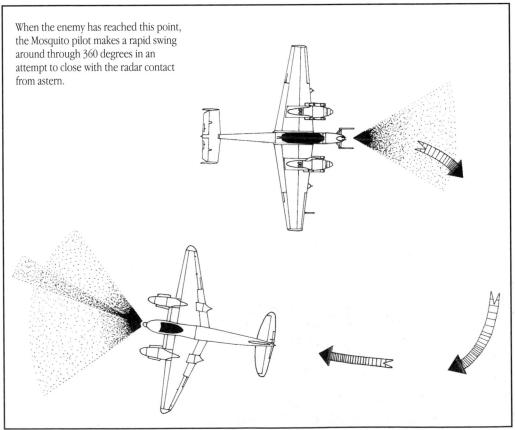

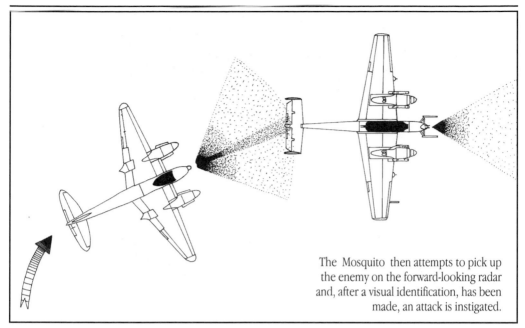

The Mosquito then attempts to pick up the enemy on the forward-looking radar and, after a visual identification, has been made, an attack is instigated.

The 'Serrate' display. The distinctive 'herringbone' pattern on the 'Serrate' CRT gives an indication of relative altitude and bearing of the German night fighter when using its radar. The more numerous and longer images on the lower part of the elevation and to the right of the azimuth displays indicate that the target is to the right and flying at a lower level. The 'Serrate' display's limitation was that it could not give the range, so could only be used in conjunction with the AI radar to achieve a successful interception.

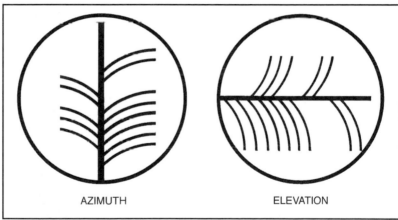

AZIMUTH   ELEVATION

It was decided to make use of technology to exploit the fact that German aircraft had no rearward-facing radar. Two Mosquito NF.Mk.IIs were equipped at the Fighter Interception Unit with a second radar transmitter, codenamed *'Monica'*, which faced aft to establish rear contact and enable the pilot to use his speed to sweep round and hit the enemy from behind, a manoeuvre known as *'Whiting'*. Special sorties or *''Mahmoud'* flights were undertaken to capitalize on this German vulnerability; during such flights a single aircraft would wait at a known Luftwaffe fighter assembly point in the hope of catching enemy fighters before they reached the bomber streams.

'Serrate' was the code-name for another state-of-the-art device which allowed the RAF to home in on enemy transmissions from as far as 100 miles away. While 141 Sqn awaited its new Mk.XVI Mosquitos it was given a number of NF.Mk.II fighters fitted with long-range fuel tanks to fly their missions with the Mk.II

'*Serrate*' equipment. This was designed to intercept signals from the German FuG 202/212 airborne radars and was effective at a range of 50 miles when the transmission source was aimed directly at it, or 10 miles when the enemy transmitter was facing away from the receiver. The intercepted signals were displayed on a CRT in the cockpit and later versions, in particular the Mk.IV, gave an audible indication with either 'dots' or 'dashes' to indicate the direction of the interceptor.

DD723, a NF.Mk.II fitted with experimental Lancaster-type power units with underslung 'chin' radiators instead of the normal wing leading-edge ones. This aircraft was tested by Rolls-Royce at Hucknall during the latter part of 1943 in an attempt to cure the over-heating and exhaust problems.
(© BAE SYSTEMS)

'*Serrate*' was issued to three squadrons in 100 Group - 141, 169 and 239. These squadrons were fitted with obsolete AI radar which enabled them to fly deep into Germany and their navigators were given special training for forthcoming operations. The fighter patrols could be divided into three types:

1.   Fighters flown in the general bomber target area during or after a bomber raid to await enemy night fighters. (This proved to be more successful after a raid because the concentrated activity of the attack brought the German night fighters to the area.)
2.   Flights of Mosquitos despatched to patrol around the known enemy night fighter assembly points.
3.   Escort patrols given to the bomber stream from about 40 miles away.

It soon became evident that the Mosquito F.IIs received by 100 Group were badly worn; trouble was encountered with the radar, but the main cause lay in the condition of the Merlin engines which frequently cut out on take-off. It was decided to reduce operational flying while the entire fleet's engines were changed to Merlin Mk.22s which cured much of the trouble.

In mid-1944 the order was given for all Mk.II aircraft to be replaced by '*Serrate*' equipped Mk.VIs, but the operational demands with the imminent invasion of Europe up and coming, the Mk.IIs were forced to remain in service for a while longer. Keeping possibly dangerous aircraft in service had its drawbacks, not to mention the operational limitations of its crude electronic equipment, as is illustrated by the experiences of Flying Officer A. C. Gallacher and Warrant Officer G. McLean flying Mk.II DD736 on a '*Serrate*' patrol to Aachen and Bourg-Leopold in May 1944.

A quick clean of the nose gun bay. Armourers took care with this task, for accumulated dirt could easily lead to the guns jamming.

Lapping in the .303 ammunition. Each box could hold 1000 rounds, usually of mixed types with day or night tracer spaced to individual tastes. *(both Simon Peters Collection)*

They took off at 0110 hrs and crossed the coast 45 minutes later; just a few minutes afterwards, when flying at 28,000 ft, a *'Serrate'* indication showed to port and below. They turned to intercept on 060 deg and had chased for four minutes when the contact dived off to starboard. Immediately a rearwards AI contact was made, slightly to port and at 5,000ft range on the same level. They turned to starboard but the contact did not reappear. At 0220hrs three more *'Serrate'* contacts were made at 22,000ft, apparently coming from Bourg-Leopold. The aircraft was turned on to the contacts and singled one out. They had been chasing it for eight minutes, and were almost within AI range, when the starboard engine cut out with the propeller feathered. Worryingly, they now picked up one AI contact forward and one to the rear at about 2,000ft range; their radar then suddenly went out of service too and they took the safety option of peeling off down to 12,000ft and returning to base on one engine, where they landed at 0340hrs.

These operations were generally unspectacular but they played an important part in dislocating German night fighter operations by posing a grave threat to all the German night fighters, either while they were seeking the British bombers or when they returned to base and attempted to land.

While engines and airframes deteriorated, the search never let up for greater Allied knowledge of German radio broadcasts across the entire frequency range. This work led to the creation of an early form of ELINT (ELectronic INTelligence) gathering using three Mosquito Mk.IVs (DZ375, DZ376, and DZ410) delivered to 1474 Flight. These aircraft were fitted with a special radio-countermeasures system, code-named *'Boozer'*, which allowed them to detect and record the enemy's radio and radar transmissions up to 3,000 Mhz. They operated throughout 1944 snooping on signals, broadcasts, investigating, identifying and then plotting the position and wavelengths of the enemy's radar stations. They gathered vitally important information on the *Würzburg* ground-controlled interception radar and the FuG.216 airborne radar, data which was used to develop Allied counter-measures equipment and tactics. Examples of such important developments were the RAF jammer systems used to support main force bombing raids such as *'Dina'*, aimed at radar in the 95-210 Mhz range, and *'Piperack'*, targeted specifically at the German SN-2 radar.

Meanwhile, despite the technological advances, Bomber Command experienced mounting losses to enemy fighters. To counter this, two more Mosquito squadrons, 85 and 157, were transferred to 100 Group operations. 85 Sqn was the first to receive the advanced night fighter variant, the Mk.XIX equipped with either the AI Mk.VIII, AI Mk.X or SCR720 airborne interception radar and powered by two Rolls-Royce Merlin 25s. Although this particular variant was more of a night

A 'Boozer' unit developed to detect the which allowed them to detect and record the enemy's radio and radar transmissions up to 3,000 Mhz. The Mosquito-equped 1474 Flight gathered vitally important information on the *Würzburg* ground-controlled interception radar and the FuG.216 airborne radar, data which was used to develop Allied counter-measures equipment and tactics.

fighter than a specialized machine for bomber support operations, such a long-endurance aircraft possessing the latest radar was a considerable asset in Bomber Command's efforts to counter the successful German night fighters. The new radar projected a beam for over five miles ahead of the fighter, instead of in all directions as with the old Mk.IV which could be badly affected by ground returns. The radar screen also provided the navigator with information on the position of his aircraft relative to the foe.

As the Allies had instigated *'Window'* to confuse German radar, it was expected that the Germans would retaliate, which they duly did with *'Duppel'*. The AI Mk.VIII radar proved vulnerable to this material and the decision was taken to replace it with the more resistant American SCR-720 radar, then becoming available under Lend-Lease. Now designated AI Mk.X, the new radar was promptly fitted to the Mosquito Mk.XIX; unfortunately it had no rearward-looking facility and therefore *'Monica I',* devised by 100 Group's own Bomber Support Development Unit, had to be fitted. The Germans themselves were not idle in this field. On 13 July 1944 a Ju 88G-6B night fighter, belonging to 7 Staffel of NJG 2 operating from Volkel in Holland, landed by accident at Woodbridge in Suffolk. Before they could destroy anything, the crew and aircraft were captured by Sergeant K. E. Clifton. Subsequent investigation revealed that the Ju 88 carried *'Lichtenstein SN-2'* radar plus *'Naxos'* and *'Flensburg'* devices. The SN-2 radar, referred to earlier, was used by the Germans to jam the AI Mk.IV radar and it was the successful use of this instrument that led to the fall-off in the *'Serrate'* Mosquitos' own success rate and prompted development of *'Serrate'* Mk.IV. *'Naxos'* was used to home in on Allied H2S sets while *'Flensburg'* homed in on the *'Monica'* tail-warning radar.

It was very much a 'stroke and counter-stroke' game, with the Allies developing *'Perfectos'* to home in on the enemy IFF equipment installed in German fighters, the FuG 25a *'Erstling'*. Switching off the radar to avoid being picked up by a *'Serrate'* Mosquito was no guarantee of immunity once *'Perfectos'* was brought into use. It sent out an interrogation pulse and, if the German pilot was following the correct procedure by having his identification equipment switched on, any contact provoked an involuntary response which was displayed on the cockpit CRT of the Mosquito, allowing the pilot to home in on an accurate bearing and range. A side benefit was that the nature of this response provided the Mosquito pilot with positive proof that the target was the enemy. Of course, the Germans became aware of this and resorted to switching off their IFF to avoid betrayal; but this then had the unfortunate effect of making them appear as enemy aircraft on their own ground defenders' radar screens, and therefore liable to attack from their own radar-directed flak batteries and other night fighters.

Conclusions

The Mosquito was one of the most devastating fighting machines of the Second World War. The number of enemy aircraft destroyed by Mosquito fighters will never be accurately known, although it is thought that the night fighter alone accounted for some 600 German raiders in its three years' service. It is safe to say, however, that the rapid development of variants to counter the threat of either high speed or high-flying enemy aircraft coupled with tremendous developments in the use of both ground-based and airborne radars played a vital part in creating an almost impenetrable Mosquito 'umbrella' which prevented large-scale night attacks against Britain and the Allied forces in Europe and the Middle East from 1943 onwards.

The specialized use of the Mosquito, not only as a pure night fighter but, when used by 100 Group, also as a machine fitted with a veritable battery of electronic equipment to counter, confuse and deceive the enemy, was vitally important in assisting Bomber Command during the latter stages of the war in Europe.

	F/NF.II	NF.XII	NF.XIII	NF.XV	FB.VI	NF.XVII	NF.30	NF.38
FIGHTER/NIGHT FIGHTER DATA								
Span	54ft 2in	54ft 2in	54ft 2in	52ft 6in	54ft 2in	54ft 2in	54ft 2in	54ft 2in
Length	40ft 6in	40ft 6in	40ft 6in	44ft 6in	40ft 6in	40ft 6in	40ft 6in	40ft 6in
Height	12ft 6in	12ft 6in	12ft 6in	12ft 6in	12ft 6in	12ft 6in	12ft 6in	12ft 6in
Tare weight	13,431lb	13,696lb	15,300lb	13,746lb	14,344lb	13,224lb	13,400lb	16,000lb
All-upweight	18,547lb	19,700lb	20,000lb	17,600lb	22,258lb	19,200lb	21,600lb	21,400lb
Max speed	370 mph	370 mph	370 mph	412 mph	378 mph	370 mph	407 mph	404 mph
Cruising speed	255 mph	255 mph	255 mph	230 mph	255 mph	255 mph	250 mph	
Initial climb	3,000ft/min	3,000ft/min	3,000ft/min	3,500ft/min	2,850ft/min	3,000ft/min	2,850ft/min	
Ceiling	36,000 ft	36,000 ft	34,500 ft	43,000 ft	33,000 ft	36,000 ft	38,000 ft	36,000 ft
Max range	1,705 miles	1,705 miles	2,450 miles	1,030 miles	1,855 miles	1,705 miles	1,300 miles	
Engines RR Merlin	Mk.21 or 23	Mk.21 or 23	Mk.21 or 23	Mk.72 &73	Mk.21, 22,25	Mk.21 or 23	Mk.113 &114	Mk.113 &114
Armament	4xmg 4x cannon	4x cannon	4x cannon	1 x57mm 8xRP,or combination	4xmg 4x cannon	4x cannon	4x cannon	4x cannon

Performance data charts are for main types of fighter and night fighter variants incorporating known data
Note. While early marks could have a range of engine marks fitted, later machines were fitted with 'handed' (i.e., rotating in different directions), hence two consecutive marks
Note. FB.VI could carry a combination of 2mg+57mm cannon and RPs under wings or4mg+4 cannon+RPs under wings

SQUADRONS THAT USED FIGHTER VARIANTS OF THE MOSQUITO

SQN	CODE	VARIANT	FROM	TO	REMARKS
23	YP	F.2	7/42	9/45	Initially based at Ford; moved to Malta 12/42. Moved to Italy following
		FB.6			invasion before return ing to UK(Little Snoring) 5/44 on intruder work.
		NF.30			Disbanded 25/9/45 at Little Snoring. Re-formed at Wittering as night
		NF.30	9/46	5/52	fighter sqn. To Coltishall 2/47. To Church Fenton 11/49. To Coltishall
		NF.36			9/50. Re-equipped with Vampire NF.10
25	ZK	F.2	5/42	11/51	Initially based at Church Fenton but moved through a number of
		FB.6			British airfields. Used on intruder/defensive and bomber support until
		NF.17			end of war. Retained as night fighter sqn post-war until re-equipped
		NF.30			with Vampire NF.10
		NF.36			
27	-	F.2	5/43	3/44	Based at Agartala, India. Operated in Burma. Later Parashuram 2/44.
		FB.6			Re-equipped with Beaufighters
29	RO	NF.12	10/42	10/50	Initially based at Bradwell Bay. Used for Air Defence of Great Britain.
		FB.6			To Ford 9/43. To Drem 3/44. From 5/44 until 2.45 used on intruder
		NF.13			work from West Malling, Hunsdon and Colerne. To Mansion 4/45.
		NF.30			Retained as a night fighter sqn post-war. Re-equipped with
		NF.36			Meteor NF.11.
36	-	FB.6	10/46	10/47	Renumbered from 248 Sqn at Thorney Island 10/46. Disbanded 14/10/47
39	-	FB.6	2/46	9/46	Based in Sudan until disbanded 9/46. Re-formed at Fayid, Egypt, as sole
		NF.30	3/49	3/53	nightfighter unit for defence of Suez Canal.
		NF.36			Re-equipped with Meteor NF.13.
45	OB	FB.6	2/44	5/46	Initially based at Yelahanka, India, then moved through several Far East
					bases. Re-equipped with Beaufighters 12/45.
46	-	NF.12	7/44	12/44	Based in Eastern Mediterranean until returned to UK 9/1/45 and re-
					equipped with Short Stirling V as a transport unit
47	KU	FB.6	10/44	1/46	Initially based at Yelahanka, India, then moved through several Far East
					bases. Disbanded at Butterworth, Malaya, 21/1/46
55	-	FB.26	6/46	11/46	Based at Hassani, Greece, where disbanded 1/11/46
68	WM	NF.17	7/44	2/45	Initially based at Castle Camps. Used for interception of V-1 flying bombs and
		NF.19			counter-intruder work along east coast. To Coltishall 10-44, to Wittering 2/45,
		NF.30			to Coltishall 2/45. To Church Fenton, where disbanded 20/4/45.
82	UX	FB.6	7/44	3/46	Operated in Burma and later India until disbanded at St. Thomas Mount
					(Madras) 15/3/46.
84	PY	FB.6	2/45	12/46	Based throughout Far East, buttook no part in war with Japanese using
					Mosquitos. Re-equipped with Beaufighters 12/46
85	VY	F.2	8/42	7/43	Initially based at Hunsdon. Intruder missions began 3/43.
		NF.12			Used the experimental high-altitude Mk.15 Mosquito.
		NF.13			Transferred to West Mailing and 100 Group 1/5/44 for bomber support
		NF.15			missions. Retained as a night fighter sqn post-war at Tangmere, later
		NF.17			West Mailing. Re-equipped with Meteor NF.11
		NF.30			
		NF.36			
89	-	FB.6	2/45	3/46	Based in Ceylon. Aircraft were transferred 3/46.
		NF.19			Disbanded at Seletar 1/5/46
96	2J	NF.12	6/43	12/44	Initially based at Honiley. To Church Fenton 8/43.
		NF.13			Operated as night fighters and against V-1 s. To Drem 9/43, to West
					Malling 11/43, to Ford 6/44. To Odiham 9/44 where disbanded 12/44.
107	OM	FB.6	2/44	10/48	Initially based at Lasham. Used on night intruder work. Moved through
					several UK bases before moving to Germany 11/45. Re-numbered 11 Sqn
					4/10/48
108	-	NF.12	2/44	7/44	Based at Luqa, Malta. Supplemented Beaufighters
125	VA	NF.17	2/44	11/45	Initially based at Valley. Moved to Hum, later Middle Wallop. Covered
		NF.30			European invasion and participated in V-1 patrols. Disbanded 20/11/45,
					with aircraft passing to 264 Sqn.

SQN	CODE	VARIANT	FROM	TO	REMARKS
141	TW	F.2	10/43	12/43	Initially based at Wittering. Transferred to 100 Group on bomber support work
					To West Raynham 12/43. To Little Snoring 7/45, where disbanded 7/9/45.
		NF.36	6/46	10/51	Re-formed at Wittering as night fighter sqn. Re-equipped with Meteor NF.11
143	NE	NF.2	10/44	5/45	Formed part of Banff Strike Wing. Disbanded 25/5/45, became 14 Sqn
		FB.6			
151	DZ	NF.2	4/42	10/46	Used on intruder work from Colerne. Moved to Cornwall on same duties.
		NF.13			Moved to East Anglia on bomber support duties 10/44 from Castle Camps.
		T.29			To Hunsdon 11/44, Bradwell Bay 3/45, Predannack 5/45, Exeter 6/46,
		NF.30			Colerne 9/46. To Weston Zoyland, where disbanded 10/10/46.
157	RS	NF.2	1/42	8/44	First Mosquito nightfighter sqn. Based initially at Castle Camps.
					Transferred to 100 Group for bomber support work.
169	VI	F.2	10/43	8/45	Formed at Ayr. Moved to Little Snoring under control of 100 Group for bomber
					support duties 12/43. To Great Massingham 6/44, where disbanded 10/8/45.
176	-	NF.19	6/45	6/46	Based in India. Never listed as operational. Disbanded at Baigachi 1/6/46
199	-	NF.36	7/51	3/53	Re-formed at Watton as part of 90 Signals Group on radio counter-
					measures work. To Hemswell 4/52. Mosquitos phased out by 3/53
219	FK	NF.17	2/44	9/46	Initially based at Woodvale after re-equipment. To Honiley 2/44, Bradwell Bay
		NF.30			5/44, Hunsdon 8/44 as part of 2 Tactical Air Force. Moved into Europe 10/44.
					Disbanded at Acklington 1/9/46
235	LA	FB.6	6/44	7/45	Initially based at Portreath. Moved to Banff 9/44 on anti-shipping strike duties.
					Disbanded at Banff 10/7/45
239	HB	NF.2	12/43	7/45	Initially equipped at West Raynham. Formed part of 100 Group on bomber
		FB.6			support work. Flew occasional day bombing raids in last stages of war.
		NF.30			Disbanded at West Raynham 1/7/45
248	DM	FB.6	12/43	9/46	Initially equipped at Predannack. Anti-shipping and fighter-reconnaissance
	WR	FB.18			missions. To Portreath 2/44, Banff 9/44, Chivenor 7/45. Disbanded and
					re-numbered 36 Sqn at Chivenor 30/9/46
254	QM	FB.18	4/45	5/45	Initially equipped at North Coates as anti-shipping sqn.
					Re-equipped with Beaufighters
255	YD	NF.19	1/45	4/46	Initially equipped in Sicily, to Rosignano 2/45. Movedto
		NF.30			Malta 9/45, then Egypt 1/46. Disbanded at Gianaclis, Egypt, 30/4/46
256	JT	NF.12	5/43	9/45	Initially equipped at Ford. Detachment to Malta 7/43 to cover invasion of
		NF.13			Sicily. Entire sqn moved to Malta 10/43. Moved to Algeria 4/44,
		FB.6			to Sardinia 6/44, Italy 7/44. To Egypt 9/45 where a Met Flight operated. To
		NF.19			Cyprus 7/46 where disbanded at Nicosia 12/9/46
264	PS	F.2	5/42	8/45	Initially equipped at Colerne. Used on intruder duties until 11/43.
		FB.6			Used for defensive patrols until 5/44, when covered D-Day landings,
		NF.13			then returned to intruder work. Disbanded 25/8/45
		NF.30			
		NF.36	11/45	2/52	125 Sqn renumbered 264 Sqn 20/11/45. Re-equipped with Meteor NF.11
268	EG	FB.6	9/45	3/46	Disbanded 31/3/46
307	EW	NF.2	12/42	1/47	Polish night fighter sqn, named 'Lwowski'. Initially equipped at Exeter.
		FB.6			To Fairwood Common and Predannack 8/43. Used on intruder duties. To Drem
		NF.12			11/43. To Coleby Grange 3/44. Transferred to bomber support missions.
		NF.30			To Church Fenton 5/44, to Castle Camps 1/45, to Coltishall 5/45, to Horsham St.
					Faith 6/1/47, where disbanded 6/1/47.
333	KK	NF.2	5/43	11/45	Norwegian sqn. Formed from 1477 Flt with Norwegian crews on shipping
					reconnaissance duties at Banff. Used as anti-shipping pathfinders. To Norway
					6/45, passing to Royal Norwegian Air Force 21/11/45.
334	VB	FB.6	5/45	11/45	Norwegian sqn. Formed from Mosquito Flt of 333 Sqn at Banff. To Royal
					Norwegian Air Force 21/11/45
404	EO	FB.18	4/45	5/45	Royal Canadian Air Force ('Buffalo') Sqn. Based at Banff, forming part of Strike
					Wing. Disbanded at Predannack 25/5/45
406	HU	NF.12	4/44	8/45	Royal Canadian Air Force ('Lynx') Sqn. Initially based at Winkleigh. To Colerne
		NF.30			9/44, to Mansion 11/44 on coastal before switching to bomber support. To

SQN	CODE	VARIANT	FROM	TO	REMARKS
					Predannack 6/45, where disbanded 1 /9/45.
409	KP	NF.13	3/44	7/45	Royal Canadian Air Force ('Night Hawk') Sqn. Initially based at Acklington before moved to other UK bases and then Europe. Used against V-1s. Disbanded at Twenthe, Holland, 7/45.
410	RA	NF.2	12/42	6/45	Royal Canadian Air Force ('Cougar') sqn. Initially based at Acklington
		NF.13			before moved to other UK bases, then Europe.
		NF.30			Disbanded at Gilze-Rijen, Holland, 9/6/45
418	TH	NF.2	2/43	9/45	Royal Canadian Air Force ('City of Edmonton') Sqn. Initially based at Ford
		FB.6			before moved to other UK bases, then Europe. Disbanded at Volkel, Holland, 7/9/45.
456	RX	NF.2	12/42	5/45	Royal Australian Air Force sqn. Initially based at Valley,
		FB.6			Middle Wallop 4/43, Colerne 8/43, Fairwood Common
		NF.17			11/43, Ford 2/44, Church Fenton 12/44, Bradwell Bay
		NF.30			3/45, where disbanded 15/6/45
464	SB	FB.6	9/43	9/45	Royal Australian Air Force sqn. Initially based at Sculthorpe, moved to other UK bases, then Europe. Disbanded at Melsbroek, Belgium, 25/9/45
487	EG	FB.6	7/43	9/45	Royal New Zealand Air Force sqn. Initially based at Sculthorpe, moved to other UK bases, then Europe. Re-numbered 16 Sqn, RAF, 19/9/45, then retrospectively renumbered 268 Sqn, RAF, 10/45.
488	ME	NF.12	8/43	4/45	Royal New Zealand Air Force sqn. Initially based at Ayr,moved to other UK
		NF.13			bases, then Europe. Disbanded at Gilze-Rijen, Holland, 26/4/45
489	P6	FB.6	5/45	8/45	Royal New Zealand Air Force sqn. Initially equipped at Banff, where disbanded 1/8/45.
500	RAA	NF.30	4/47	10/48	Post-war RAuxAF Sqn. Based West Malling. Re-equipped with Meteor F.3.
502	RAC	NF.30	12/47	6/49	Post-war RAuxAF Sqn. Based at Aldergrove, N. Ireland. Re-equipped with Spitfire F.22.
504	RAD	NF.30	4/47	8/48	Post-war RAuxAF Sqn. Based at Syerston. Re-equipped with Spitfire F.22
515	3P	NF.2	2/44	6/45	Initially equipped at Hunsdon as part of 100 Group for
		FB.6			bomber support work. Disbanded at Little Snoring 10/6/45
600	BQ	NF.19	1/45	8/45	AuxAF Sqn. Initially equipped at Cesenatico, Italy. Disbanded in Italy 21/8 45
604	NG	NF.12	2/44	4/45	AuxAF Sqn. Initially equipped at Church Fenton. Part of 2 TAF. To several
		NF.13			UK bases, then moved to Europe. Disbanded at Lille, France, 18/4/45
605	UP	F.2	2/43	8/45	AuxAF Sqn. Initially equipped at Ford. To several UK bases, then moved to
		FB.6			Europe. Used on intruder duties. Renumbered 4 Sqn 31/8/45.
	RAL	NF.30	5/46	1/49	Re-formed as post-war RAuxAF Sqn at Honiley. Re-equipped with Vampire F.1
608	RAO	NF.30	7/47	8/48	Re-formed as post-war RAuxAF Sqn at Thornaby. Re-equipped with Spitfire F.22
609	RAP	NF.30	6/47	9/48	Re-formed as post-war RAuxAF sqn at Church Fenton, later Yeadon. Re-equipped with Spitfire LF.XVI.
613	SY	FB.6	11/43	8/45	AuxAF Sqn initially equipped at Lasham, later Sculthorpe, Hartford Bridge 10/44 and Epinoy, France, 11/44. Re-numbered 69 Sqn 8/8/45.
616	RAW	NF.30	9/47	4/49	Post-war RAuxAF Sqn at Finningley. Re-equipped with Meteor F.3

Note. This chart details only the main variants used. It does not include training variants that were supplied to many squadrons. Fighter-bomber variants used in the chart were mainly used in the fighter role.

In addition to the units listed above. No 133 Squadron of the Royal Canadian Air Force, based at Patricia Bay, British Columbia, was equipped with Mosquito FB.26s — replacing Kittyhawks - in order to attain the speed and altitude necessary to intercept Japanese 'Fugo' fire balloons (launched during favourable winds). The Mosquitos served with 133 from April to September 1945, but no victories were recorded.

FIGHTER-BOMBERS

The first fighter-bomber variant of the Mosquito was the FB.VI which, while retaining the use of its eight guns, could also carry four 500 lb bombs, giving Fighter Command crews a much greater flexibility in choice of armament. Facilities were built into the wing structure to allow the carriage of either bombs or drop tanks to increase the aircraft's operational radius, which brought much of Europe within its reach.

The prototype, DZ434, first appeared in May 1942 and was delivered to A & AEE on 13 June, but was wrecked the next month after an engine failure on take-off. This, together with changes brought about in production planning, meant a delay until February 1943 when the first production FB.VI was rolled out. 418 Sqn (RCAF) at Ford, Sussex, received the first examples from Hatfield on 11 May 1943; they were powered by Merlin 25s to increase low-level speed. 605 Sqn received its FB.Mk.VIs soon after and these fighter- bombers gradually took over much of Fighter Command's *'Ranger'* and *'Intruder'* operations, harassing the enemy wherever he could be found for the remainder of the war. A number of FB.Mk.VIs arrived in the Middle East during May 1943 for use with 23 Sqn and were soon put to good use ranging out over the Balkans, mixing weather-reconnaissance flights with day and night fighting.

A number were also used on similar duties in the Far East, where in 1944 1672 Conversion Unit began to train crews from 45 and 82 Sqns to operate the FB.Mk.VI; they were joined later by 47 Sqn. All these squadrons were tasked with the destruction of Japanese road, rail, waterway and airfield targets throughout Burma, meeting and overcoming sporadic opposition from the Japanese Air Force.

The 'Big Gun' Mosquito
The Mosquito fighter, as explained earlier, had been planned in two forms: a home defence variant and a convoy escort type requiring greater endurance and long

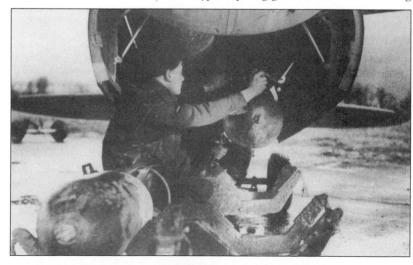

Crouched under the belly, these armourers load a Mosquito FB Mk.VI with a pair of 250 lb bombs. A further two bombs could be carried on the wing racks - later increased to 500 lbs on the Series II machines. *(Simon Peters Collection)*

range. The convoy escort type was typified by the FB.Mk.VI, which first went into service with 333 (Norwegian) Sqn of Coastal Command. An important duty falling to Coastal Command was the destruction of enemy submarines entering or leaving the Bay of Biscay ports to attack Allied convoys. This was a growing menace, that required considerable firepower to combat it. Therefore, on 19 March 1943, J E Serby from the Ministry of Aircraft Production asked Ronald Bishop at De Havilland to investigate the possibility of installing a six-pounder cannon, weighing 1,800 lb, in the Mosquito.

This request originated from discussions within the Air Ministry for a replacement of the 40mm anti-tank gun fitted with such success to the Hawker Hurricane IID used in North Africa. Under the leadership of GF Wallace, a series of ground firing tests was carried out by the RAF's Gun Section. The gun was found to be trouble-free, although feed unit problems were feared under the

A shot of a FB.Mk.XVIII on a test flight from Hatfield prior to delivery to the RAF.
(© BAE SYSTEMS)

The business end of a Mk.XVIII showing the four machine guns and end of the 57mm barrel sealed over for protection.
(Molins Machine Co. Ltd, via author)

Air Marshal Sir Ralph Swirc Sorley (*b.9* Jan 1898 *d.* 1974), Controller of RAF Research and Development.

What sat inside the fuselage of the Mk.XVIII Mosquito - the 57mm Airborne Six-Pounder Class M' gun *(Molins Machine Co. Ltd, via author)*

stress of actual combat. The head of the department sent a favourable report to the Controller of RAF Research and Development, Air Marshal Sir Ralph S. Sorley, who was instructed by the Air Staff to make the necessary requests to the aircraft manufacturers.

The gun intended was an adaptation of a weapon designed originally for naval use, with the addition of an automatic feed. It was designed and manufactured by Molins Machine Company, one of the world's leading manufacturers of cigarette-making, packing and handling equipment. Desmond Molins had already done considerable work on the automatic feed, intending to adapt the gun to be fitted to a tank-busting armoured car.

The automatic feed mechanism was to store rounds in groups of four or five, with an electrical drive to move the next group into position over the breech feed. The upward angled magazine took up relatively little space, and allowed the heavy shells to be fed automatically into the weapon without the use of case links. While working on the gun's feed unit, Molins discovered that the gun needed modification to allow the recoil mechanism to operate the magazine. In time this gun became known as the 'Molins Gun' or, in official parlance, the 'Airborne Six-Pounder Class M Gun'.

Bishop, while knowing little of the Molins gun, stated that rough calculations indicated that few problems would be encountered in dealing with the envisaged 8,000lb recoil reaction. De Havilland had already studied the mounting of a 94mm/3.7 inch anti-aircraft gun in the Mosquito and, during December 1942, had already made detailed weight estimates for a ground-attack version with extra armour plating.

Serby therefore gave instructions in April 1943 to proceed with the prototype installation. De Havilland had previously adopted policies to ensure that every modification of the Mosquito family was developed as rapidly as possible. Illustrating the excellence of their system, just one day later they had cut the nose from a crashed machine, installed a normal six pounder gun measuring over twelve feet in length, and fired the weapon into the Hatfield butts to study the blast effects on the nose. During the first week of May another mock-up was made to see how the ammunition would be placed and, later the same week, a FB.Mk.VI, HJ732, was taken into the experimental shop for the first 'big gun' to be installed. This task was completed on 6 June, allowing the test firing of all 22 rounds in the magazine in one burst into the sand of the stop-butts; when fired into a jump-card set at 400 yards range, the mean point of impact was ten inches.

This adaptation of the Mosquito design was allocated the designation

Mk.XVIII and the code-name of 'Tsetse' after the African tsetse fly, an insect that causes human sleeping sickness and animal trypanosomiasis. To fit correctly, the gun had to be mounted four inches to starboard of the aircraft's centre-line, and aligned to fire at a slightly downward angle of 3 $^3/4$ degrees to the aircraft's horizontal datum. It was not overlooked that when fired, the gun emitted a flame between 15 and 30 feet long and therefore required a flash-eliminator.

The aircraft made its first flight two days later. No difficulties were encountered with either recoil or blast, so the machine was passed to A&AEE Boscombe Down for air firing trials. In the first week alone 100 rounds were fired into the butts to try to cure the problem of overpowering the feed unit drive during combat, a problem that had been predicted by the RAF's Gun Section. These stoppages occurred because rounds failed to reach the correct position when the feed mechanism was subjected to loads over 2.5G on the final run. On 22 June the aircraft was returned to Hatfield for further modifications.

Another problem arose during the testing of the gun. It was known that when any weapon was mounted in the closed compartment of an aircraft, and most especially if the barrel was facing forward directly into the airflow, some of the gases produced from firing were blown back when the breech was opened to eject the spent shell case. However, the 'blow through' created by the six-pounder when the breech was open was incredibly powerful; it could be likened to a 57mm-diameter column of air moving at up to 350 mph into

Above: three poor quality stills taken from a test-film showing the 6-pound cannon. The top view shows the barrel fully extended - the bottom, fully recoiled. Distance of travel is about 18 inches and the time taken between firings is 1.5 seconds.

Opposite page, above: the oft-shown picture of an armourer holding a 6 lb shell under the nose of a Mk.XVIII Mosquito.

Lower picture: the 'magazine' that was also the auto-feed mechanism holding 22 shells.
(all Molins Machine Co. Ltd, via author)

the fuselage of the Mosquito. It was discovered that the intense air pressure was enough to hinder the operation of the automatic loading mechanism, not to mention the effects of gas fumes on the crew in the cabin. To overcome this problem - which existed on all guns but was particularly noticeable on the Class M gun because of the barrel diameter - Desmond Molins set about devising a solution. The result was a blast tube that contained a multi-sectional, spring-steel muzzle cap that screwed on to the end of the barrel that was provisionally patented under No.581817 on 12 January 1943. This date is interesting, for it demonstrates that research into fitting large bore guns into the fuselages of aircraft must have been going on for some time before the Ministry of Aircraft Production notified De Havilland of its thoughts on 19 March 1943.

The muzzle cap was connected to the automatic loading mechanism, and only closed when the breech was actually open. It was also designed failsafe, in that if the mechanism did jam in the closed position, it was possible for the shell to be fired through the spring steel strips.

HJ732 returned to Boscombe Down for further trials, during which the valuable prototype was nearly lost to the Germans when navigational errors were made one weekend. Wing Commander Garland, accompanied by David King of De Havilland, was conducting tests over Lyme Bay in the West Country when the pilot contacted Boscombe Down for a fix and course to steer after the air firing trials had been completed. He was given it, and set the course on his compass. As they flew out to sea they saw haze on the horizon, which turned out to be the French coast! It seems that the corporal on radio duty had given them not a course to steer, but the reciprocal. Luckily the Wing Commander made a successful, if later than planned, landing at Boscombe Down.

Meanwhile a second machine had been fitted with extra armour around the nose and cockpit, weighing 900 lb in all. The first accuracy shoot took place two weeks later against a tank target at Larkhill on Salisbury Plain. The 57mm cannon could be fired either single shot or, with the automatic feed engaged, one shell could be fired every one and half seconds. Many people observing the tests wondered how the Mosquito structure could stand up to such stresses and still stay together the answer of course lay in the fact that the wooden structure was flexible and therefore absorbed shocks safely and efficiently.

Following this successful testing, work began at Hatfield to convert 30 Mosquito FB.Mk.VIs into Mk.XVIIIs. Crates containing Molins Guns were received and placed in secure storage until needed.

The firing trials continued, however, and in July and August HJ732 was back at Boscombe Down to help devise and practise operational tactics, using a dummy submarine conning tower built of wood and rigged up on the ranges. It was found that if a straight and level run-in at 50 to 100 feet altitude was made, it was possible for the pilot to fire off around seven shots during the mile-long approach. The

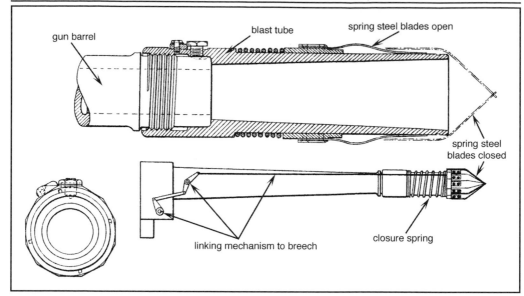

gun was exceptionally accurate, with an average of six out of the seven shots finding the target. The rifling of the barrel began to show signs of wear and tear after 300-500 rounds had been fired, but this was considered acceptable if it translated, as expected, into 20 sorties each expending a full load of ammunition. A more worrying sign was the damage which 450 rounds - regarded as 'excessive use' - inflicted on the undersurface of the inner flaps of the aircraft, notably to the starboard side. This 'sucking away' effect was cured by fitting a heavier skin and by adding strengthened longitudinal ribs to the existing flap structure.

The blast tube and muzzle cap of the 57mm cannon.

Blast effect problems also affected the nose area, with cracks appearing between the 'Big Gun' and the four Browning 0.303in machine guns. It was decided to remove the outer pair of machine-guns and strengthen the area with tie-rods fitted between the gun mounts and nose cone. A drop in fire-power was averted by enlarging the ammunition tanks and thus doubling the firing time of the remaining machine-guns.

Desmond Molins OBE, seen in the 1960s (Molins PLC).

By October three production aircraft had reached Boscombe Down. A minor modification, the fitment of 65 gallon fuel tanks in the fuselage, allowed the aircraft to range out far over the Bay of Biscay. A big-gunned, long-range Mosquito offered plenty of promise.

With many of the technical problems overcome, operating procedures could now be worked out. It was thought that the Barr and Stroud Mk.IIIa reflector sight, normally mounted in turrets and on free guns, could be used since it gave a better peripheral view and, when fitted with a dimming screen to reduce the reflections from the surface of the sea, it would be better than the larger GM2 fighter gunsight. The alignment of the Brownings and the six-pounder was not the same and therefore two graticules, or aiming dots, were incorporated

in the sight with the central one for the Molins Gun and a slightly higher one for the machine-guns.

The 'Big Gun' in Combat

To operate this new variant a special detachment was formed from 618 Sqn. The squadron had originally been formed in April 1943, to use a variant of the Barnes Wallis 'bouncing bomb', code-named *'Highball'*, but had been left waiting endlessly while the bomb underwent prolonged testing. Under its commander. Sqn Ldr Charles F. 'Charlie' Rose, DFC, DFM, the five aircrews and 30 ground staff and armourers received a morale-boosting crash-course on the operation of the six-pounder gun. Two Mk.XVIIIs, HX902 and HX903, were taken from A&AEE where they had performed altitude measurements and overload handling trials and were moved, in October 1943, to Predannack in Cornwall where they were placed under the control of 248 Sqn, which at that time operated Beaufighters.

Operations began in earnest just two days later when the two Mosquitos set off over the Bay of Biscay, having been briefed to attack U-boats but not surface shipping because of the top secret nature of their weapon.

This first mission was uneventful but on 7 November the *'Tsetse'* scored its first success. Flying Officer A. L. Bonnett, RCAF, flying HX903, found a surfaced U-boat heading for its base south of Brest. He fired several shells, but the crew had seen him during his approach and given the alarm to their commander who crash-dived; nevertheless, the shells managed to strike the conning tower, producing a plume of black and yellow smoke. Ideally the spot to aim for was the pressure hull rather than the more heavily armoured conning tower; the hull was vulnerable to penetration even after the shell had passed through three feet of water. This attack came just three days after a disastrous attack by HX902 on two armed trawlers escorting a suspected submerged U-boat. As the *Tsetse*, flown by Sqn Ldr Charlie Rose with Flight Sergeant Cowley navigating, made

Another view of a Mk.XVIII, showing the effects of blast on the nose of the aircraft The end of the 57mm gun shows the mounting flange and screw-threads to locate the muzzle-cap which, as far as can be gathered was never fitted in service. Clearly visible also is the bulge for part of the recoil mechanism. *(via Martin Bowman)*

its second pass, it was hit and forced to try to ditch, but tragically, it disintegrated on impact with the water and the two men were killed.

On their first missions the Mosquito Mk.XVIIIs were escorted by Beaufighters of 248 Sqn but from December onwards the Beaufighters were replaced by Mosquito FB.Mk.VIs. As further aircraft arrived and built up a combined striking force, they gained confidence and sought out more and more German shipping. Intelligence gained from breaking Germany's '*Enigma* ' cypher code allowed Coastal Command to direct the '*Tsetses*' far more efficiently in their attacks on U-boats.

The effectiveness of the '*Tsetse*' forced the Germans to provide both surface ship escorts and further cover for their U-boats. Admiral Donitz of the German Submarine Command even issued an order that: '*...owing to damage caused by enemy aircraft mounting heavy calibre guns, surface passage will only take place during the hours of darkness*'.

The first major action involving the Mosquito Mk.XVIII occurred on 10 March 1944 when two of these machines and four Mk.VIs, acting as escorts, found a German naval force protected by ten Ju.88s off the northern coast of Spain. Four Ju.88s were engaged in a number of individual combats, with one falling in flames and another listed as a 'possible'. Meanwhile, the two Mk.XVIIIs attacked the convoy, paying particular attention to a U-boat and a destroyer, and for good measure Sqn Ldr Tony Phillips fired five rounds, eventually shooting down a Ju88 with a single shell.

There was intense Mosquito activity during this period - on 25 March two '*Tsetse*' Mosquitos crewed by Flying Officer Turner, DFC, with Flying Officer Curtiss as a navigator in one, with Flight Lieutenant Jack 'Hilly' Hilliard and navigator Jimmy Hoyle in the other and escorted by four FB.VIs came across a flotilla of armed minesweepers, a destroyer and, in the middle a single U-Boat. which was returning to St Nazaire. Two of the escorting Mosquitos attacked the

A standard FB.VI cockpit layout. The instrument panel were either finished in a matt black or a special baked-on crackle finish.
(© *BAE SYSTEMS*)

escorts, while Turner opened his attack in the U-Boat, getting off five rounds. Turner made four attacks until all his ammunition was expended. Then it was Hilliard's turn. He attacked the U-Boat, aiming for the base of the conning tower. About ten rounds were seen to hit the area, and the U-Boat was seen starting to sink. German records show that the U-boat -U-976, a 769 ton Type VIIC - under the command of Oberleutnant sur see Raimund Tiesler, was sunk on 25 March 1944 in the Bay of Biscay near St. Nazaire, in position 46.48N, 02.43W, by gunfire from two British Mosquito aircraft. There were 4 dead and 49 survivors.

Two days later there was almost a repeat performance. At 0700hrs on 27 March 1944 two Mk.XVIIIs with the same crews of 248 Sqn on board took off from Portreath with an escort of four FB.Mk.VIs to undertake a U-boat reconnaissance patrol in the Bay of Biscay. They flew along the U-boats' safety lane, some 20 miles from the submarine base at St. Nazaire, at an altitude of 500 ft. The weather was fine and sunny, although haze reduced forward visibility to 2,000 yards maximum, and as they neared the end of the line just off Ile de Yeu they saw enemy shipping ahead. The lead aircraft of the formation, piloted by Turner, began to climb for height and then Turner transmitted the order to attack. The second Mk.XVIII Mosquito began its climb at full power too. Flight Lieutenant Jack Hilliard and navigator Jimmy Hoyle noticing that the thirteen-strong convoy had two surfaced U-boats in its midst. When they reached 2,000 ft heavy flak began bursting very close. Hilliard banked to port in preparation for the attack. A FB.Mk.VI escort Mosquito targeted a flak ship to the left of one of the U-boats while Hilliard fired off seven shots at the submarine. Five of his shots hit. He then swooped low over the submarine at periscope height, sustaining a hit in the nose from a 37mm shell which forced open all the machine-gun inspection hatch. Luckily the armour plate behind the instrument panel had done its work and they managed to return to base by 1115hrs.

The submarine they had attacked was later captured in the Mediterranean, whereupon during interrogation, the U-boat crew talked of having been hit by an aircraft carrying a big gun which emitted a long flame. It seems that Hilliard's Mosquito had severely damaged the U-boat, injured fourteen of its crew and led to its withdrawal from the war.

The success of 248 Sqn led to the formation of a second Coastal strike squadron in June, for this is what they had become. 235 was also equipped with

A poor quality, but unique photograph of U-976 under attack from *'Tsetse'* Mosquitos while returning defensive fire. survivors from the U-boat were later picked up by the minesweeper V604 just visible on the right. *(Des Curtiss via Martin Bowman)*

FB.Mk.VI and Mk.XVIII Mosquitos and flew a number of successful anti-ship missions before operations were wound down in the wake of the D-Day landings. 235 Sqn moved to Banff in Scotland from where large-scale attacks were made on shipping and coastal installations in Norway. The Banff Wing became quite famous; it included 'B' Flight of 333 (Norwegian) Sqn, whose pilots knew the coastal waters well and could act as outriders for the rest of the Wing. The nature of the terrain, particularly the restricted airspace of the fjords, led to the tactic of the line-astern attack being adopted. The Germans placed gunners on the shore and cliffs of the most frequently used waters, which meant that many of these attacks were pressed home through intense flak at low-level. The Mosquitos though, with their machine-guns, cannon, six pounder gun and now rockets, made formidable opponents.

In March 1945 248 Sqn's coastal strike unit or at least its aircraft were transferred to 254 Sqn. They continued to fly anti-submarine patrols for several months but generally their role, like the war itself, had come to an end. These heavily armed aircraft, with rockets now supplementing their 57mm cannon, had been a definite success; their Molins guns were in some ways a disappointment, but they did force the German naval forces to take great care when entering or leaving port. This caution, at a time when the U-boats were still a menace, diluted their operational capabilities, forcing them to stay submerged for longer than they wanted, and thus the Mosquitos made a further contribution to the Allied war effort on the high seas.

The Molins Gun in the Mosquito Mk.XVIII was tested in the USA in 1945, when after storage at 27 MU, Shawbury, PZ467 was allocated to the US Navy. The aircraft arrived at Patuxent Naval Air Station on 30 April and was given the US Navy serial of 91106. This allowed the Mosquito to be flown in direct comparison with the nearest American equivalent, the manually loaded 75mm AN-Mk 5 gun fitted in the North American PBJ-1H Mitchell. This comparison was more valid than the difference in calibre might suggest, for the 75 x 350R ammunition used in the American gun (the same as was used by the M4 tank gun in the Sherman) was

It is not often that there are ways of verifying the historical record.

In the mid-1980s the author arranged for a surviving Molins Gun kept with the Mosquito Aircraft Museum at Salisbury Hall to be restored by the company apprentices. During this process Flt Lt Jack Hilliard got in touch and brought along with him this nose panel from Mosquito HX903 'I' which shot up the U-boat in the story told here. The damage was done by a German 37mm shell fired at them in return! *(author)*

Nose panel of
MOSQUITO AIRCRAFT
damaged by 37mm shell
from GERMAN "U"BOAT
off ILE DE YEU
27-3-44

'THE 750 MOSQUITO MK XVIII
LETTER 'I' - HX903
CARRIED 57mm. MOLINS CANNON
U/OR U/BO PORTSMTH LANDED 1115.
HIT U/B WITH 5 SHELLS —
DAMAGED U/B TOWED INTO PORT.
PERISCOPE SHOT AWAY'S 16 CREW
INJURED
PILOT. F/O HILLIARD.   613 Sqdn.
NAV. F/LT HOYLE.   DETACHMENT
                       TO
27-3-44   248 Sqn.

about the same overall size as the 57 x 441R, and the 6lb and 75mm tank guns were effectively interchangeable in the later British tanks. The Molins Gun impressed the Americans with its performance and reliability and was considered superior to the 75mm as it could achieve a much higher rate of fire. It was noted that fairly violent evasive action and 2.5 positive Gs did not cause stoppages - which could not be said for manual loading! The Americans recommended that the Molins autoloader could be considered as suitable not just for conventional guns but also for recoilless weapons and spin-stabilised rockets.

Rocket Projectiles

Rocket projectiles were used by Mosquitos for the first time on 26 October 1944, and greatly increased the aircraft's firepower. De Havilland had studied the possibility of fitting rocket projector rails under the Mosquitos wings, between the engine nacelles and the drop tank/bomb shackle position, in the autumn of 1943. The Air Ministry gave its approval in September for four circular section rails to be carried under the wing, each with a 60 lb rocket on it. Flight testing at Hatfield followed by further work at Boscombe Down in an FB.VI, HX918, revealed

An armourer loading the .303 machine guns on an FB.Mk.VI of 333 (Norwegian) Sqn.

that the best angle for a diving attack was 20 degrees. Many pilots were later to have a line painted on the cockpit canopy the correct distance up from the normal horizon position when flying level so that without taking their eyes off the target the correct dive angle to be used during an attack could be achieved simply be realigning the horizon to the painted mark.

Mosquito FB.Mk.VI NS623 NE:D of 143 Sqn fitted with rocket racks and underwing fuel tanks. *(© BAE SYSTEMS)*

An RP round comprised a rocket motor tube of $3^{1/4}$ inches diameter and $55^{1/4}$ inches length, which contained a single 21lb cruciform stick of cordite as the propellant charge. The stick incorporated an electrical igniter wired to long leads protruding from the rear of the tube, inside which was a venturi arrangement. Simple plate fins could be slotted externally on to the rear of the motor tube, with suspension sleeves clamped around the tube permitting easy attachment to the fixed launching rails under the wing. At the nose of the motor tube a standard screw thread allowed for the following variety of warheads to be fitted:

60 lb shell. High-Explosive/Armour-Piercing (HE/AP)
60 lb shell. High Explosive/General Purpose Hollow Charge (HE/GP)
60 lb shell. Practice, Concrete head (Training)
25 lb shot. Armour-Piercing (AP)
25 lb head. Solid Anti-Submarine (A/S)
25 lb shot. Practice (Training)
18 lb shell. High-Explosive (HE)
12 lb head. Practice

Laden with rockets and long range tanks, Mosquitos thread their way to the runway at Banff in May 1945 *(via Chas Bowyer)*

The front and rear view of the three-inch rocket projectiles as fitted under the wings of the FB.Mk.XI Mosquito.

The upper view shows the rockets fitted with 60 pound high explosive heads.

The middle view shows rockets fitted with 25 lb armour-piercing heads.

The long centre body of the projectile was its individual rocket motor - a 21 lb stick of cordite that was electrically ignited and thrusting out through a tube at the end.

Below: a broadside of eight rockets just after launch.

Two types of projector rails could be used, the Mk.IB and Mk.IIIA. Both types could be used for single or multiple (tier carriage) round installation. The rockets were installed on the projector beams, working from the inboard beams outwards. Just before take-off each igniter lead was plugged into the aircraft's electrical system via a Niphan socket on the rear strut of each projector rail. A rocket was launched by the pilot using the appropriate switch in the cockpit and aiming with the normal gun sight. Normal procedure was to launch the rockets in pairs, one from each wing or, if required, a salvo of all eight at once. The relatively low-velocity projectiles did not compare well for accuracy with the impressive high-velocity 57mm cannon; they

The Strike Wing at work - a U-boat under attack in the Kattergat on 2 May 1945. Just visible in the middle of all the spray is the submarine's conning tower. *(G Lord via Martin Bowman)*

would decelerate once the propellant had burnt up and then adopt a parabolic trajectory. These were of course early days in rocket technology; none of the modern inertial guidance systems had been developed for missile fitment. However, the rocket remained a useful weapon for its explosive power.

The stabilizing fins tended to do what they were meant to prevent, leaving the rocket at the mercy of the wind once it was free of the support rails. Similarly, if the aircraft was being flown with any yaw, the projectile would steer itself into the wind in an opposite direction to that of the yaw. If the aircraft accelerated, the trajectory was affected by positive G forces giving a steepness to the missile's flight; conversely, deceleration and negative G forces caused overshooting.

A further, and crucial, complication resulted from the fact that the rocket rails supporting the weapons were fixed to the aircraft's wings; thus the angle of attack to the airflow changed with the speed flown. The lower the speed, the greater the angle of attack. It was clear that for a given range there could only be one speed or angle of attack at which a direct hit could be achieved. If, at the moment of firing, the speed was higher than specified for the range, the rocket would

FB.Mk.VI Mosquito attack U-boats in the Kattergat. Note the Mosquito climbing away from the attack in the top left of the picture. *(G Lord via Martin Bowman)*

Above: Mosquitos from 143 Sqn, lead by Wing Commander Christopher Foxley-Norris pulls up and away from the *Lysaker* at Tetgenaes on 23 March 1945.
Below: An attack on shipping in Sandefjord, Norway on 2 April 1945 by 143 Sqn. *(both © BAE SYSTEMS)*

undershoot the target. This meant that the pilot had simultaneously to acquire the specified speed at the correct range from the target and without yaw or acceleration, all at the moment of firing. This was far from easy, even under ideal conditions. Under operational conditions, or in turbulence, there was every possibility that there would be more misses than hits.

Despite all these problems the installation was incredibly successful for it allowed future Mosquito fighter-bombers and bombers to fire the equivalent of a broadside from a naval cruiser, with no recoil stress on the airframe. Thus, within a very short period of time, a small force of Mosquitos could be called upon to deliver the same fire power as a naval force but over a distance of many hundreds of miles and they could then repeat their attack a few hours later on either the same target or another in a totally different location. If the aircraft was required to fly without the rocket projectors for any reason, they could be removed by two armourers in thirty minutes. The holes in the skin were then covered with doped patches and all protruding bolts covered with fairings normally neatly stowed in the front rocket projector strut.

Eight roket rails, four 20 mm cannon and four .303 machine guns - no wonder a Mosquito attack was said to be a broadside from a battleship!

The Banff Wing Mosquitos sometimes carried close-in attacks too far. This is the result of what happened when a FB.Mk.VI of 248 Sqn struck the mast of a vessel in the Kattergat on 4 May 1945.

The 'Opposition'

Throughout the Second World War the armed DH.98 design encountered little sustained opposition from enemy aircraft. The Germans had developed several machines possessing roughly the same forward-facing fire power. The Dornier Do 217J carried four 20mm cannon and four 7.9mm machine-guns, as did the later (and lighter) Do 217N version, but both were considerably slower than the Mosquito fighters. The Bf 110F-4 and the Ju 88C-6 were the most widely used German night fighters during the 1942-3 period, but, again, both these machines suffered a distinct lack of speed. The Germans did develop a specialized and highly effective night fighter, the Heinkel He 219, but conflict within the German High Command limited its production and operational use. The Focke-Wulf Ta 154, intended as a 'Mosquito Hunter', and even named *'Moskito'* according to some sources, never entered service.

In terms of speed, the Focke-Wulf Fw 190 came very close (within 5 mph in the worst possible scenario) to the Mosquito, but the greatest threat came from the Messerschmitt Me 410, which first appeared over Britain in June 1943. This twin-engined fighter was armed with a pair of 20mm cannon and two 7.9mm machine-guns facing forward and a further pair of 13mm machine-guns in rearward-facing side fuselage barbettes. With a top speed of over 380 mph at around 22,000ft, the Me 410 was marginally faster than the early Mosquitos. However, there were two drawbacks with this aircraft: the ammunition runs to the rear barbettes caused many Me.410s to disintegrate if hit by fire; and the Luftwaffe had relatively few of these fast and nimble machines in service.

Towards the end of the European conflict, the Mosquito came up against some of the German jet and rocket-powered fighters in the form of the Messerschmitt Me 262 and Me 163 Komet. The Me 163 was used in daylight against the large bomber formations, for it was restricted in range because of its rocket engine. The Me.262 could have been a totally different story. If Adolf Hitler had not intervened in November 1943 to demand that the design be used as a bomber not a fighter early in the machine's development, the Me 262A-la would have made a formidable adversary for the Mosquito. The German jet had a far higher speed than any other operational fighter in any air force during the war; it also carried a greater fixed-gun punch than any Allied

A T.Mk.29 two-seat trainer - converted from a FB.Mk.26 is towed away after a test flight. The picture is thought to have been taken at Downsview, Toronto. A few of these machines were used in Europe. *(National Museum of Science and Technology)*

The Bondi Blonde - a FB.Mk.VI, A52-518 of 1 Sqn RAAF. The starboard engine cover, and the covers on the four machine guns were essential in wet or dusty conditions. *(via Stuart Howe).*

fighter. Indeed, this machine, if originally allowed unrestricted development and production, would probably have out-flown and out-gunned the Mosquito. Instead, Hitler was forced into a compromise fighter-bomber design as a result of the devastating USAAF raids on Germany, a decision which lost a vital six months and caused unnecessary dissipation of the development and production team's energy. By the time the fighter version was complete, with four 30mm cannon installed in the nose, German manufacturers could not produce enough of these aircraft. The Allied land advances created shortages of spares and fuel which aggravated the situation, so there were never enough Me 262s to make much of an impression on the Mosquito, which by now, had almost total air superiority over Europe.

Conclusions
The adaptability of the Mosquito design was so ably shown by the Fighter-Bomber variant. The ability of the airframe to absorb the recoil of the 57mm cannon, the tremendous offensive fire-power that could be aimed at the enemy with both guns and rockets that could at the same time be coupled with the destructive effects of a bombload was never more clearly on display. Truly it was the first Multi-Role Combat Aircraft.

BOMBERS

During 1941 RAF Bomber Command faced accusations that it seemed unable to inflict significant damage on Germany by bombing. There was also the distinct possibility that some of its squadrons would be reallocated to Coastal Command to help counter the threat of Germany's U-boat attacks on Britain's supply lines across the North Atlantic.

Into this delicate atmosphere W4064, the first Mosquito bomber for Bomber Command was delivered on 15 November 1941 to 105 Sqn at Swanton Morley. The aircraft, one of nine machines initially known as the PR/Bomber conversions but changed to B.Mk.IV Series I, was flown in from Hatfield with Geoffrey de Havilland Jnr at the controls; he ended the delivery flight with a series of high-speed runs interspersed with sparkling aerobatics. The squadron's excitement was short-lived however, for the next day the machine developed oil feed and hydraulic troubles which forced a return to the manufacturers. Nevertheless, two days later, W4066 was delivered, followed shortly by three more before the squadron moved to its new home at Horsham St. Faith near Norwich. It was here that the testing began.

A series of high-altitude round-Britain flights was undertaken to check fuel consumption, and almost immediately there was a crash. On 27 November Sergeant Swann was returning in W4070 from a trip that had reached 30,000ft when bad weather forced a diversion to Portreath in Cornwall where he overshot the runway. As this was the first machine to be damaged in such circumstances, Hereward de Havilland hurried to inspect the wreckage from which the crew had escaped uninjured. Repairs looked as if they would take months, just at a time when the company had been proclaiming the ease with which wooden structures could be mended. De Havilland saw a beneficial side to the incident: it provided the impetus for a Mosquito repair organization.

The Unarmed Bomber Enters Service

The higher echelons of Bomber Command were still very sceptical about the unarmed bomber, even though 105 Sqn had demonstrated that the type could use its superior speed for crew safety in the best way possible by a series of mainly low-level attacks against heavily defended targets. High-ranking RAF staff officers did not

A pleasing study of B.Mk.IV DZ313 in flight. (Simon Peters Collection)

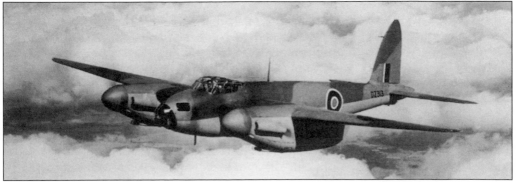

A line of Percival built
B.Mk.XVIs awaiting
collection for delivery to
the RAF with PF563
closest to the camera.
*(Simon Peters
Collection)*

think that this was the best method of employment for the Mosquito and they instructed that practice bombing be conducted from around 26,000 ft. This resulted in an average error of 400 yards, a margin that was improved to around 150 yards when the MR. XVI bombsight was used, which was then being tested on DK286.

De Havilland also investigated various means of stepping up the efficiency of each sortie by increasing the bomb load. A more definitive version of the early Mosquito bomber had been developed, the B.IV Series II, but there were still problems to be ironed out: although the aircraft had the capability to lift a greater weight, its bomb bay was too small to carry four 500 lb bombs with standard fins. De Havillands experimented first with bombs fitted with telescopic fins, and later with simpler, rigid 'short' fins, much to the alarm of the traditionalist ballistic experts. DK290 began stability tests on 23 May carrying four 500 lb bombs that gave the aircraft an increased all-up weight of 20,700 lb, the same as that of the planned B.V (of which only one example was built). The weight was then increased to 21,300 lb by the addition of two 250 lb bombs in underwing racks. The tests proved successful. The bomber was now put into service with another squadron. 139 Sqn also based at Horsham St. Faith, but due to a shortage of aircraft the early operational sorties were flown by both squadrons using 105 Sqn aircraft.

Pilots soon began worrying about the rate of interceptions they were experiencing, mostly by Focke-Wulf Fw.190s. The Mosquitos usually managed to escape, but the crews quickly learned that visibility was not all that it could be and they suggested that the cockpit canopy roof be modified to include a Perspex blister so that the navigator could kneel on his seat for a better view rearwards to spot oncoming fighters. Two other problems came to light at this early stage: wing-tip damage and engine coolant leaks. As the wing was a one-piece unit, it caused on-site repair difficulties and A. J. Brant, De Havilland's Service Engineer, worked with the design department and others to devise a simple procedure that would do away with traditional scarf or feather-edge joints; these were normally applied to every stringer and area of skin. In its place a simple butt-joint was substituted, with the damaged area being sawn off and a standard wing-tip end taken from stock and attached with screwed and cemented overlapping patches, both inboard and outboard of the joint. This procedure greatly simplified wing repairs throughout the life of the Mosquito.

A pair of B.Mk.IVs -
DZ353 and DZ367 of 105
Sqn caught over the
clouds.
(Author's Collection)

Early variants of the Merlin suffered from leaks when fitted in the Mosquito because of the engine's installation design which reversed the coolant's direction of flow. This was due to the position and location of the wing-mounted radiators, which meant that the liquid had to be pumped through instead of drawn through as with other types of Merlin-powered aircraft. It was eventually discovered that long periods of taxi-ing before take-off lay at the root of the problem for the leading-edge radiators were not able to receive a large enough flow of cooling air and thus overheated. This was overcome by changes in ground handling techniques.

Increasing Performance
The search for greater performance was increasing. De Havilland had experimentally polished DK290, but despite the high-gloss finish only 5mph was gained. The removal of the side blister windows from the canopy gained a further 3 mph. These were minor bonuses and a more substantial boost was expected if the saxophone flame-damping exhausts were replaced by the stub type. Trials had taken place at Martlesham Heath with DK336 fitted with open stubs, but the exhaust flames had produced too much glare which made night landings hazardous. A far more serious problem as far as operations were concerned was that the exhaust glare revealed the position of the Mosquito to any enemy fighters. The glare was reduced without impairing the engine's efficiency when the stub ends were closed to form an oval section; in fact, as an added bonus, this produced a jet propulsion effect. The net gain was a maximum 13 mph, depending on the

DK308, a Hatfield-built
B.Mk. IV.
*(Simon Peters
Collection)*

altitude flown. Nothing else produced such a worthwhile increase, despite efforts to reduce the area of the radiator opening and removal of the aerial mast and wing root leading-edge fillets.

Of course, the bomber remained unarmed and it was not long before the issue of fixed rear guns raised its head again, despite potential lost performance. A 'scare' gun in the tailcone was considered but rejected, along with a Browning machine-gun in the rear of each engine nacelle to fire aft. The idea had been successfully tried out in a trial installation by Rose Brothers at Scampton, but was soon dropped, for alternative gains in performance made the risk of interception less likely. One simple scheme that was adopted, however, was the painting of some unarmed bombers with a 'sky' band around the rear fuselage and 'sky' propeller spinners in the same manner as Mosquito fighters (which already had a formidable reputation) in the hope that from a distance the bombers would be mistaken for fighters and thus frighten the enemy away.

The high performance of the Mosquito was at least partially negated if the correct tactics and operating procedures were not adopted. The testing of aircraft radios by Bomber Command engineering staff on the ground and the number of machines taken up on air tests before a raid, often alerted the German radio and radar monitors that a raid was about to take place. Steps were taken by the RAF to prevent this concentration, but the problem was never completely solved. Even if precautions were taken to ensure that a forthcoming bombing raid was not revealed, the German coastal defence radar was able to detect the oncoming raiders at nearly 100 miles range if they flew at medium altitude. This gave plenty of warning for both ground and airborne forces to prepare their defences. However, at sea-level the radar was ineffective, so the Mosquito squadrons adopted the tactic of crossing the Channel into enemy territory at wave-top height. It was a daring move that created a new problem of bird strikes, for when the leading aircraft of a formation inevitably roused the birds, they would then fly up into any following aircraft. Leading edges of the wings had to be strengthened, for such was the impact that it was common for birds to penetrate both webs of the front spar. Even bullet-proof windscreens - which were fitted later - were not immune, as many squadron records testify.

The bomb bay of an unidentified B.Mk.IV Mosquito. The item just in front of the starboard door is a flare tube. *(Authors Collection)*

First Daylight Operations

With the bomb carriage problem resolved, Bomber Command planners began to think that the Mosquito bomber could be used on targets that would receive wide acclaim and thus boost civilian and service morale. Six aircraft from 105 Sqn left Horsham St. Faith on 19 September 1942 on an audacious daylight raid on Berlin the first of the war, all previous attacks on the German capital having been at night. It was aborted, however, due to bad weather but it would be repeated. Meanwhile other tempting targets presented themselves. Armed resistance in occupied Europe was growing and acts of sabotage increased as Britain helped supply groups with arms and agents; in return the Resistance helped downed Allied airmen to escape and return to their bases in Britain. Naturally such activities attracted the attention of the German *Sicherheitspolizei* or Security Police, in particular the members of Division IV, the *Geheime Staatspolizei* or Gestapo. They were highly efficient and methodical in gathering vast amounts of documents and dossiers to help maintain their intelligence efforts. The RAF was therefore asked to organize several air raids against such targets, either to destroy the evidence or free the prisoners.

On the morning of 25 September 1942 105 Sqn was briefed to bomb the Gestapo headquarters in Norway, housed in the former Foreign Ministry building in Victoria Terrasse. By 1400 hrs they were ready to go, each of the four Mosquito B.IVs loaded with two 1,000 lb bombs. Thirteen minutes later the four machines took off in pairs, with the course set from Leuchars to the Norwegian coast. Sqn Ldr George Parry, the squadron's CO, was flying DK296 GB:G flying with navigator Flg Off 'Robbie' Robson. Pilot Officer Rowlands was aboard DK313 GB:U with Flg Off Richard Reilly. The second pair consisted of DK328 GB:V flown by Flg Off Alec Bristow and Pilot Officer Bernard Marshall and Flt Sgt Carter and Sergeant

William Young in DK325 'GB:S. As the aircraft crossed the mouth of the inner Oslo Fjord they dived from their cruising height to about 100ft then, following a turn to port, swept over the capital directly on target for the Gestapo Headquarters, where all four aircraft dropped their bombs. Unfortunately two Fw.190 fighters from 3 Staffel I/JG 5, temporarily based at Fornebu to protect a major party convention of Norwegian Nazis, managed to close on the British aircraft and attack them. They were unable to maintain contact for any length of time because of the Mosquitos' high speed, but the fighters did manage to hit and damage DK296 with several shells; more seriously their gunfire set DK325's starboard engine ablaze. Carter radioed to the others that he would try to make neutral Sweden, but his aircraft crashed into a lake on the western outskirts of Oslo, killing him and his navigator. The remaining machines returned to Scotland, landing at Sumburgh airfield in the Shetlands with no further trouble.

The bombs the four aircraft dropped on Oslo hit five different buildings around Victoria Terrasse, but the building itself survived and the Gestapo continued to interrogate and torture Norwegian citizens. Although the raid had failed to achieve its main objective, it was considered dramatic enough to be used to reveal the existence of the Mosquito to the British public, and the following day to the BBC Home Services learned that a new aircraft - the Mosquito - had been revealed for the first time by the RAF, and that four had made a low level attack on Oslo. A further raid was planned, but it took a full eighteen months for these plans to be put into action.

On 30 January 1943 105 and 139 Sqns conducted a daylight bombing raid deep into Germany - their target was finally Berlin. The raid was timed to coincide with a tenth anniversary speech to be given by Adolf Hitler at the Sportspalast and broadcast live on the radio. (In the event, Reichsmarschall Hermann Goering, Air Minister and Commander-in-Chief of the Luftwaffe, stood in for Hitler who was feeling unwell.) The Germans had made no secret of the rally, confident that the Allies could not strike Berlin during daylight hours. Of those tuned in to listen, only the people 'in the know' understood the reasons for the muffled noises and cries, followed by martial music as the speech was delayed. Three Mosquitos from

Just visible on the left of the picture is the moment that a stick of bombs entered the Gestapo Headquarters at Victoria Terrasse, Oslo, Norway.
(DH/BAE/Hatfield)

Russian Mosquito. This B.IV, DK296, served with 105 and 139 Sqns before being flown to Russia in April 1944 by a Soviet crew for evaluation. It was the lead aircraft in the famous raid on the Gestapo Headquarters in Oslo on 25 September 1942, when flown by Squadron Leader D A G Parry, DSO, DFC. Although little is known about Russian operations with Mosquitos, it is thought that they used only a small number of machines.
(both © BAE SYSTEMS)

105 Sqn had arrived perfectly on time to bomb the German radio station on Wilhelmstrasse in central Berlin, just as the announcer went on air at 1100. Several hours later at about 1600hrs, two Mosquitos from 139 Sqn repeated the act to coincide with Dr Joseph Goebbels' speech (a third aircraft was lost en route). The raids were primarily for propaganda purposes, but they also indicated what a fast, unarmed Mosquito bomber could achieve; and the crews involved brought back detailed timings and fuel consumption figures that were of the greatest use for future raid planning on the German capital, as well as other long-range operations.

The development of such attack techniques, evolved and polished by the RAF during 1942 and early 1943, vindicated the faith shown in the design by all involved during the early days. It was possible to take a small unarmed, high-speed bomber deep into enemy territory at low-level in daylight to attack a defended target of medium size without excessive risk, while maintaining surprise and accuracy. Although many of these targets were beyond the range of single-engined fighter-bombers, the twin-engined Mosquito could reach them with a sizable load. Time and time again, the combination of Mosquito photographic reconnaissance, effective intelligence interpretation and Mosquito bombers to carry out the attacks proved a lethal and almost unbeatable team.

'Oboe', Pathfinders and the Light Night Striking Force
Although Air Chief Marshal Sir Arthur Harris opposed the idea of taking the best of his bomber crews to form a corps d'elite in the shape of a separate Pathfinder Force (preferring instead the suggestion of "raid leaders' or 'target finders'), he was ordered to do so by Prime Minister Winston Churchill in August 1942. Thus four squadrons were placed under the command of Air Commodore Donald C. T. Bennett, headquartered at RAF Wyton near Huntingdon. 7 Sqn equipped with Short Stirlings, 35 Sqn with Handley Page Halifaxes and 83 Sqn with Avro

Lancasters. The fourth squadron was 109 that had pioneered the use of '*Oboe*' navigation equipment; it was supposed to equip with the pressure-cabin version of the Vickers Wellington VI but thought that the Mosquito would be a much better machine for the task. Although Bomber Command and the Air Ministry were strongly against the squadron using the Mosquito, pressure from Don Bennett eventually resulted in a number of aircraft being transferred. The four squadrons of the new Pathfinder Force (PFF) were placed initially under the control of 3 Group, but in January 1943 the PFF was elevated in status to 8 Group. In June it was bolstered by the addition of 105 and 139 Sqns which were soon equipped with Mosquito B.IXs specially fitted with '*Oboe*' Mk.II.

'*Oboe*' had been developed in 1941 by Alec H. Reeves of Standard Telephones and Cables Ltd in partnership with Frank E. Jones at the Telecommunications Research Establishment (TRE) with a system of two Type 9000 ground stations called 'Cat' and 'Mouse'. The stations were 100 miles apart and each transmitted pulses at different rates to the receiving aircraft. The concept was for the aircraft to fly at a constant range from one station while receiving pulses sent from the ground which the aircraft would amplify and return. The ground station would then find the aircraft's range from the time it took for the pulses to make the two-way journey. The constant range path would form part of a circle, centred on the ground station, with its radius calculated so that the edge passed slightly short of the target, since when the bombs were released they went off at a tangent. All this data could be accurately calculated so long as the aircraft's height and speed were known. The second ground station also determined the range of the aircraft, so that the moment the aircraft was at the correct range (when the two arcs intercepted) it was ordered to drop its stores in a position to hit the target. The radio signals travelled at a tangent to the earth's surface, therefore limiting the range to that of the altitude at which the aircraft could be flown the greater the height, the greater the distance possible from the transmitting stations.

The usc of the high-flying Mosquito as a target-marker was therefore vital for

Inside a '*Oboe*' ground
station.
*(Simon Peters
Collection)*

When 109 Sqn converted several Mk.IVs for Pathfinder work, DK500 was the first to receive attention. Here work is being done on the starboard engine to increase its electrical power output to drive the pathfinder equipment.

When DK500 was converted, much work was done on the nose to allow the fitment of H2S radar. This shows the housing constructed.

many important Bomber Command raids. The aircraft's design suited the requirements of *'Oboe'* to a unique degree, for it could carry the equipment necessary with just enough crew to operate it. It had the desired range and it could be flown at speed through heavily defended areas on an accurate track, a matter of vital importance for pathfinder operations.

Initially, only one aircraft at a time could be guided by the *'Oboe'* system; this meant about six machines an hour, allowing four minutes for the run-up to the target and then the dropping of markers that would burn for about six minutes. The system could be used at a range of up to around 275 miles with the target-marking aircraft flying at around 28,000 ft. Later, more sophisticated models of the equipment allowed four aircraft to be guided at a time, but these did not come into use until 1944. Obviously it was a disadvantage to have only a small number of aircraft using the system at any one time, but if, as a result, the Pathfinders used their time to drop their target-markers accurately, it served to increase the accuracy of the main force following behind.

The range of *'Oboe'* could be increased if *'Repeata'* aircraft were used to re-transmit the signal; this development, very significant in its implications, was first tested at A & AEE in a Mosquito B.XVI, ML926/G, during June 1944. The aircraft was a standard model with the enlarged bomb doors replaced by modified doors to which was attached a blister of transparent plastic (painted externally) some 8.5ft long by 2.5ft wide by 2.5ft deep, and used to surround and protect the radio gear. Before the tests could be completed the blister was damaged during dive tests at around 250 mph, but enough data had been gained to demonstrate that such a large shape underneath the aircraft only created minor changes to the type's handling characteristics: there was a loss of elevator effectiveness and a minor increase in elevator buffet, a tendency to skid slightly in both climb and level flight, and a slightly higher stalling speed. Boscombe Down cleared the

installation for service use after the manufacturers strengthened the blister.

'*Oboe*' was the most accurate bombing system used during the war. It was so precise that the scientists who developed it were forced to investigate the accuracy of the geodetic alignment between England and the continent of Europe as previously calculated by the Ordnance Survey. This alignment relied on accurate triangulation across the Straits of Dover, which in turn required calibration raids to check, and therefore make adjustments to, the calculations that aligned the system. All this meant getting very precise information from the ground as to where the bombs fell, and it eventually came from two totally different sources.

It was known that the Germans had a sector headquarters for their night fighter control network near Florennes in Belgium, so this was selected as one of the targets. Contravening all security procedures of the time, a radio message was sent to members of the Belgian Resistance to inform them, in advance, of the time, location and aiming point of the raid so that they could observe and later

Armourers loads bombs aboard B.Mk.IV DX367 of 105 Sqn in December 1942. Note how the shrouded exhausts have scorched the cowlings. (© BAE SYSTEMS)

Navigator Flt Lt D W Allen DFC and pilot Flt Lt T P Lawrence stand in front of LR503, a B.Mk.IX of 105 Sqn on the occasion of its 203rd mission. The aircraft has a painted-over nose containing the 'Oboe' navigation equipment. (via Martin Bowman)

report on the exact fall of the bombs from the small Mosquito force. Two days after the operation, the scientists at the TRE had reports of where all the bombs had gone with distances from the aiming point in yards. It seems that, at great danger to themselves, the Belgians had paced out the fall of each individual bomb!

Other calibration raids were still needed to make the system scientifically accurate. On the night of 21/22 December 1942 six aircraft from 109 Sqn, each carrying four 500 lb high-explosive bombs, attacked the coking plant of a power station at Lutterade in Holland from an altitude of around 8,000 ft. Two nights later, on Christmas Eve, the target was the Ruhort Steel Works. Confirmation of the accuracy of this attack was provided by an unexpected source: the traitor and propagandist William Joyce, known in England as 'Lord Haw-Haw' He announced during a routine German propaganda broadcast that some British aircraft had '...broken the peace of the Christmas night and destroyed several graves by bombs in a remote cemetery in southern Germany'.

This news was received with much gratification by scientists at the TRE near Malvern, for they knew that a small graveyard was situated just to the south of the Mosquitos' aiming point.

A total of thirteen Mosquito squadrons operated with 8 Group; these were 83, 97,105, 109, 128,139,142,162,163, 571, 608, 627 and 692. Later 83, 97, and 627 Sqns were transferred to 5 Group to assist them with pathfinding techniques.

The PFF Mosquito force was divided into two main sections: the target-marking force with the two 'Oboe' squadrons formed part of the PFF proper; while the remainder constituted what Bennett referred to as the Light Night Striking Force (LNSF) whose chief role was 'nuisance bombing'.

The successful results of the early long-range flights to targets such as Berlin were repeated when these 'nuisance' raids began in April 1943 with another raid on Berlin to 'celebrate Hitler's birthday'; it was flown by nine aircraft from 105 Squadron and two from 139. These raids developed into operations that caused far greater disruption than could normally have been expected from such a small force. A typical air raid warning in Germany could, for example, indicate at one extreme a

A bombing photograph taken during a precision raid on the Stork Engineering and Diesel Works at Hengelo, Holland on 10 October 1942. (© BAE SYSTEMS)

thousand-bomber raid saturating a target or a small raid undertaken by just a few Mosquitos. Either way, civilians were forced to take to the shelters, resulting in a loss of war production, an erosion of home front morale and the sowing of much confusion in the defenders' minds as to where the main target lay. As more and more Mosquitos became available, they were organized into 'Siren' tours the bombing of several targets on one mission so named after the air raid warning sirens which could be triggered all over Germany by such a sortie. The LNSF was thus quickly making its presence felt, but there were even bigger things to come.

The 4,000 lb Bomber

Increasing the all-up weight, and therefore the potential combat load, of the Mosquito was vitally important. Three production B.Mk.IXs (LR495-497) fitted with two-stage Merlins were completed by March 1943. LR495 went to Farnborough where it took off at 23,000 lb, the highest Mosquito weight so far. The load included 200 lb of desert equipment, four 500 lb bombs in the fuselage, a 500 lb bomb on each wing rack and 540 gallons of fuel.

These high-weight tests were of critical importance, for in April 1943 it was decided that the Mosquito would carry the 4,000 lb bomb, commonly known as the 'Blockbuster'. (A mistaken impression has grown up over the years that the weapon was code-named 'Cookie', a name in colloquial use with the squadrons at the time. This was actually the official designation for any bomb load incorporating the 4,000 lb bomb.) Air Chief Marshal Harris took the view that if it was possible it would be the only light bomber capable of such a delivery it would be a further blow to German morale. His decision was made against the wishes of the experts on his staff, who believed that the normal load of four 500 lb high-explosive bombs produced a greater destructive effect. He overruled them and the Ministry of Aircraft Production began discussions with Hatfield on how to adapt the airframe.

The changes needed to the B.Mk.IV appeared to be straightforward, with modification to the bomb doors to take the extra diameter of the bomb and some work on the main supporting structure. Two of the bombs arrived at Hatfield in order to test it all; one was medium-skinned, the other thin-skinned for greater blast effect. A simple loading arrangement was designed whereby the bomb was slung in from a hook which was fitted to a bridge of two spruce beams fixed to the front and rear wing spars. The redesign of the bomb doors with a fairing aft meant that the new fuselage belly was slightly swollen, and this made the aircraft identifiable to keen-eyed observers.

The trial installation of a B.Mk.IV with the bulged bomb-bay doors in November 1943.
(© BAE SYSTEMS)

Loading a 4,000 lb bomb aboard a Mosquito - this was the heaviest single item the aircraft was to carry. (© *BAE SYSTEMS*)

DZ594. the first of the modified B.IVs made its maiden flight in early July but could not be fully tested at Hatfield because the all-up weight of around 21,500 lb was too heavy for a take-off from the Hatfield runway. The subsequent load trials at Boscombe Down were a success, although there were some minor troubles that were cured.

The aircraft (now known as the B.IV Special) were a little unstable in flight but their handling was greatly improved when the elevators were fitted with larger horn balances. DZ594 had flown at an all-up weight of 25,200 lb and was still reasonably stable, but more improvement was required before the variant could enter squadron service. The obvious sign that the limit had been reached on increasing all-up weight was the unsatisfactory nature of single-engined directional control. Boscombe Down provisionally passed the modified B.Mk.IV with the larger elevator horn balance, the rear camera removed, and 60 lb of ballast fitted in the nose. Stability problems remained with the 4,000 lb bomb conversion of the B.IV and the later B.IX that were never really cured, a fact that resulted in very few being modified. The first examples reached 8 Group in February 1944 and on the night of 23/24 February three aircraft -DZ534, DZ637 and DZ647 - from 692 Sqn made their operational debut against Dusseldorf.

To cure these stability problems, the Mk.XVI, equipped with a pressure cabin and Marshall's blower, was designed to take full advantage of the Merlin 72 engines and was intended to carry 4,000-pounders to an altitude of 35,000ft. This powerful aircraft had the ability to reach Berlin with its 4,000 lb load and carry enough fuel internally and in two externally mounted 50 gallon drop-tanks for a 1,200 mile mission. The worst moment for the crew was during take-off: if anything happened to cause an abandonment, a bomb of such size would go off on impact, fused or unfused. Pilots therefore evolved a safety-first take-off procedure in which the aircraft was kept on the runway until about 200 yards from the end, even if the runway was

2,000 yards long, to allow the speed to build up and so give a better chance of take-off in the event of an engine failure. Even that technique was not without risk, especially if done at night or in bad weather. Ironically, it was equally as dangerous to return to base with the weapon on board, for the 4,000 lb bomb could not be dropped 'safe'. A special jettison area was therefore allocated in the Wash for this purpose. If all this proved impossible, a very careful landing was necessary.

A perfectly timed picture of a 4,000 lb bomb just having been released from MM200 'X' of 128 Sqn.
(© BAE SYSTEMS)

Mighty Range of Weaponry

The RAF's bombers and fighter-bombers could carry an enormous variety of weaponry in bomb form, as the table shows. Much of this material, although not all, could be used with Mosquitos. All RAF ordnance was grouped into specific classes. The largest of these was high-explosive (HE) and this in turn was sub-divided into categories arranged by gross weight and charge/weight ratio (CWR), which gave the percentage of explosive as a portion of the stated gross weight. For example, General Purpose had a CWR of 30-35 percent; Medium Capacity had one of 40-50 per cent; while High Capacity had a mighty one of 75-80 per cent. Several other categories existed, including Armour Piercing (AP), Deep Penetration (DP) and Fragmentation.

The main explosive charge was, in general terms, insensitive to both heat and shock, which allowed the weapons to be handled safely in the less than perfect conditions found in service use. To initiate the explosive process there was a built-in pocket in the nose and/or tail which contained a mildly sensitive explosive and provision for a detonator. Detonators came in many categories, depending on what delay, if any, was required before initiating the explosion. Two principal devices were used to prime the bomb. The first was the fuse, which contained a small amount of highly sensitive explosive triggered off at a certain point. The second was a purely mechanical striker device, the pistol, which was screwed into the detonator pocket by hand. Both, as stated, could be set with time delays and

BOMB TYPES IN RAF USE DURING THE SECOND WORLD WAR

Type	Weight	Period of Use	Total Dropped	Total Weight
Fire	20 lb	1945	14	280 lb
Float	250 lb	1944	32	256,000 lb
Fragmentation	20 lb	1944	532	10,640 lb
High-explosive (AP)	40lb	1944	104	4,160 lb
High-explosive (AP)	20 lb	1943	72	1,440 lb
High-explosive (GP)	1,000 lb	1940-45	2	2,000 lb
High-explosive (GP)	500 lb	1939-45	11,763	5,881,500 lb
High-explosive (GP)	250 lb	1939-45	778	194,500 lb
High-explosive (HC)	4,000 lb	1941-45	776	3,104,000 lb
High-explosive (MC)	4,000 lb	1943-45	141	564,000 lb
High-explosive (MC)	500 lb	1942-45	31,357	15,678,500 lb
High-explosive (MC)	1,000 lb	1943-45	12	12,000 lb
High-explosive (MC)	250 lb	1944	4	1,000 lb
High-explosive (M2)	4,000 lb	1943-45	7,469	29,876,000 lb
Incendiary (explosive)	4 lb	1943-45	280	1,120 lb
Incendiary	250 lb	1940-45	62	15,500 lb
Incendiary	4,000 lb	1942-43	8	32,000 lb
Incendiary	30 lb	1941-44	128	3,840 lb
Incendiary	4 lb	1940-45	18,866	75,464 lb
Incendiary (Type 14)*	4 lb	1944-45	6,678	26,712 lb
Incendiary (Type 15)*	4 lb	1944-45	3,160	12,640 lb
Spot Fire	250 lb	1944-45	396	99,000 lb
Smoke	500 lb	1944	17	8,500 lb
Smoke	100 lb	1944	10	1,000 lb
Target Indicator	250 lb	1943-45	16,632	4,158,000 lb
Target Indicator	1,000 lb	1942-45	347	347,000 lb
Napalm (in gallons)	-	1945	11,000	-

*Type 14 and 15 Incendiary bombs were used in clusters of 106, 110, 158, and 236, including a mix of 10 per cent explosive incendiaries

both set in motion a chain reaction which led to the larger explosive going off. Some of the later fuse types incorporated anti-handling devices, which were intended to prevent enemy bomb disposal squads from rendering the weapon safe. Unfortunately, these devices were a double-edged sword, in that they created yet another hazard for the RAF's armourers to handle if any bomb so fitted had to be brought back from a sortie.

Other groups included incendiary, practice and pyrotechnics. The latter were the most multi-purpose; they were used for target-marking, illumination and identification, photographic flashes, marine markers (used to mark targets and to check wind drift when flying over water), and flares. The need for photographic flashes arose from an operational requirement to record exactly where each aircrew had dropped their weapons. The flash was released at a pre-set time after the explosive store and set to explode at a predetermined height above the target, yet in a position outside the angle of view of the aircraft's camera. This allowed a clear target photograph to be taken without displaying the flash-bomb in the picture. These 'fireworks' ranged in weight from a few pounds up to the size of a 4,000 lb 'Pink Pansy'.

Improving Raid Effectiveness

By mid-1943 RAF heavy bombers were operating beyond the range of 'Oboe' so the Mosquito squadrons were allocated the new task of attacking specialized targets such as manufacturing complexes in western Germany. They started with a raid on Emden, during September, flown by B.Mk.IXs carrying six 500 lb bombs (four in the fuselage and two on wing-points). From a release height of around 30,000ft they achieved an accuracy of 80% of the load placed within 100 yards of the aiming point. This was very impressive for its time.

Such results meant that, in due course, the German V-1 flying bomb launch sites could be targeted for destruction with some confidence. The failure to close down the sites totally in 1944 revealed that the Mosquitos and 'Oboe' were not nearly accurate enough. Admittedly the sites were difficult ones to hit; they were small and awkwardly constructed, as well as being located in Occupied Europe, thus endangering local civilians should misses occur. But this prompted further research into the accuracy of delivery systems.

A Mosquito was tested at RAE Farnborough while equipped with an experimental auto-pilot and bomb-release mechanism. The idea was that the unit would receive a series of 'Oboe' signals from the ground which allowed the aircraft to be directed automatically to the correct point over the target. On receipt of a further signal, the stores would be released. This entirely automatic process was intended to remove the lag created by the human operators, who took time to interpret the signal before releasing the stores.

This clever system was also used in reverse for pathfinder operations when Mosquitos were fitted with *Gee-H* and later *H2S* radar for pathfinder operations. *Gee-H* was a beam radar system used for navigation or blind bombing. In this instance an airborne transmitter in a Mosquito interrogated two ground beacons to obtain a fix. The system demonstrated good accuracy, with a range of about 300 miles but was found to be susceptible to jamming. The more sophisticated *H2S* was also a ground scanner but this 'S' band (10cm) radar utilized a revolving antenna within the aircraft to feed signals into a cockpit radar screen which presented images of the ground terrain. The system freed the aircraft from the range limitations of *'Oboe'* and *'Gee-H'*, but it did not have the accuracy. Many of the *Gee-H* and *H2S* Mosquitos were used on the 'Siren' tours mentioned earlier, ranging far and wide over Germany and hitting special targets.

Low-Level Target Marking

As we have seen, the Pathfinder Force used electronic equipment from high altitudes to help it with its target-marking. Other, perhaps more skilful, techniques were used by 627 Sqn which preferred to rely on low-level, human visual methods, combined with excellent flying.

Under the command of Wing Commander R. P. Elliott, DSO, DFC, the squadron began dive-marking practice on the Wainfleet Sands ranges, with the intention of placing a marker within 50 yards of any given target. Initially, practice dives began at 18,000 ft down to a height of 12,000 ft for release, but it was discovered that the accuracy was not good enough and the aircraft's speed at the end of the dive was far too high. Dives were then started at lower and lower levels until the optimum was found: dive commencement at 3,000 ft with stores release

With bulged bomb-bay and wing-mounted drop-tanks, this is a fine study of B.Mk.XVI ML991 in flight.
(Authors Collection)

The damage done to the Phillips factory at Eindhoven, Holland on 6 December 1942. The photograph was taken from Mosquito DZ314 of 139 Sqn, the unit which led the raid by 2 Group aircraft.

(© BAE SYSTEMS)

at 1,000 ft. In combat this technique was dependent on prevailing weather conditions, for an aircraft's crew had to identify the target and make a shallow dive ending in a low-level run, before the target markers were released from as low as 100 ft. It was generally used to great effect. Group Captain Leonard Cheshire of 617 'Dam Busters' Sqn flew a Mosquito using the same target-marking technique on several of the squadron's raids, but eventually 627 took over much of 617's marking work.

As many raids were in Occupied Europe rather than Germany concern was expressed that the civilian population should be affected as little as possible. The use of 627's technique could minimize any danger to the local population by very accurately marking both ends of the target under attack, so that the heavy bombers which followed could drop their bomb loads in between the two sets of target indicators. One such example was a small factory that had been subjected to a USAAF daylight attack from high level that had left the target untouched. The Mosquitos were called in and 627 Sqn marked the target with ease, although a minor problem occurred when the first markers were dropped with such accuracy that they fell through the glass roof of the factory, becoming almost invisible.

Towards the latter part of the war those aircrew who had gained most experience were used to great effect by 627 Sqn which employed these men in a 'Master Bomber' role. They directed the attack from the Main Force via a VHF radio link as they orbited, often at low-level, and would call in more target indicators if they deemed it appropriate. It was while engaged on one such sortie that 627 Sqn's Base Operations Officer, unofficially taking the role of Master Bomber to direct the attack against Rheydt in the Ruhr valley, met his death while flying in a Mosquito B.XX (KB267 'E') during the night of 29/30 September 1944. The officer's name was Wing Commander Guy Gibson, VC. He had volunteered for the operation in order to relieve the boredom of his desk job.

Second Tactical Air Force Operations

From June 1943 onwards when the Allies were beginning to prepare for the invasion of France, 2 Group, Bomber Command's light and medium bomber force, was transferred to Fighter Command control. This then evolved through several stages into the Allied Expeditionary Air Force (AEAF) that officially came into being on 13 November 1943 as a joint air force, separate from existing commands, for the exclusive use of the Allied Expeditionary Force. This new air arm was made up from three main components: the USAAF 9th Air Force (which already existed), and the former RAF Fighter Command which was divided into the Second Tactical Air Force (2TAF) and the Air Defence of Great Britain (ADGB) A number of the squadrons in the AEAF were equipped with the fighter-bomber Mosquito Mk.VI, some of which operated mainly in a fighter role (already mentioned in the 'Fighters' chapter) while others tended to specialize in bomber operations.

Their first significant action was the famous Amiens Prison raid led by Group Captain Percy Charles Pickard, DSO, DFC. In January 1944 London received intelligence that indicated that over 100 members of the French resistance, many of whom had helped downed Allied airmen to escape, were being held in the gaol awaiting execution, together with several hundred non-political prisoners. In response to a desperate plea from the French Marquis to rescue their countrymen, the French Government in exile requested that the RAF break down the walls and other sections of the prison, as this seemed to be the only possible method of enabling a mass break-out to be made. The task was accepted and provisionally planned for 17 February. 140 Wing of the 2nd Tactical Air Force was given the job. Dense cloud and heavy snowstorms unfortunately delayed proceedings by 24 hours. The 18th finally dawned, misty and snowy as the crews awoke for what was then still a secret briefing. Six crews

from 487 Sqn, RNZAF, at Hunsdon were given the lead part (in an effort to raise morale following a serious accident at their base), six crews were chosen from 21 Sqn RAF and another six from 464 Sqn RAAF. Also detailed was Mosquito DZ414 of the RAF Film Production Unit flown by Flt Lt Tony Wickham to record the sortie with the aim of bringing back enough footage of the raid to allow the propaganda experts to produce a morale-boosting film.

Detailed planning in the short time available had been conducted in great secrecy, using an intricately made plaster of paris model of the cruciform building, to be studied by the crews at great length. The prison was surrounded by a wall 20ft high by 3ft thick and the six machines from 487 Sqn, forming

Above: Group Captain Percy Charles Pickard DSO, DFC, leader of the legendary jail-busting raid against the Amiens prison.

Left: HX917 EG:E of 487 Sqn RNZAF who was one of the participants in the Amiens Raid.
(both © BAE SYSTEMS)

A model used for briefing the aircrew before the attack on the Amiens prison.
(© BAE SYSTEMS)

the first attack wave, were to breach this on the east and north sides. A second wave, from 464 Sqn, was then to open up either end of the prison building proper, destroying the German garrison quarters in the process. The third wave, the RAF one, was to stand by until needed, while the photographic Mosquito was to take still and cine photographs of the action. Exact timing was essential, both to avoid collisions over the target as the Mosquitos flew over it at right-angles, and to ensure that the French resistance members gathered outside the gaol would be ready to assist the prisoners in making good their escape. It was an attack that was almost custom-designed to test the Mosquito's ability, not in the usual destructive sense but in an attempt to save as many lives as possible.

The nineteen aircraft, each carrying a pair of 500 lb bombs, left Hunsdon in a snowstorm a few minutes before 1100 hrs, heading for a point on the Sussex coast

Smoke and dust pour from the prison buildings during the raid. Rubble from the hole in the perimeter wall is clearly visible against the snow on the ground..
(© BAE SYSTEMS)

Above: One of the Mosquitos seen during the attack, showing the prison on what was then the outskirts of the town.

Right: Damage to buildings and the prison walls are clearly visible in this view.
(both © BAE SYSTEMS)

near Littlehampton where they were to meet up with twelve Hawker Typhoons of 198 Sqn which were to act as their escort. Four Mosquitos became detached from the formation, two from 21 Sqn and two from 464 Sqn, together with four Typhoons which failed to link up in the bad weather. These eight aircraft returned to base. The remainder crossed the Channel at wave-top height before climbing to 5,000 ft as they crossed the French coast into better weather. As the force swept to the north of Amiens in order to approach the prison along the straight poplar-lined road leading to the target, the winter sun was casting shadows across the snow-covered landscape. Working to the briefing, the force split into three sections flying at tree-top height. The first wave, led by Wing Commander T.S.

Smith, attacked the eastern wall from a very low height but failed to breach it. The second wave made a 90 degree sweep to the north, then dropped their bombs deliberately short, neatly blowing holes in the northern wall. Two aircraft from 464 Sqn then bombed the guards' dining room at the base of the main prison structure, where it was thought that the majority of the German guards would be at around midday. This was successful and left two aircraft from the same squadron to bomb the main building. Seeing that the attack had been successful in breaching both the compound and prison, Group Captain Pickard, acting as Master Bomber, called off the remaining four aircraft belonging to 21 Sqn that left the area.

The Film Unit Mosquito, which had been orbiting to the north, then made three runs over the target to film the results. All the Mosquitos then had to leave for home very quickly, for a group of Fw.190s had already been engaged by the escorting Typhoons. Pickard, having observed the success of the attack, left the area at low-level, but it seems that his machine was damaged by ground fire. A few moments later a pair of Fw.190s attacked and shot off the tail of his machine, HX922, EG:F, which crashed near Montigny.

Of the nineteen aircraft that left Hunsdon, three were damaged, one totally beyond repair, and two failed to return. It was later learned that out of the 700 prisoners held in the gaol, 258 had escaped, many of whom were due to be executed; about 50 of their German captors were killed in the bombing. However, the miracle that the planners hoped for did not occur; indeed quite the opposite. Some bombs had fallen outside the prison, causing widespread damage to the hospital at St. Victor and about 30 domestic houses. On top of this, 150 prisoners were lying dead or wounded in the rubble of the prison block, killed either by the bombing or subsequent German machine-gun fire.

Despite the apparent failure to save the lives of many of the prisoners, five days later a message was received in London from the French Resistance which read: *'I thank you in the name of my comrades for bombardment of the prison. The*

A post raid reconnaissance photograph of the Amiens prison. The damages wall at the lower right was one area where the prisoners escaped.
(© BAE SYSTEMS)

delay was too short and we were not able to save all, but thanks to the admirable
precision of attack the first bombs blew in nearly all the doors and many
prisoners escaped with the help of the civilian population. Twelve of these
prisoners were to have been shot the next day'.

The next special daytime low-level raid took place on 11 April 1944, when six
machines of 613 Sqn attacked the Kunstzaal Kleizkamp Art Gallery in The Hague.
This building was being used by the Gestapo to store the Dutch Central
Population Registry and was located in the Scheveningsche Weg in the Hague.
Again, this was to destroy Gestapo records on the local population, with only one
five-storey building targeted.

The formation, led by Sqn Ldr Bateson in LR255 SY:H left Lasham at 1305 hrs
and flew via Luton to Swanton Morley where the Mosquitos refuelled and then
took off again to cross the Suffolk coast at Southwold, heading out over the North
Sea at 50ft to prevent detection by enemy radar. Before the squadron reached
the Dutch coast at Overflakkee, it climbed to 4,000ft, then descended again to
very low level and made its way to Gouda and from there to Delft, where flood
water made map-reading (and therefore navigation) difficult. While the first two
machines attacked the target with 500 lb delayed-action bombs, the other four
circled a lake to the east of the target. The third and fourth aircraft carried
incendiaries, but by this time the target was covered in smoke and difficult to
locate. The fifth aircraft dropped two delayed-action HEs and two incendiaries, but
the sixth machine encountered trouble and failed to attack; nevertheless it did
photograph the burning building. All six aircraft returned safely, with only one
machine (NS844 SY:A), flown by Sqn Ldr C. W. M. Newman, damaged by light flak.
The Air Ministry was later to call it a '*...brilliant attack on a very difficult and*
important target'.

Later that year, on 31 October, the Gestapo headquarters in Jutland, Denmark,

The results of the low-level attack by 613 Sqn on the Kinstaal Kleizkamp Art Gallery building in the Hague, being used by the Gestapo as the Dutch Central Population Registry. *(© BAE SYSTEMS)*

housed in two buildings of Aarhus University, received attention from twenty-four Mosquitos of 21, 464 and 487 Sqns. As with the earlier Oslo and Hague raids, the intention was to destroy German records that were used for the persecution of Danish patriots. The aircrews' briefing was similar to that of the Amiens raid, conducted in great secrecy with the aid of a plaster model. The attack formation led by Group Captain Wykeham-Barnes comprised four sections of six aircraft, each carrying bombs fitted with 11-second delay fuses, so that each section could bomb without risk, but leave as little time as possible between section attacks.

On the run-in to the target the weather was poor, but it cleared enough over Aarhus so that the bombs were well placed. Such was the level of surprise achieved by the Mosquitos that it was some while before any German anti-aircraft guns opened up. As the formation flew over Denmark, many Danes waved or saluted the attacking aircraft; one man, standing close to the target, was seen to duck as the bombs whistled overhead! The raid was not, however, without incident. Squadron Leader Denton of 487 Sqn in PZ332 EG:A returned with only half the tailplane and tailwheel and a damaged engine nacelle after he flew so low that his aircraft brushed the ground. Another aircraft from the same squadron (PZ164 'EG:K) forced-landed in Sweden and two others returned with bomb-blast damage. Numerous other machines received bird strike damage during the sea crossing.

Contemporary newspaper reports stated that *'The first formation was over the target a few minutes before noon, said another pilot. There was low cloud and light very bad. In fact, it was getting so dark that lights were in the rooms of the*

The Mosquito attack on the Aarhus University in Denmark, showing two Mosquitos, taken from a third as the bomb the already over the burning buildings.
(© BAE SYSTEMS)

University when we approached the target. Some of our fellows could see people dashing across the rooms, apparently rushing for shelter. The leading navigator said that everything went according to plan, the weather was pretty dirty just before we reached the target, but it cleared to give us a good run up, he added. I could see the bombs of the first section go squarely into the middle of the left-hand building. The pilot of a Mosquito, whose task it was to take photographs said, "I made three runs across the target, the bombing was very accurate". "I did not see any bombs outside the target area, although there appeared to be some damage to neighbouring buildings, probably owing to blast or flying debris. The attack had all the appearance of a surprise assault, for it was not until it was nearly over that the enemy woke up and then the last section had to make their run up in the face of fairly intense flak". Another pilot said "We

could see lots of people giving the 'V' sign and waving, one man who was ploughing in a field on the way to the target, came to attention and saluted as we passed. Some of the Mosquitos were less than ten feet above the buildings and I saw a man duck as the bombs from the Mosquitos ahead of me passed over his head on their way into the building". A pilot going into the attack at low level saw "someone squirting at him with a machine gun through the windows of one of the building". He resolved to squirt back so went down still lower and as a result left his tailwheel behind him on the roof.

In December 1944 627 Sqn staged a repeat of 105 Sqn's 1942 attack on the Gestapo headquarters in Norway. The twelve aircraft, in two groups of six, took off from Woodhall Spa in Lincolnshire just before 0930 hrs on 31 December and headed for Oslo. Led by Wing Commander G. W. Curry, they had difficulty in finding the target, for as with

the first raid, the weather was good. However, they failed to achieve surprise and were met with heavy fire from flak batteries on the ground and ships in the harbour. All the aircraft returned, landing at Peterhead airfield, but every machine had been damaged in some way by the flak. The Gestapo headquarters building received only minor damage, but it was estimated that around 1,000 civilians had been made homeless, with 77 killed and 58 wounded. Two years apart, neither raid had been completely successful, but they did provide a great morale boost, for they were undertaken in full daylight against an objective that was loathed and feared by the Norwegian population.

Two more albeit poor quality, but highly important photographs showing the Mosquito attack on the Aarhus University in Denmark. The upper photograph was taken of a bomb exploding just as a Mosquito overflies. In both photographs, a number of German vehicles can be seen on the ground. *(all © BAE SYSTEMS)*

The Gestapo were again the target in the next low-level precision raid of this type, in March 1945. The former Shell building in Copenhagen, taken over by the Germans, was believed to contain some forty Danish secret army chiefs, held in custody on the top floor. These included Dr Mogens Fog, political chief of anti-Nazi operations of the Freedom Council, and Professor Brant Rehberg, a scientific colleague of the Danish physicist Niels Bohr. It was hoped that they might escape along with their comrades. Gestapo files held in the lower part of the building had also to be destroyed before an in-depth study could be made of them by the Germans. With these aims in mind the Mosquitos would have to operate at very low-level to get under the German radar screen and then sweep into Copenhagen's streets for an opportunity to take just one shot per aircraft.

Audacious Danish resistance workers stole a boat and photographed the building from the sea approach, providing a view of the target exactly as the crews could expect to see it during the last stage of the attack. Old tourist photographs and travel brochures were located and used to create a large model of Copenhagen, so that the men could study it from the correct angle - by crouching down beside the table. There were considerable risks to the local population, because the HQ was in a densely populated area of the city and a large convent school adjoined it. Even with everything going perfectly to plan, it was expected that there would be some Danish casualties. It was believed that the benefits of the attack outweighed the potential drawbacks and the go-ahead was therefore given.

Shortly before dawn on 21 March 1945, eighteen Mosquitos drawn from the three squadrons of 140 Wing (21, 464 and 487) and the Film Production Unit took off from Fersfield, Norfolk, and were joined by a fighter escort of 64 Sqn's North American Mustangs. Each Mosquito was carrying bombs fused with an 11-second delay to allow each machine to escape its own bomb blast. The first and third waves carried incendiaries, while the second carried high-explosive. Group Captain Robert Bateson was the formation leader in RS570 'X', with Ted Sismore as the master navigator leading the aircraft directly for Jutland. They flew so low over the North Sea that the windscreens became coated with salt-spray. Flying in the 3 position off Bateson's port side was a certain Wing Commander 'Smith'. This was in fact Air Vice-Marshal Basil Embry who had instigated the raid and obtained authorization for it to take place from Churchill himself. The records are confusing in that some state that Embry had been forbidden to take part by his superiors because his knowledge of future war plans was too great for him to risk capture; others state that Embry had a price on his head for he had been charged with murder by the Germans back in 1940 when he killed three people while escaping dressed as a civilian and

It looks like a low-level photograph of a city - until you notice smoke above the building on the centre right and the Mosquito in the bottom right of the photograph!

It is in fact a photograph taken during 140 Wing's attack on the former Shell Building in Copenhagen. (© BAE SYSTEMS)

would have been a prime target if he was sot down and captured. Whatever the real reason, he had secretly gone on the mission regardless.

The Germans had attempted to camouflage the building, but as it was the only one painted green and grey it stood out! *'It was...',* according to Bateson, *'...a case of bowling right down the alley, releasing the bombs at the right moment, and pulling away in a tight turn up a side street'.*

At the height of the raid the worst possible thing happened. A Mosquito from 21 Sqn, DZ977 YH:T flown by Wing Commander Peter A Kleboe, along with his navigator Flying Officer Reg Hall, was caught up in a sudden melee of aircraft when the second wave of machines, confused by the fires, decided to make another run on the target. Kleboe's wing caught a flagpole, which spun his aircraft into the Catholic school, killing nuns and children in the resultant explosions. Unfortunately the smoke and flames from the crash led to following pilots mistaking the school for the Gestapo HQ and hitting it again.

The six-storey Shell building was set ablaze, many Gestapo officers were killed and their records had been largely destroyed. In the chaos some thirty leading Danish resistance members escaped from their interrogation cells. The cost was ten airmen, 27 teachers and 87 children killed with many more civilians injured.

None of these precision raids could be described as totally successful for with the benefit of hindsight, inadvertently they killed or injured many civilians, or the people they were supposed to rescue. The planners must have expected a certain number of casualties, having weighed this possibility against the value of such attacks on these very important targets. Nevertheless, every raid of this nature gave the message to friend and foe alike that in the Mosquito the Allies possessed an aircraft that could and would make precision attacks with impunity.

Anti-Shipping Roles

The Mosquito bomber airframe was capable of lifting a large amount of standard explosive ordnance, but there were other, more unconventional, weapons in the RAF's armoury. On the night of 16 May 1943, 617 Squadron led by Wing Commander Guy Gibson, used a special mine or 'bouncing bomb' code-named *'Upkeep'* to breach a number of German dams in the Ruhr valley. The weapon had been designed by Dr Barnes Wallis but there was also a parallel, although less well publicized weapons system developed in the form of *'Highball';* this was a smaller anti-shipping mine designed to sink the German battleship *Tirpitz* in the Norwegian fjords. It was delivered in the same manner as 'Upkeep', was highly secret and intended for daylight use.

'Highball's' origins date back to November 1942 when the Bristol Beaufort was selected as the machine to carry two of the spherical mines in tandem. The aircraft was to descend to 25ft and release the mines nearly a mile from the target. They would then bounce along the water one behind the other, having been backspun to nearly 1000 rpm by an air turbine- driven belt. It was expected that the spinning mines would leap over the battleship's defensive booms and nets, strike the hull, rebound and then sink to a preselected depth where a hydrostatic pistol would detonate the mine's 600 lb charge of Torpex.

The performance figures for the Mosquito soon revealed that this aircraft would be a better carrier of the weapon, so on 24 March 1943 a Mosquito B.IV (DK290) was flown to Heston for the trial installation of a modified bomb bay minus the weapons drive. On arrival at the Heston Aircraft Company, the aircraft was stripped of surplus equipment and a heavy electrical generator was fitted which would spin up the relatively massive '*Highball*' bombs, half-housed in the open bomb bay. Target date for the raid, launched from Sumburgh, was set for 15 May.

618 Sqn, commanded by Squadron Leader Charles F. Rose, had been specially formed to use the mine and just nine days later it borrowed a number of Mosquitos from RAF Marham in order to train at Manston, Kent. The unit practised its drops at Reculver on the north Kent coast and had varying degrees of success with a series of wooden skinned development weapons.

By 5 May the Ministry of Aircraft Production decreed that trials of steel-cased weapons should begin immediately. The attack procedure called for the stores to be spun up to 700 rpm, then released at an altitude of between 50 and 60ft 1,200 yards from the target while flying at 360mph. Squadron Leader Rose made ten drops of mines on 10 May but half of them failed to operate correctly, due to a failure of the release mechanism. It was now obvious that the target date for the raid could not be met, but it was decided that the trials would continue, since it was thought that the Germans would be unlikely to learn the secrets of the novel system of delivery from the dams raid. Indeed, after the war it was discovered that the Germans thought that rocket-propelled bombs had been used to breach the dams.

618 Squadron received its first modified B.Mk.IVs on 14 May and by the end of the month had fifteen. The stores release problems were overcome in early July and attention could now be devoted to the problem of sighting. During August a completely unexpected decision was announced: the squadron was told that in order for them to get operational experience, the stores were to be used as simple depth-charges. Trials were hurriedly arranged for later that month, but as suddenly as the order came, it was rescinded. To 618 Sqn it appeared that the end was near, for on 13 September it was ordered to dispatch its aircraft for storage, despite the fact that only a week earlier the '*Highball*' stores were beginning to perform as planned. The recent performance increases were then taken into account and the entire programme was reconsidered. 618 Sqn was reassembled at Wick in Scotland and on 12 November 1943 Vickers received an order for 250 steel-covered weapons. Six of the squadron's aircraft continued to train with some of the old mines at RAF Turnberry.

In an attempt to assist with sighting, a ring aperture was designed to fit on to the pilot's helmet. Hand sights, and a fixed one for the navigator, were also developed, but good height judgment was the main requirement. Problems continued to arise though, with companies unable to meet their supply dates. Then, in early 1944, it became obvious that low-level Merlin 25s were needed for the remaining eleven Mosquito B.Mk.IVs.

This extended period of development reduced the level of operational flying, which began to affect squadron morale. Detachments were therefore made to 248 Sqn where 618 Sqn crews could fly Mk.XVIII *Tsetse* Mosquitos.

On 9 July 1944 orders were given to reconstitute 618 Sqn at Wick before the squadron was sent on anti-shipping operations in the Pacific theatre from aircraft-carriers under the code-name of Operation '*Oxtail*'. Airspeed and Marshalls of Cambridge re-engined the aircraft with Merlin 25s, installed air turbines to set the stores

spinning, fitted armour plate (which had previously been removed), new windscreens and arrester hooks to allow carrier borne operations. While the conversion programme was carried out, the squadron moved to Beccles in Suffolk during August.

On 10 September 1944 a Mosquito FB.MkVI (DZ537/'G') arrived at RAE Farnborough to have its unstrengthened fuselage tested with up to 1.9g retardation to ascertain the type's suitability for carrier-based work. Ten Mk.VIs were sent to Beccles and Captain Eric Brown, RN who had been the first pilot to land a Mosquito on a carrier that January arrived with just two days to instruct the squadron's pilots in the art of deck landing, on a specially painted runway; they also carried out practice attacks using a sashlite-bulb acting as the bomb to allow the aircraft's height and run to be checked. Meanwhile 68 test drops of the stores were made at

Top: A B.Mk.IV seen during the *Highball* trials at Loch Scriven in Scotland.

Above: A *Highball* weapon is loaded into the front position of this Mosquito. Note the fairing ahead of it on the fuselage.
(© BAE SYSTEMS)

Wells-Next-the-Sea on the north Norfolk coast where a vast area of beach was exposed at low tide, thus allowing the stores to be salved and inspected later.

In October 618 Sqn moved to Turnberry again for live weapons training. The crews were meant to perform their deck landings at Scapa Flow, but the tests was abandoned and the 25 Mosquitos, equipped with five 'Highballs' each, were loaded on to the escort carriers HMS *Striker* and *Fencer* at Glasgow docks, destined for Australia; they arrived at Melbourne on 23 December. The aircraft now went to Narromine, NSW, for 'more training' while the stores went to Sydney for storage. Squadron members whiled away their time on training, for despite strenuous efforts no progress could be made on integrating the unit into the Allied sea campaign. Finally the inevitable occurred on 29 June 1945 when the squadron was disbanded and its entire stock of 'Highball' mines was statically blown up for security reasons.

The ill-fated 'Highball' thus never received the acclaim that 'Upkeep' did after its spectacular raid on the German dams. The trials of the weapon had however demonstrated that the two mines carried in the belly of a Mosquito would have been a very valuable and effective anti-shipping weapon system. Indeed, later developments upgraded the weapon into the Mk.II form, creating a mine that was designed to fit into an easily removed crate on Mosquito Mk.33 and Sea Hornet operations.

A significant conventional mining attack was made in the early hours of 13 May 1944 when ten Mosquito B.Mk.IVs and three B.Mk.XVIs from 692 Sqn set off to raid the Kiel Canal at low level. The bombers would attack after Mosquitos of 100 Group who had first shot up ground defences. The canal was one of the most important waterways in Germany, connecting the Baltic with the North Sea ports. It was particularly important for the carriage of heavy submarine parts from the Baltic to areas such as Bremen, Hamburg and Wilhelmshaven. The mines were carried internally and were dropped on timed runs made from ground markers. They were all released into the narrow strip of water from below 250ft and resulted in complete closure of the canal to traffic for ten days. As this operation was conducted at the height of the ice-free summer, months, when river traffic was at its highest, around a million tonnes of overseas cargo and 230,000 tonnes of coastal cargo was held up for a considerable time. It therefore constituted an important blow to the German war effort. (Another attack on Kiel by Mosquitos on 2 May 1945 was to be the last Bomber Command raid of the war.)

The search for new ordnance and means of delivery continued at A&AEE during 1944 and a Mosquito FB.Mk.VI (HR 135) was tested for the external carriage of naval depth-charges and mines from the under-wing hard points. Suitable fairings were required for the wing carriers, but when installed the aircraft was rapidly cleared to carry stores up to 450mph and drop such stores from low altitude up to a speed of 250mph; above this speed it was discovered that due to airflow pressures there was a tendency for the weapons to 'hang-up' (that is, remain on the carriers). Actual combat reports resulting from these trials are not recorded in A&AEE records, but it is known that naval mines were later used under the wings of aircraft by air forces in other wars.

An earlier, but certainly unofficial, use of this idea occurred shortly after the invasion of France. To supply the invasion troops with some of life's little luxuries, several Mosquito bombers were 'converted' to carry barrels of beer (which are, after all, similar in shape and size to a naval mine) into the forward airstrips behind the advancing forces. No official records of these trips seem to have survived, but it does appear that the Mosquito could reach the parts that other aircraft could not!

Conclusions

Without doubt Geoffrey de Havilland's concept of the unarmed Mosquito bomber proved itself in combat right from the start of operations. But how effective was it as a bomber? This, after all, was the task it was specifically designed for; all the other variants which derived from it were an added bonus. The somewhat intangible yardstick of 'effectiveness' can be drawn against several different sets of data, but perhaps the most graphic illustration is provided by comparing the Mosquito with another Allied bomber type when flown against just one target: the famous American B-17 Fortress and target Berlin.

When I was researching this book, I came across an interesting comparison that I had not seen anywhere else but one that was later often quoted by airshow commentators when BAe's Mosquito RR299 was displaying. During the early part of

Bombing up a Mosquito! In this case it is a B.Mk.35 of 139 Sqn at Hemswell in 1950 and the 'bombs' are in fact 250 lb target indicators. *(DH/BAe/Hatfield)*

the USAAF's campaign against the 'Big City' the 8th Air Force's B-17s were only capable of carrying a 3,500 lb bomb load, due to the routeing they used and the large amount of ammunition which they needed for protection against German day fighters. Each B-17 had a crew of ten men. In comparison, just two men flying the much faster Mosquito could take a 4,000 lb bomb load to Berlin with ease. It also should be noted that Boeing's own figures quote a cruising speed of 150 mph - a figure that compared to the Mosquitos of 265 mph. This suggests that it may have been theoretically possible - but certainly highly improbable - for a single Mosquito with two men on board to make two trips to Berlin delivering 8,000 lbs of ordinance in the same time it took ten men aboard a B-17 to deliver one 3,500lb bombload!

Other interpretations of data produce equally startling results. When one considers the percentage loss rate per sortie, the Mosquitos was considerably lower than that of any other RAF machine. As can also be seen from the chart opposite, the same applies to the bomb load carried per sortie not to mention per man. Although this load was obviously not as high as that of the heavy bombers, the Mosquito was top of the light/medium bombers by a considerable margin. It must be remembered that these figures can only be regarded as minima, for they were compiled using only information obtained from aircraft crews who returned to the United Kingdom after a sortie. At the time of compilation (or even to this day) it was not possible for Air Ministry recorders to know accurately the tonnage of bombs dropped successfully by aircraft on the intended target, if they then failed for whatever reason to make it back to Britain.

It is possible to derive from this chart a 'theoretical average life expectancy' of a typical crew member, simply by dividing the potential crew loss figure by the number of sorties flown. The chart does not take into account the fact that the Mosquito did not serve through the entire period of the conflict (as did some of the others), was fastest of all listed and, because of the Mosquito's speed, in many cases conducted two sorties a night against one for all the others.

As can be seen, these figures provide proof positive of how good a bomber the Mosquito was.

MOSQUITO BOMBERS COMPARED WITH OTHER RAF BOMBER TYPES

Type	Normal Crew	Sorties Flown	Total Tonnage Delivered	Average Tons Dropped per Sortie	Average Tons Dropped per Man	Failed to Return	Potential Crew Losses	Loss Rate per Sortie Ratio (%)
Blenheim	3	12,214	3,028	0.2479	0.1239	443	1,329	3.6269
Halifax	7	82,773	224,207	2.7086	0.3869	1,830	12,810	2.2108
Lancaster	7	156,192	608,612	3.8965	0.5566	3;340	23,380	2.1383
Stirling	7	18,440	27.821	1.5087	0.2155	606	4,242	3.2863
Ventura	5	997	726	0.7281	0.1456	38	190	3.8114
Wellington	5	47,409	41,823	0.8821	0.1764	1,332	6,660	2.8095
Mosquito	2	397,895	26,867	0.6751	0.3375	254	508	0.6382

BOMBER PERFORMANCE DATA

	B.IV	4,000lbconv.	B.XV	B.35
Span	54ft 2in	54ft 2in	54ft 2in	54ft 2in
Length	40ft 9.5in	40ft 9.5in	40ft 6in	40ft 6in
Height	12ft 6in	12ft 6in	12ft 6in	12ſt 6in
Tareweight	13,400 lb	13,400 lb	14,635 lb	14,180 lb
All-upweight	21,462 lb	22,570 lb	23,000 lb	22,100 lb
Maximum speed	380 mph	380 mph	408 mph	425 mph
Cruising speed	265 mph	265 mph	245 mph	300 mph
Initial climb	2,500 ft/min	-	2,800 ft/min	2,000 ft/min
Ceiling	34,000 ft	25,000 ft	37,000 ft	43,000 ft
Maximum range	2,040 miles	1,430 miles	1,485 miles	3,340 miles
Engines: RR Merlin	Mk.21 or 23	Mk.21or 23	Mk.72 & 73	Mk.113 & 114

Performance data for main types of bomber variants, incorporating known data
Note. B.IV & 4,000lb bomb conversion 3.5in longer

SQUADRONS THAT USED BOMBER VARIANTS OF THE MOSQUITO

SQN	CODE	VARIANT	FROM	TO	REMARKS
4	UP	FB.6	9/45	7/50	Renumbered from 605 Sqn, based at Volkel, Holland. Used aircraft in bomber role. Moved to several bases in Germany before re-equipped with Vampire FB.5
8	HV	FB.6	8/46	4/47	Renumbered from 114 Sqn, based at Khormaksar, Aden. Used aircraft in bomber role. Re-equipped with Tempest F.Mk.6.
11	OM	FB.6	10/48	9/50.	Renumbered from 107 Sqn, based at Wahn, Germany. Moved to several bases in Germany before re-equipped with Vampire FB.Mk.5.
14	CX	FB.6 B.35	4/46	7/48	Re-numbered from 128 Sqn, based at Wahn. Re-equipped with Vampire FB.Mk.5.
18	WV	FB.6	3/47	11/47	Re-formed at Kabrit, Suez Canal zone. Moved to Far East and renumbered 1300 (Met) Flight.
21	YH	FB.6	10/43	11/47	Initially based at Sculthorpe. Used on daylight raids, including Amiens Prison attack. Moved through several English bases before moving to France 2/45, then Belgium 4/45, Germany 11/45. Disbanded in Germany 7/11/47
22	-	FB.6	5/46	8/46	Renumbered from 89 Sqn at Seletar, Singapore. Disbanded 15/8/46

SQN	CODE	VARIANT	FROM	TO	REMARKS
69	Wl	FB.6	8/45	3/46	Based at Cambrai, France, after renumbering from 613Sqn. Disbanded 28/3/46
		B.16	4/46	11/47	Based at Wahn after renumbering from 180 Sqn. Disbanded 6/11/47
98	VO	B.16	11/45	2/51	Retained as post-war sqn in Germany. Re-equipped with Vampire FB.5
		B.35			
105	GB	B.4	11/41	2/46	Initially based at Horsham St. Faith. First RAF sqn to receive Mosquitos.
		B.9			Began operations 5/42. Moved to Marham 9/42. Transferred to 8 Group for
		B.16			Pathfinder duties. Moved to Bourn 3/44. To Upwood 6/45. Disbanded 1/2/46.
109	HS	B.4	8/42	9/45	Initially based at Wyton. Used to develop 'Oboe' for Pathefinder duties. To
		B.9			Marham 7/43. To Little Staughton 4/44. Disbanded 30/9/45
		B.16			Renumbered from 627 Sqn at Woodhall Spa. To Wickenby 10/45. To Hemswell
					11/45. To Coningsby 11/46. Re-equipped with Canberra B. Mk.2
110	VE	FB.6	11/44	446	Initially based at Yelahanka, India. Moved through several bases in Far East until disbanded at Labuan, Borneo, 15/4/46
114	RT	FB.6	11/45	9/46	Based at Khormaksar, Aden. Renumbered 8 Sqn 1/9/46
128	M5	B.20	9/44	3/46	Re-formed at Wyton under 8 Group for Pathfinder work. To Warboys 6/45.
		B.25			Transferred to 2 Group 9/45 in Europe. Disbanded 1/4/46 and retitled 14 Sqn
		B.16			
139	XD	B.4	9/42	11/53	Initially based at Horsham St. Faith using 105 Sqn aircraft. Detached Oulton
		B.16			6/42 for one month. To Marham 9/42. To Wyton for 8 Group Pathfinder
		B.20			duties 7/43. Retained as post-war bomber squadron. Re-equipped with
		B.25			Canberra B.2 11/53.
		B.35			
142	4H	B.25	10/44	9/45	Part of 8 Group's Light Night Striking Force. Based at Gransden Lodge. Disbanded 28/9/45
157	RS	FB.6	8/44	8/45	Joined 100 Group on bomber support work 8/44 at Swannington. Disbanded 16/8/45
162	CR	FB.6	1/44	7/46	Part of 8 Group's Light Night Striking Force Based at Bourn. Transferred to Transport Command 7/45 on fast courier work. Disbanded at Blackbushe 14/7/47
163	-	B.25	1/45	8/46	Formed at Wyton as part of 8 Group. Disbanded at Wyton 10/8/45.
		B.16			
180	EV	B.16	9/45	3/46	Based at Wahn, Germany. Renumbered 69 Sqn 1/4/46
211	-	FB.6	6/45	3/46	Based in Burma. Intended for use in invasion of Japanese mainland, but surrender came too soon. Disbanded at Don Muang, Thailand, 28/2/46
305	SM	FB.6	12/43	1/47	Polish sqn, named 'Wielkopolski'. Initially based at Lasham. Used against low-level targets. Disbanded at Faldingworth 6/1/47
502	RAC	B.25	7/46	12/47	Post-war RAuxAFsqn. Based at Aldergrove,NI. Re-equipped with Mosquito NF.30
527	WN	B.35	8/52	8/58	Formed from 'N'and'R'Calibration squadrons at Watton. Renumbered 245 Sqn and re-equipped.
571	8K	B.16	4/44	9/45	Initially equipped at Downham Market. Detached to Graveley, before moving to Oakington as light bomber unit (8 Group). Disbanded Warboys 20/9/45
608	6T	B.20	8/44	8/45	Initially equipped at Downham Market as part of 8 Group's Light Night
		B.25			Striking Force. Disbanded at Downham Market 24/8/45
617	-	B.16	8/43	3/45	Used some as pathfinders, including three as a detachment from 418 Sqn, RCAF.
618	-	B.4	4/43	6/46	Used to carry 'Highball' bouncing bomb. Based at Skitten 4/43, to Benson 9/43,
		FB.6			to Wick 6/44, to Fishermans Bend (Australia) 12/44, to Narromine 2/45. Disbanded at Narromine 29/6/45.
627	AZ	B.4	11/43	9/45	Formed as a part of Light Night Striking Force. Initially equipped at Wyton,
		B .16			later moved to Oakington 11/43, Woodhall Spa 11/44. Transferred to 5 Group
		B.20			where carried out target-marking work. Renumbered 109 Sqn at Woodhall
		B.25			Spa 1/10/45
692	P3	B.4	1/44	9/46	Initially equipped at Graveley. To Gransden Lodge 6/45.
		B.16			First sqn to carry 4,0001b bomb. Disbanded at Gransden Lodge 20/9,45

Note. This chart details only the main variants used. It does not include training variants that were supplied to many squadrons. Fighter-bomber variants used in the chart were used mainly in the bomber role

AN INFINITELY ADAPTABLE AIRCRAFT

Although the main basic types of combat requirement - bomber, fighter, fighter-bomber and photographic reconnaissance had been catered for in the Mosquito design, these were by no means the only uses to which the aircraft was put.

Other branches of the armed forces, and even civil airlines, wanted to use the aircraft, either by specialized adaptation of the design, or just because it was simply the best machine for the purpose. The post-war years brought a plethora of adaptations of the Mosquito airframe that the original designers could never have envisaged.

Civilian Interlude

Throughout the Second World War the British Overseas Airways Corporation (BOAC) struggled to maintain as much as possible of their pre-war long-range airline route network. One of their tasks was to conduct a regular air service between Scotland and neutral Sweden, but it became more difficult and dangerous as German fighters swept northwards into Norway and Denmark after the invasion of those countries in April 1940.

Daily contact with Stockholm was of vital importance, from both the strategic and political points of view, for the Swedes were trading legally with both sides and wished to maintain their contact with London without offending the Germans. It was a delicate situation. The German propaganda machine, under Doctor Joseph Göebbels, painted a black picture to the Swedes of Britain's impending defeat, one that could partially be countered by flying over British newspapers and magazines. These same flights brought back small, but specialized engineering products, such as tool steel, ball bearings, fine springs and electrical resistances. Much of this Anglo-Swedish co-operation took the form of personal negotiations, so many important passengers were flown along with the mail. A further and important part of this transport service was the carriage of additional freight which passed through Sweden bound for the Soviet Union. These flights led to the strange situation where BOAC and Deutsche Lufthansa aircraft often shared the same airport apron at Bromma. Many of the aircrew involved had previously been friendly during the pre-war years at London's Croydon Airport. Now, instead of friendly conversations, they would just exchange a curt nod.

BOAC operated several Lockheed Hudsons and Lodestars and the occasional Douglas DC-3 on the route in conjunction with the Swedish airline AB Aerotransport, who also operated DC-3s. The service was fraught with danger, both natural and man-made. The aircraft had to avoid daylight, moonlight, clear weather and the Northern Lights in an attempt to evade German interceptors. Cloudy weather was also disliked by the crews for it meant the increased risk of icing and navigational errors, while the light summer nights of almost continuous daylight made the route virtually inoperable between May to August.

After the German invasion of Norway, the Royal Norwegian Air Force in Britain used Lockheed Lodestars to assist Norwegians who had escaped to Sweden and wanted to come over to the Allies to fight.

Increased German activity in the Skagerrak during late 1942 meant that an even more northerly route was needed. Identification and navigation in the narrow Swedish corridor was difficult, radio navigation aids were unreliable and there existed no direct contact between Leuchars, whence most flights departed, and Stockholm. Radio silence was kept at all times, and although a single high-frequency transmission would serve to identify an aircraft to the Swedish anti-aircraft gunners, it could also be received by the Germans and was therefore prohibited. The Germans would not allow the Norwegian bases at Stavanger and Bergen to broadcast, but the Norwegians often managed to get around this by leaving the transmitters switched on so that a carrier-wave was broadcast to assist BOAC and RAF crews. Keeping radio silence almost certainly resulted in an aircraft being fired upon by the Swedish anti-aircraft gunners, although almost always the shells went conveniently wide of the target!

To reduce the hazards a faster aircraft was needed, and one that could fly much higher than the 20,000ft then available using the Hudsons and Lodestars. The solution came when the RAF was asked to deliver a quantity of top-secret mail to Sweden on 6 August 1942. One of 105 Sqn's aircraft was chosen, Mosquito DK292 which had all its RAF roundels and markings removed and the crew, Flight Lieutenant Parry and Flying Officer Robinson, dressed in civilian clothing before they flew the diplomatic bag over to Stockholm. They landed there only a few minutes ahead of the Junkers Ju.52 used by Göebbels and his staff! The crew stayed the night and the aircraft was placed under a joint British and Swedish guard. After this incident an immediate request was made by BOAC to the Air Ministry for a number of Mosquitos. Eventually two Corporation pilots were allowed to go to Lyneham to learn to fly the type.

It was decided that Mosquito B.Mk.IV DZ411 would be allocated for conversion into a form of an airliner/mailplane by De Havilland. Long-range tanks were installed in the bomb bay, leaving little space for payload; and, to ensure as high a speed as possible, separate ejector exhausts were fitted. The finished aircraft was delivered to BOAC wearing standard camouflage but with the British civil registration G-AGJV on 15 December 1942. The pilots were quick to express their concern at the lack of de-icing equipment, which was eventually fitted to all BOAC Mosquitos.

Mosquito G-AGFV of BOAC. It was in this aircraft that Captain Rae made a forced landing at Barkaby, Sweden on the night of 22/23 April 1943 after being attacked by German fighters.
(© BAE SYSTEMS)

Mosquito HJ720 - now marked as G-AGGF taxies out at Leuchars ready for a flight to Stockholm early in 1943. The two lines of dark writing at the base of the fin states the ownership 'British Overseas Airways Corporation'.
(© BAE SYSTEMS)

After a short period of training, the first Mosquito flight to Stockholm was made on 4 February 1943, crewed by Captain C.B. Houlder - who was later to become BOAC's Mosquito Training Captain - and radio-operator F. Frape. Radio and fuel system troubles, along with further crew training, delayed operations somewhat, but on 12 April it was decided that BOAC were to receive six more unarmed Mosquitos; this time they were FB.Mk.VIs. These were all civil-registered and delivered to Brammcote near Nottingham between 16 April and 2 May 1943. The chief project engineer at Hatfield, C. H. Clarkson, wrote to BOAC explaining the differences in performance: the B.Mk.IV had unshrouded multiple ejector exhausts which, compared with the saxophone exhausts of the FB.VI, gave an increase in top speed of 12 mph and 9 mph in the cruise. The external wing tanks of the Mk.VI cost a further 5 mph, thus making the B.Mk.IV a favourite with crews in terms of speed, but not range.

Following the USAAF 8th Air Force raid on the German ball-bearing production plant at Schweinfurt near Frankfurt in mid-1943, it became vital for Britain to purchase Sweden's entire ball-bearing output to prevent it from falling into enemy hands. In a matter of hours two Mosquitos were modified to carry a single passenger each in cramped conditions in their bomb bays. This allowed the British negotiators to reach Sweden an hour or so ahead of the Germans, and later led to a similar journey for many important people on a regular basis. Much propaganda was made of this event, so much so that the popular press of the day dubbed BOAC's Swedish air service the 'Ball Bearing Run' Although many ball bearings were carried in the Mosquitos - up to 1,300 lb, due largely to the compactness of the packing - far more bearings were brought out by fast motor boats from Gothenburg to ports in Scotland.

A typical Mosquito 'passenger' reclined on a mattress in the plywood-lined bomb bay and wore a flying suit, boots, Mae West and parachute harness. As the hydraulic jacks used for closing the bomb doors were inside the bay, they folded into the 'passenger compartment' as the doors closed. To avoid having his legs trapped, the unfortunate passenger had to tuck his knees up under his chin as the doors closed; then he could relax and stretch out under the closed jacks. The passenger had a small reading lamp, a temperature control and could adjust the oxygen flow to his mask when ordered to do so by the pilot via the intercom.

BOAC MOSQUITOS

Mk.IV DZ4II/G-AGFV

Received 15 December 1942. Forced-landed at Barkaby, Sweden 23 April 1943 with hydraulic trouble, following enemy attack. Repairs took until 10 December 1943 when the aircraft was returned to service. The machine swung off the runway at Stockholm 7 April 1944 when the airspeed indicator went unserviceable, forcing the undercarriage to collapse. Temporary repairs were completed to allow the aircraft to be flown back to Leuchars. The machine was returned to RAF service on 6 January 1945.

Mk.VI HJ680/G-AGGC

Received 16 April 1943, when delivered to BOAC at Bramcote. Withdrawn from use on 30 November 1944, but retained at Leuchars for emergency use. The aircraft was despatched to Croydon for Certificate of Airworthiness 14 March 1945 before being returned to the RAF 9 January 1946.

Mk.VI HJ681/G-AGGD

Received 17 April 1943, when delivered to BOAC at Bramcote. Following radio trouble, the machine forced-landed at Satenas, Sweden on 3 January 1944, and was damaged; the propellers were bent and the undercarriage damaged, but the crew escaped unhurt. Aircraft then scrapped.

Mk.VI HJ718/G-AGGE

Received 23 April 1943, when delivered to BOAC at Bramcote. Damaged on landing at Stockholm on 15 August 1944, when the propellers touched the runway. Returned to the RAF 22 June 1945.

Mk.VI HJ720/G-AGGF

Received 24 April 1943, when delivered to BOAC at Bramcote. The aircraft was lost on service '11B452' 17 August 1943 when it crashed at Invermairk, Glen Esk, Scotland; it was destroyed by fire and the crew, Captain L. A. Wilkins and radio-operator N. H. Beaumont, were killed. Soon after take-off the pilot radioed that he was returning to Leuchars, but nothing more was heard. The aircraft was not found until 8 September 1943, by a gamekeeper.

Mk.VI HJ721/G-AGGG

Received 2 May 1943, when delivered to BOAC at Bramcote. The aircraft crashed about a mile from Leuchars on 23 October 1943 following failure of the

port engine when returning from Stockholm on service '12B5517'. The crew, Captain Martin Hamre and radio-operator Serre Haug (both ex- members of the Royal Norwegian Air Force), were killed.

Mk.VI HJ723/G-AGGH

Received 2 May 1943, when delivered to BOAC at Bramcote. Due to crew shortages, the aircraft was withdrawn from use but retained at Leuchars until 30 November 1944. Returned to the RAF on 22 June 1945.

Mk.VI HJ667/G-AGKO

Received 27 April 1944, when delivered to BOAC at Bramcote. Withdrawn from use 30 November 1944 due to crew shortages. Returned to the RAF on 22 June 1945.

Mk.VI HJ792/G-AGKR

Received 11 April 1944, when delivered to BOAC at Bramcote. The aircraft departed Gothenburg heading for Leuchars 28 August 1944, but failed to reach its destination - presumed to have crashed into the sea, but no trace has ever been found. Captain J. H. White and radio-operator J. C. Gaffeny lost.

Mk.VI LR296/G-AGKP

Received 22 April 1944, when delivered to BOAC at Bramcote. Crashed into the sea 9 miles off Leuchars on the night of 18/19 August 1944 in good weather. Captain G. Rae, OBE, radio-operator D. T. Roberts and Captain B. W. B. Orton killed.

Mk.III HJ898

Received 19 August 1945, when delivered to BOAC for use as crew trainer. The aircraft swung off the runway on to grass while landing at Leuchars during acceptance test. The port wing, propeller and undercarriage were badly damaged and the starboard undercarriage bent. Returned to the RAF on 12 May 1945.

Mk.III HJ985

Received 28 November 1943, when delivered on loan to BOAC for crew training at Leuchars. Returned to the RAF on 26 January 1944.

Mk.III LR524

Received 21 January 1944, when delivered to BOAC for crew training. Returned to the RAF on 4 December 1944 following the suspension of BOAC's Mosquito operations.

BOAC Mosquito G-AGFV, - note how the civilian registration is outlined in silver and underlined with red, white and blue on both the fuselage and upper surfaces of the wings as an aid to show that this was a civilian aircraft.
(© BAE SYSTEMS)

Passengers were usually supplied with refreshments and reading material to pass the time; the flight to Sweden normally took around three hours (against nine in a slower aircraft). Crews were not normally told the identity of their passengers; usually they just saw a shadowy figure in flying clothing being bundled by the ground crew into the converted bomb bay. Some distinguished people travelled in this manner, including Niels Bohr, the Danish physicist who worked for the Allies on the atom bomb.

Often the flights were fraught with danger, particularly as German intelligence agents at Bromma reported the departures of British aircraft to the German fighter squadrons in Denmark, which then intercepted them. Captain Rae and radio-operator Payne had a nerve-racking time on the night of 18 July when, just after leaving the Swedish coast, they spotted two contrails thought to belong to a pair of Fw.190s at 23,000ft on an interception course. Rae remembered only too clearly the night a few months previously when he had been attacked and forced into an emergency landing at Barkaby near Stockholm. His escape hatch had been shot out and the aircraft's wings and hydraulic system damaged. It had been a lucky escape.

How the lucky travelled - a priority passenger in the converted bomb bay, with his own oxygen supply and an intercom to the crew.
(© BAE SYSTEMS)

The rule at the time was to return to Sweden if the aircraft was still in the Skagerrak so as to avoid running out of fuel in a long chase back to Britain. However, in this instance Rae elected to continue for Leuchars because his passenger was an important man who the Germans had already asked the Swedes to hand over. Another reason for Rae's decision was that Captain Steen and radio-operator Omholdt were following a short distance behind with a similar passenger and Rae did not want to lead the enemy on to the second Mosquito. Rae turned, weaved, dropped his wing tanks and dived down almost to sea-level. The Mosquito's airspeed indicator was put out of action by a high-speed stall but finally the German aircraft gave up the chase after about 30 minutes, probably because they had reached the limit of their range. When the Mosquito was examined later it was discovered that the elevator had been deformed by the high-speed manoeuvring. It was taken to Hatfield for further examination because the RAF had had similar experiences. This led to a modification replacing metal skin for fabric.

BOAC were already looking forward to getting bigger aircraft on the route. Yorks, Lancasters and Liberators were all considered, but none of these had the high speed of the Mosquito, nor could they use the runway at Bromma until it was extended beyond the existing 1,200 metres. Around Christmas 1944 a period of bad weather led to cancellations and diversions, which created a build-up of passengers. This forced BOAC to adopt the Pathfinder technique of an advance aircraft radioing back a single code letter (changed every night for security reasons) indicating that tactical and weather conditions were 'suitable' or 'unsuitable'. On a night when any RAF photo-reconnaissance machines were operating in the Scandinavian area they would undertake the task, but when there were none BOAC undertook the job themselves. They viewed the loss of one aircraft's payload on the easterly flight as being more than made up by the increase in frequency. The faster Mosquito Mk.IV, G-AGFV, was preferred as the advance aircraft, for on the northern route it could reach the Norwegian mountain area, or could get to within a couple of hundred miles of Bromma, and still return if required.

Captain Gilbert Rae, BOAC Mosquito Captain who was killed when G-AGKP crashed into the sea off Leuchars on 19 August 1944. His radio Operator D. T. Roberts and passenger Capt B W B Orton were also killed.

As the summer of 1944 beckoned, thoughts were given to obtaining later marks of the Mosquito such as the B.IX and XVI, with which to replace lost aircraft, for they could fly higher and had a better performance. The idea was soon dropped owing to the problems of operating a fleet of mixed aircraft and engines within such a small organization. That spring, three more Mk.VIs joined BOAC and three non-civil-registered T.Mk.IIIs were used for crew training at different times from November 1943 onwards.

All these Mosquitos wore standard RAF camouflage but had their civil registrations outlined in white - or possibly silver - in the normal positions, and underlined in red, white and blue with an RAF flash on the fins. Operations continued until 17 May 1945, by which time 520 round trips - equal to around 784,000 miles - had been made since the Mosquito was first brought into use with BOAC on 3 February 1943. Three aircraft (G-AGKO, 'GE and' GH) were handed back to the RAF on 22 June. Shortly afterwards the operational terminal was transferred from Leuchars to Croydon. Just a few Mosquitos had played a vital part in keeping the lines of communication open to Sweden while at the same time playing a crucial part in the denial of important materials to the Germans.

In the Navy!

The British Admiralty had a requirement for an aircraft that could provide a greater range and a higher speed of striking power than was currently available. It was thought that this could be met by the Mosquito, but there were reservations as to the strength of the wooden airframe and whether it could withstand the forces involved in an arrested deck landing. Theoretically, there was no reason why the Mosquito should not be able to operate from a carrier.

To test this, LR359, a Mosquito FB.Mk.VI was 'semi-navalized'. The programme involved deletion of the guns, an internally strengthened rear fuselage reinforced with additional longerons to accept an arrester hook; and experimental non-feathering four-bladed de Havilland propellers cropped to 12ft 6in diameter and fitted to new Merlin 25s, which could then be run at increased boost levels to give a 5-10 per cent increase in power.

Trials began in November 1943. Meanwhile the Admiralty wrote the official specification around the machine. A few weeks later Captain Eric Brown, then serving as a test pilot with 'C' Squadron at A & AEE Boscombe Down, received a telephone call from the Admiralty asking him if he thought that he could deck-land a Mosquito. After some consideration he said 'yes' and was transferred to RAE Farnborough on 17 January 1944 for duties with the Aerodynamics Flight, the section given the task of conducting the deck- landing trials which were scheduled to begin in March.

Captain Brown: *I suddenly found myself whisked off to Farnborough, and then, I had to build up some twin-engined time (of which I had very little), and finally on the great day a different than normal Mosquito VI arrived, in that on the rear fuselage a Barracuda-type arrester hook was fitted and the rear fuselage itself was strengthened on either side by reinforced longeron ribs.*

Captain Brown made his first flight in LR359 on 25 January, accompanied by Bill Stewart of the Aerodynamics Flight. In naval circles the project was prestigious, for it was thought that this would be the first time that a twin-engined aircraft had landed on a carrier. The problems associated with twin-engined aircraft for carrier operations were numerous: *the speed and weight of the Mosquito was way beyond anything we had dealt with before on an aircraft carrier. One must realize that in 1944 the arrester gear on an aircraft carrier had limitations in that it could only absorb an entry speed of about 65 kts, and that for an aircraft of some 10,000 lbs weight or so. Here we were talking about an aircraft that in, the official pilots' notes said the approach speed was 125 mph, and the weight for the first landings we were going to make was 16,000 lbs.*

So we had a problem, we had to get the speed down somehow or other, and of course here we would be helped by the carriers speed to create wind over the deck. The other problem was pure dimensions: the flight deck of the carrier we

LR359, the modified FB.Mk.VI that was the first twin-engined aircraft to land on a carrier, piloted by Captain Eric Brown, The upper surfaces were naval grey/green and the undersides yellow.
(© BAE SYSTEMS)

were going to use had a flight-deck length of 766 ft, and a width of 95 ft. But that width diminished as you came to the island, which intruded into the main area, leaving only about 80 ft. So here we were with an aircraft with a span of 54 ft, and we had 80 ft space - that was another little one we had to think about.

Another problem was would the undercarriage, which had not been modified, take the vertical velocities which arc normally extremely high in deck landing? Or would it collapse under the strain? Also we were of course very nervous about the fact that the whole construction was wood. The decelerations that I have experienced in a deck landing were such that many predicted that the whole thing would be torn in two as the hook caught and the deceleration came on.

Another problem - the crash barrier. Normally when one landed - this was before the days of the angled deck - on a carrier, if you missed the wires or anything went wrong, you went forward in to a crash barrier. This was two steel ropes raised off and strung across the deck with criss-crossed steel wires in it The idea was that as you went into this in your single- engined aeroplane, your propeller chewed it up and wound it round the engine so that it was all over before it got to you. With the Mosquito you have to admit that the pilot is sitting pretty close to the accident!

Finally there was the matter of single-engined deck landings - was this going to be a possibility? Or, were we even going to be able to go round again if we had an engine problem?

The barrier was not ready by the time the deck- landing trials began but the design was proceeding apace. It featured strips of nylon tape strung vertically between two widely spaced steel hawsers attached to the ship's arrester gear through the normal crash barrier supports. A gap was left in the middle of the nylon strips to allow the nose of the aircraft to pass through while the nylon tapes wrapped around the wings. There remained the constant worry that the fuselage, despite strengthening, would not prove strong enough for the task.

The preparations involved take-off and stall measurements, single-engined approaches and simulated deck-landings at both Farnborough and RNAS Yeovilton, with the aircraft flying at various weights from 16,000 to 20,000 lb. The stall tests revealed that with the undercarriage down and flaps at various settings, the stall was unexpectedly vicious. If the control column was slammed hard over to one corner the ailerons locked, which nearly caused the aircraft to turn over on to its back. It soon became clear, however, that it was possible to reduce the aircraft's approach speed to around 90 knots, with the actual touch-down speed some 9 knots lower, by keeping the engine power on until a height about three feet above the deck and then cut the engines. The limiting factor of the landing run was the lack of aileron effectiveness in correcting any error of line. The landing tests once again revealed the cleanness of the Mosquito's design and offered much encouragement in terms of contemporary entry speeds for arrester gear use and the desirability of increasing the landing weight to 20,000 lb. They also resulted in a much flatter approach line than was normally seen on carrier operations.

Eric Brown: *First thing was to ensure that we could get the aircraft off in the shortest possible space. So in our experiments the technique we finally adopted was to have 25° of flap on, hold the aircraft on the brakes, wind up the Port engine to +4 lb boost, the Starboard engine to +2 (the brakes could just hold that) release the brakes, ram on full power and away we go. We found that in the standard atmospheric conditions of pressure and zero wind, we could get the Mosquito VI off at 16,000 lbs in 620 ft and at 20,000 lbs in 820 ft.*

We then went on to check on the stall and see how that behaved. Contrary to a nice clean ordinary stall, the stall of the Mosquito with power on was quite something else, and we started doing the stalls from zero boost with increments +2 and +4. When it stalled at these power settings the stick clacked hard over in the cockpit to the left with such violence that you could not hold it and the aircraft dropped its wing violently to over the vertical. So it was quite clear that if we got low and slow on the approach it was going to be a fatality.

However, we did find that we could hold the aircraft at +4 lbs boost and get the speed down to something we felt would be less than a hundred miles an hour. So the approach, we determined, would have to be made at this boost, literally hanging on the props the whole way in, finally cutting the engines three feet above the deck and letting it just fall on. That way we would probably arrive without any risk of a wing drop and also probably we would not impose too heavy loads on the undercarriage.

So, we had our approach weighed up, now it was a question of single-engine approaches. With the non-feathering propellers we found we could not even go round again, far less make a single-engined approach. We could not really go below 500ft, because the aircraft could not be held at any speed below 170mph with one propeller wind-milling and the other actually operating at full boost You ran out of rudder, so you never could get up to full boost, since you could not hold it anyway. Single-engine landings were absolutely out and so was going round again.

So, we went on to the first check of the landing into the wires and took the aircraft up to Arbroath, where there are a set of arrester wires laid out on the runway, and conducted a number of run-ins there, really to prove the installation - that is the hook installation – there were no great problems involved at all.

A second machine, LR387, was delivered to Farnborough as a back-up aircraft, so that by mid-March all was ready for arrester gear proofing runs at RNAS Arbroath and familiarization landings at East Haven, where Lieutenant-Commander Bob Everett, Commanding Officer of the Deck Landing School, was to act as batsman for the trials. The landings at East Haven proved their use by revealing that during the final approach the batsman disappeared from the pilot's view behind the port engine, a fact that forced the batsman to change his position and stand further inboard than the usual deck-edge.

First Carrier Landing

On 25 March word came to Machrihanish in Strathclyde that all was ready to proceed, with HMS *Indefatigable* steaming off Ailsa Craig with her deck cleared. Captain Brown took off in LR359 at 1330hrs with just enough fuel for 25 minutes' flight so that the aircraft's weight would be down to around 16,000 lb for the first landing. After arriving over the carrier he was told that there was 40 knots of wind over the deck, so after a low pass he turned into the circuit to be 'batted in' on the final approach by Bob Everett. Brown crossed the carrier's stern with 69 knots indicated airspeed, he received the 'cut' signal and touched down firmly on the deck, picking up the number two arrester wire. A camera fitted in the cockpit recorded the instrument readings and showed a touch-down speed of 68 knots, which was well below what was expected.

Eric Brown again: *All went well until the eighth landing which was at the weight of 18,000 lbs, and when at touch-down I felt the deceleration start, which is normal when you catch a wire, then suddenly it stopped, and the aircraft began to move forward again. Well, I had to make a lightning assessment - one of two things could have happened: either the hook had broken in which case we had to go on - incidentally there was no crash barrier of course because we hadn't developed a specialised crash barrier -I am going to come to that later. We just hadn't had time to develop an adequate crash barrier, so I could take off again if the hook had actually broken. If the wire had broken however, which was quite possible with these higher weights, which were unusual on carriers. Then if I opened up again too early I might cause another disaster and pull the hook out, because I had to wait to give sufficient time to get to at least one more wire. We did get to this position, when I realized that something had gone wrong that was not going to arrest us. So I had to give it the full-gun, irrespective of the swing and the torque caused, fortunately the torque in the Mosquito takes you to port, and of course by this time we were up and near the Island, and so I just let it swing straight over the side – all was well.*

What happened was to the claw of the arrester hook. The claw is held on to the frame of the hook by a couple of bolts, and the forward bolt had sheared, therefore allowing the claw to rotate and the wire was thrown out clear of the claw. Of course the hook also snapped back up into position. There was no question of stopping so we had to go on.

The aircraft was sent back to Hatfield, who very rapidly modified it, and put a strengthened bolt in and also made sure that the snap gear would not allow the hook to lock up if such an incident actually happened again.

Now with the take-off technique, of course, we could not line the aircraft on the central line of the flight deck because of the Island, so we had to put the

Captain Eric Brown brings LR359 over the end of HMS *Indefatigable* to be 'batted down' by Bob Everett on the bottom right of the photograph. This was the first ever twin engined landing on a carrier...
(© BAE SYSTEMS)

starboard wheel on the centre line, and take it from there. But it was much easier than on land in control the swing, because you already had the wind speed, and the ship's natural speed to give you some control over the rudder.

After refuelling, the Mosquito was ranged aft for its first deck take-off. Because of the span of the machine, it was necessary to position the aircraft with the starboard wheel on the centre-line of the deck to give enough wing-tip clearance from the carrier's island. This in turn created problems, for the wide track of the aircraft's undercarriage meant that the port wheel was close to the edge of the flight deck. It was thought that the normally powerful swing on take-off would have to be closely controlled, but as it turned out the swing was more easily controlled on the aircraft-carrier than on land. This was due to the existence of a slipstream effect acting on the rudder, which was caused by the carrier's speed plus the natural windspeed over the deck; it served to make the rudder much more effective during the early stages of the take-off run. As a consequence the Mosquito took off in an amazingly short distance and the swing never had time to develop.

Several more landings and take-offs were made that day, all completely successful. The following morning Captain Brown landed-on again, this time carrying Bill Stewart..

LR359 went back to De Havilland on 11 April, while LR387 went to Crail and the Navy's Service Trials Unit. A second series of shipboard trials was scheduled for early May, during which the aircraft took off at weights in excess of 21, 000lb.

During both series of tests, 24 successful landings were made and many invaluable lessons learned about twin-engined aircraft deck operations and how to handle the Mosquito at sea. Among the latter matters were the problem of rain and the difficulties encountered with spray clearance on the flat fighter- type windscreen, an excessive bounce in the rubber-in-compression undercarriage, and the size of the escape hatch which only allowed one crewman to vacate the aircraft at a time (an obvious problem if it went under water). The major worry was the swing that might be encountered on take-off, a problem aggravated by the wingspan which drastically reduced deck clearances. The only possible solution was to use

... the landing was to the left of centreline, so as to assure adequate wingtip clearance from the carrier's superstructure. This view clearly shows that Capt Brown caught the second arrestor wire. *(© BAE SYSTEMS)*

directionally handed engines (that is, engines that rotated in different directions) to remove any such possibility of swing. After it had received further extensive modifications, including the fitment of American ASH radar in a thimble radome, LR387 became the full prototype Sea Mosquito as LR359 was written off in an accident at Arbroath.

Sea Mosquito

It was one thing to be able to land on and take off from a carrier deck, but if the Mosquito was to be used operationally to good effect, its wingspan would have to be reduced to save space when ranged on a carrier's deck. Considerable

FLEET AIR ARM UNITS OPERATING MOSQUITOS		
SQN	TYPE	REMARKS
703	TR.37	
711	FB.6	
728		1948-50
728	TT.39	1948
762		2/46-11/49
711	TR.33	11/45-1950
772	TR.33	1946-47
790		10/45-11/49
811	FB.6/TR.33	9/45-7/47

modifications were needed to the single full-span wing structure to allow incorporation of manual wing-folding. This involved Alclad (aluminium clad) sheet being let into the top and bottom surfaces of the wing inboard and outboard of the fold joint; the spanwise stringers were then cut down and sandwiched between the alloy sheets. The two ribs at the fold point were made of thick Alclad-spruce- Alclad sandwich webs with laminated booms.

The outer wing panel folded on four centrally placed light-alloy hinges, with the latch pins and pick-up fittings bolted to the lower booms of the main spars. Each bolt was fitted with mechanical locks, that were withdrawn simultaneously when a large spring-loaded lever was folded down and aft from the wing joint. The aileron controls were continued past the joint by short lengths of heavy-duty Bowden cable.

The Admiralty issued Specification N. 15/44 and the aircraft eventually emerged from Leavesden as the Sea Mosquito TR.Mk.33. TW227, the first production aircraft flew on 10 November 1945, too late to see combat in World War Two. The wing-folding mechanism and long-travel undercarriage were not introduced into the Mk.Mk.33 production line until TW241, the fourteenth aircraft. The production Sea Mosquito also introduced an additional bulkhead in the rear fuselage above the arrestor hook attachment points; a pair of laminated longerons from the hook attachment points to the rear wing spar; and a long-travel Lockheed

TS449, one of the prototype Torpedo-Reconnaissance/Torpedo Fighter (TR/TF) Sea Mosquito Mk.33s used for service trials. The aircraft was built at Leavesden and delivered in 1946. It had four-bladed propellers, Rocket-Assisted Take-Off Gear (RATOG) fitted behind the wing, and - just visible in front of the tailwheel - an arrestor hook.
(© BAE SYSTEMS)

LR387, a Sea Mosquito
TR.Mk.33 converted from
an FB.Mk.VI in 1945.
(© BAE SYSTEMS)

Close-up of the Sea
Mosquito's folding wing
joint, showing how the
normally one-piece
wooden wing was split,
with the hinges
immediately outboard
of the flaps. Also visible
are the locking pins and
release mechanism, with
the locking pin release
lever in the fully
extended position.

Folding the wings on the
Mosquito was quite a
labour-intensive job - the
process required seven
men on each side!

The aircraft design had
insufficient hydraulic
power for power lifting,
and to install such
equipment would have
been a major operation.
(all © BAE SYSTEMS)

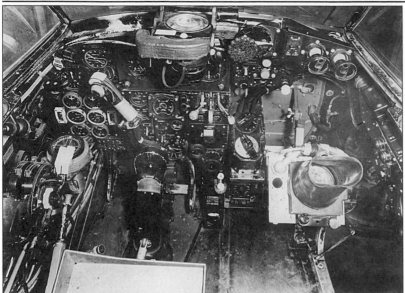

The cockpit of a Sea Mosquito TR.Mk.37, showing the somewhat cramped layout. Note the reflecting gunsight, with the padding to protect the crew in the event of a crash at top centre, with the radar scope on the right hand side.
(© BAE SYSTEMS)

Above left: a close-up of the RATOG equipment fitted to the Sea Mosquitos. Above right: A close-up of the arrestor hook fitted to LR359.

Below: another view of TS449, showing the 'thimble' radar nose and just visible the joint line of the folding wing, between the 'TS' and '449' *(all © BAE SYSTEMS)*

The 18 inch torpedo, its cradle supports, and ASH radar installed in the nose can be clearly seen in this view of LR387.

A close-up of the nose of the TR.Mk.37. Note that the inner, slightly forward pair of the four 20mm cannon ports have been faired over, indicating that the guns have been removed. *(both © BAE SYSTEMS))*

oleo undercarriage in place of the rubber-in-compression units. All production aircraft were equipped to carry an 18in aerial torpedo externally, supported by a tubular fitting bolted on the top end of the front main spar at the point of the centre of gravity. Provision was also made for the carriage of a pair of 50 gallon drop-tanks; these could be exchanged for a pair of 30 gallon tanks if a pair of rocket projectiles were also carried.

Only 50 TR.Mk.33s were built and the type first entered service with 811 Squadron of the Fleet Air Arm, shore-based at Ford, in August 1946. The squadron had earlier received a number of Mosquito FB.VIs to gain experience in September

Above: the second prototype TR.Mk.33, LR387, showing the wing folding mechanism and the arrester hook under the rear fuselage. The rubber- in-compression undercarriage legs were later changed to oleo pneumatic which stood up better to carrier landings.

Above left: VT724, the first torpedo-fighter (TF) Mk.37, fitted with the enlarged radar nose containing the ASV Mk.XIII radar scanner.

Below left: TW240 after conversion to the prototype TR.Mk.37.

Bottom: VT724, a TR.Mk.37, showing the oleo- pneumatic under-carriage legs installed *(all © BAE SYSTEMS)*

PF606, a target- towing TT.39 with dorsal cupola awaits delivery to the Royal Navy.

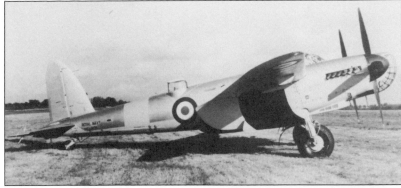

The TT.39 nose conversion of the B.XVI with optically flat glazing for observation of gunnery results, produced to meet Royal Navy Specification Q. 19/45. The work was done by General Aircraft Ltd of Hanworth. *(both © BAE SYSTEMS)*

1945. TS449, one of the two special TR.Mk.33 prototypes, was used at Farnborough during May and June 1946 for a series of RATOG (rocket-assisted take-off gear) trials; using four rockets fitted to the fuselage aft of the wing trailing edge, this allowed an increase in take-off weight to around 22,500 lb within the short distance of a carrier's deck. These tests included asymmetric firing of rockets, all of which were completely successful.

The Sea Mosquito TR.33s were also used by 771 and 772 Training Squadrons of the Fleet Air Arm and a number of T.Mk.IIIs (un-armed, dual-control trainers derived from the F.Mk.II) were allocated from RAF stock to be used by the FAA for crew conversion training.

One TR.Mk.33 was used as the prototype for the TR.Mk.37 which was basically the same aircraft but fitted with the British ASV Mk.VIII radar. The use of this scanner dictated a larger, more bulbous nose. However, only six of these aircraft were built and all served with 703 Sqn.

The FB.Mk.VIs supplied to the Royal Navy from the RAF had normal night-fighter camouflage colouring, complete with fin stripes. The PR aircraft also had standard RAF colour schemes, as did the T.Mk.IIIs supplied for twin conversion crew training. Initially all the TR.Mk.33s were painted extra dark sea grey on their

upper surfaces with under surfaces Sky Type S. This was also applied to some Mk.VIs of RAF Coastal Command during the last few months of the war.

After the war many of these aircraft were painted silver overall. The Navy also made use of the target-towing TT.Mk.39 converted from the B.Mk.XVI by General Aircraft Ltd of Feltham, Middlesex. The Mk.39 could be used tor target-towing, photographic marking and radar calibration. Structurally it had a lengthened nose with extensive glazing, a dorsal cupola added in the rear fuselage and fitment of winch gear. This variant entered service with Fleet Requirements Units as a target tug from 1948 and with 728 Sqn at Hal Far, Malta. The main difference with this variant was the fitment of hydraulically driven target-towing gear in the bomb bay, which in the main was operated by a winch operator in the rear compartment. Smaller targets could be carried internally, launched via a chute in the belly, but a target with up to 32ft wingspan could be towed without causing changes to the aircraft's handling. Rate one turns could be performed normally, but care had to be taken when climbing, diving or turning faster than rate one, as the tow cable could foul the aircraft's structure.

RS719, one of the pre-production TT.Mk.35s, showing the wind-driven target winch attached to the forward bomb bay. Note the diagonal black stripes under the wings denoting that the aircraft is a target-tug.
(© BAE SYSTEMS)

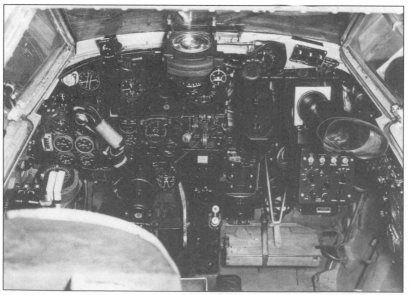

A typical late-war fighter Mosquito cockpit. Top centre is a reflecting gunsight, with the rudder trim control to the right of it. The A.I. Mk.XV CRT is on the extreme right, with the control box installed below.
(both © BAE SYSTEMS)

A pair of PR.Mk.34s fly low-level down the Suez Canal in 1949.

Post-war

When war ended in 1945, the British and Commonwealth Services that used the Mosquito suffered a drastic run-down, and many surplus aircraft were passed over or sold to foreign air forces which were struggling to rebuild after the war.

In the immediate peacetime years the RAF was charged with the role of diplomatic couriers in a similar manner to BOAC and the wartime Swedish run. 162 Sqn used its Mosquitos as mini-airliners, carrying diplomatic mail and newspapers to cities such as Athens, Copenhagen, Naples, Rome and Vienna. The RCAF also ran a daily courier service with Mosquitos from Nuremberg (where most of the war trials were being held) to Odiham, Hants.

In September 1946 an aeronautical exhibition was held in Buenos Aires, Argentina, and Ernest Bevin, Foreign Secretary in Britain's post-war Socialist government, arranged for an RAF Mosquito to be sent over on a goodwill mission, with the thought that sales of surplus equipment might also be made.

It was calculated that a PR.Mk.34, if operated at maximum cruising speed, could make the journey from Benson to Buenos Aires in 24 hours (with refuelling stops in Gibraltar, Dakar, Natal and Rio de Janeiro). Flight Lieutenant

TJ121, a Mosquito B.Mk. 35 named *'Pudukkottai'* *(© BAE SYSTEMS)*

S. McCreith as pilot with Flight Lieutenant F. Thayer in PR.Mk.34 RG300 were seen off from Benson on 22 September 1946 by Air Commodore MacDonald, AOC Benson, at around 0400hrs. Just under 3½ hours later they landed at Gibraltar to refuel, made a successful quick turn-round and were on their way again. When nearing Dakar they failed to make radio contact, so were forced to divert to RAF Yundum at Bathurst, Gambia. As soon as the Mosquito had landed it was sprayed with foam by the station fire tender; in the dark it was thought that the blue flames from the aircraft's unshrouded exhausts meant that the machine was on fire! A replacement aircraft (VL613) was sent out and went on to Argentina as planned; but no sales resulted as the Argentine airfields were not really suitable for Mosquito operations.

TT.Mk.35 TA634 of 3 Civil Anti-Aircraft Co-Operation Unit (CAACU) is caught by the camera at Exeter Airport.

The RAF may have been reduced in size, but its primary and secondary duties remained the same. Many front-line squadrons retained the type for less warlike duties. 13 Sqn (previously part of the RAF force sent to stabilize Greece during the 1945 uprising) was re-formed at Ein Shemer in Palestine by renumbering 680 Squadron and equipped with both PR.Mk.XVI and PR.Mk.34 Mosquitos. From this base it flew numerous reconnaissance sorties throughout the Middle East area, with an additional requirement to record ships that brought illegal Jewish immigrants to Palestine.

Of the RAF's secondary duties there remained a commitment to provide

TT.Mk.35 TA634 undergoes maintenance

aircraft as 'practice targets' for Army, Navy and Air Force surface forces to train against aerial attack. To this end a number of Civilian Anti- Aircraft Co-Operation Units (CAACUs) were formed, staffed in the main by ex-RAF personnel who operated under contract to the Ministry of Defence. They were tasked with testing the reactions of ground-based radar defences and providing towed drogues for target practice by anti-aircraft gunners. The CAACUs operated a number of Beaufighters before they were re-equipped with Mosquito B.Mk.35s (with target gear fitted in the bomb bays) from 1953 until as late as 1963, when they were finally retired and replaced by more modern jet aircraft.

The number of RAF squadrons that operated the Mosquito may have been reduced, but the Auxiliary Air Force (retitled Royal Auxiliary Air Force [RAuxAF] from December 1947) continued to operate the type until re-equipment and until

Two photographs believed to be of a T.Mk.III belonging to Far East Air Force Training Squadron which was at Butterworth, Malaya in 1954 and 1955.

The aircraft appears to be undergoing a tank-change and from the look on the face of the engineer, it was not a happy time!

the RAuxAF flying units were disbanded. The growth of Communism in the Far East saw 81 Sqn conducting operations against the bandits in Malaya from July 1949, under the code-name 'Firedog' (already mentioned in the Photo-Reconnaissance Chapter), until its aircraft were replaced by jets.

Deliveries Abroad

As early as April 1944 a Mosquito B.IV (DK296) was handed over to the Soviet Union and, although additional information is obviously difficult to obtain, it appears that several other machines also found their way into Russian hands.

The FB.VI variant was the most versatile of all and was subsequently sold in greater numbers than any other, although other variants were put to equally good use. Czechoslovakia purchased 26 FB.VIs in 1947, the machines serving with the Czech 'Atlantic' Squadron at Pilsen. Because of a shortage of ammunition, some of the Czech machines were converted to carry German weapons and given the local designation LB-36. Yugoslavia also operated 46 FB.VIs, together with 60 NF.38s, and some T.IIIs. It is thought that some of these aircraft operated well into the 1960s in the target- towing role.

333 (Norwegian) Squadron operated during the war as part of Coastal Command. When peace came the Mosquito Flight of 333 was redesignated No

In late 1951 the Yugoslav Air Force began receiving FB.Mk.VIs, NF.Mk.38s and a few T.Mk.IIIs. *(© BAE SYSTEMS)*

The French Air Force operated a large number of Mosquitos, represented here by FB.VI RS616 'R', seen somewhere over North Africa.

An FB.Mk.VI of the Czech Air Force, RF838 'TY-12' taxies out at Malacky airfield.
(John Stride Collection)

334 Squadron and took its FB.VIs back to Norway and obtained a further 22 in 1947 to supplement them. Also in Scandinavia, Sweden's Flygvapnet (Swedish Air Force) purchased sixty NF.XIXs, giving the type the local designation J 3U.

Another large post-war user was France who purchased at least a hundred Mosquitos, mainly FB.VIs, but also PR.XVIs and NF.30s, all of which retained their RAF scrials. The machines were put to good use during the French campaign in Indo-China when between January 1947 and July 1949, the Mk.VIs were used as strike aircraft against the Communist forces. They also formed part of the French Air Force's 19e Escadre which was based in Algeria during the immediate post-war years.

Belgium purchased two FB.VIs and 24 NF.30s which served with No 10 Squadron. During the 1950s the Union of Burma Air Force acquired a flight of FB.VIs which it used as ground support against separatist groups.

The South African Air Force continued to operate the type after reorganization for peacetime work, with a number of PR.XVIs, XIXs and NF.IIs used by the Photo-Survey Unit. The Turkish Air Force received 96 FB.VIs and ten T.IIIs, all of which were refurbished by Fairey Aviation at Ringway before delivery.

The Royal Australian Air Force kept part of the Bankstown production, supplementing stocks with FB.VIs and PR.XVIs that arrived from the UK. A Survey Flight was formed from the wartime survey squadron, with Ansons, Hudsons and a number of Mosquitos from 87 (PR) Squadron which used PR. 16s

TE603 'KP-1' a FB Mk.VI of the Czech Air Force in an all-silver scheme.
(John Stride Collection)

supplemented by PR.41s. The Flight began operations in 1946 in conjunction with the Royal Australian Survey Corps on a complete aerial survey of Australia. The task was enlivened by emergency work, mapping a number of floods that devastated much of the continent: the Murray River floods. Diamantina Georgina and Coopers Creek floods and, just for a change, the eruption of Mount Lamingham in Papua New Guinea. The Flight achieved squadron status in 1951 but was finally disbanded in 1953 after mapping two- thirds of the continent at a photoscale of 1:50,000. The remaining one-third was contracted out to civil operators who took a further ten years to complete the task.

About eighty Mosquitos from RAF stocks (many direct from Standard Motors manufactured stocks) were passed on to the Royal New Zealand Air Force who used them to equip two complete bomber-reconnaissance (BR) squadrons until replaced by De Havilland Vampire jets.

Above. Mosquito FB.Mk.VIs of the post-war Czech Air Force overfly the Czechoslovak and Yugoslav flags at their base at Pilssen. *(John Stride Collection)*

Left: Royal Norwegian Air Force RS650 AK:F was a FB.Mk.VI and served with 334 Sqn RNoAF. *(via Stuart Howe)*

This Mosquito J.30 of the Swedish Air Force was formerly NF.Mk.XIX TA281 of the RAF and was the third machine delivered to the Swedes. It crashed in May 1949. *(via Stuart Howe)*

'542' - one of the T.Mk.IIIs sold to the Turkish Air Force is seen here in the hands of Pat Fillingham on a test flight out of Hatfield before delivery. *(© BAE SYSTEMS)*

Chinese Nationalists

The Nationalist Government of China had shown considerable interest in the later stages of Mosquito production in Canada, and inspecting Chinese Air Force officers were seen regularly at the Toronto plant. With the end of the war, many surplus Mosquitos were stored at Downsview. In late 1947 the Canadian Government, represented by Roy Peers, and Lieutenant-Colonel R. P. Mow on behalf of the Chinese, concluded negotiations for the sale to the Chinese Nationalist Government of around 180 aircraft at knock-down prices, which cleared out almost the entire stock of Mosquitos held in reserve by the RCAF. Due to the politics of the time, the Canadian Government went to great lengths to emphasize that this was a purely commercial arrangement and did not imply aid for Chiang Kai-Shek against the Communists. De Havilland Canada provided planning and technical support, much of which came from Fred Plumb who, since the days of working in Salisbury Hall on the prototypes, had moved from England to become DH Canada's Works Manager. The Mosquitos were dismantled at Downsview during October 1947 and packed into crates that had previously been used to ship Vampires out from Hatfield to Canada before being transported by rail to a Canadian port and then by sea to Shanghai. From there they were transferred to Tazang Air Base for reassembly and were then test- flown under the direction of De Havilland personnel before being handed over to the Chinese.

First to arrive were several T. Mk.27 trainers, followed by considerable numbers of FB.26s and some T.29s. A fair number of aircraft sub- assemblies failed to survive the winter crossing of the Atlantic, through the Suez Canal and on to Shanghai, suffering severe salt corrosion and damage to electrical and metal parts. So bad was the damage that some aircraft could only be cannibalized for spares, and the remainder of the airframes scrapped.

Training accidents were common when the aircraft were flown by Chinese Air Force instructors and students, and many Mosquitos were written off. In an attempt to reduce these accidents, a fighter-bomber (KA252) was modified into a taxi-trainer, with the undercarriage locked down and bracing tubes bolted between each undercarriage leg, the fuselage and the outer wings. Although this machine could not be flown, the Chinese still managed to write this aircraft off when it was taxied into a hole.

It was in China that the Mosquito gained yet another nickname, 'Lin Tai Yu' after a legendary Empress who was 'beautiful but wicked'. The Chinese attempted to use the aircraft against the Communists, with possibly four lost in

A Canadian-built FB.Mk. 26, believed to be 'B-M008'. The Nationalist Chinese purchased nearly 180 FB.Mk. 26s and T.Mk.29s from surplus Canadian stocks in 1947. *(© BAE SYSTEMS)*

A Chinese Nationalist Air Force T.Mk.29 lies on the grass minus undercarriage at Hankow in 1949. *(© BAE SYSTEMS)*

combat, but in the end they were defeated by the Communist's guerrilla tactics. The situation within the country had deteriorated, and by late 1948 the Canadians were advised to leave. Finally the Communists overran the country and the remaining airworthy Mosquitos were evacuated to Formosa by escaping Nationalist pilots. There they were used for a short while against shipping, but nothing further is known of their fate.

There is the remains of a Mosquito - possibly a FB.Mk.26 - housed at the Beijing Aviation Museum, China. The aircraft appears to be a mocked up fuselage incorporating the rotting remains of a Mosquito port wing, and as such hardly qualifies as a survivor...

To War with the Israelis

During the Israeli War of Independence of 1948-49 the Israeli Air Force possessed just a single Mosquito, a PR.Mk.XVI which had been smuggled into Israel and flown in action by a young French-Jewish pilot with Second World War experience.

In addition, two ex-USAAF reconnaissance machines with the civil registrations of G-AIRT the former NS812 and G-AIRU formerly NS811 respectively, had been secretly purchased in England and registered in October 1946 to VIP Association Ltd of Gumley Leicestershire. On 1 July 1948 ownership changed to Harold Lough White, of Rodney House, Dolphin Square London. On 5 July 1948 the first of the pair was smuggled out of England but the second machine only got as far as Corsica. Ownership of 'RU never changed to Harold White. The surviving Mosquito was incorporated into the 103rd squadron at Ramat David and was operational for two months during which it flew ground attack missions as well as a pair of photo reconnaissance sorties. It crashed on September 21st 1948 and was returned to service during November. The first operational Mosquito with the IAF, it was also one of the last, retired from service in January 1957 after breaking up upon landing.

Admittedly this is not the best of photographs, but it shows Mosquito PR.Mk.XVI G-AIRT before it was smuggled to Israel in July 1948.

There was also a further Israeli Mosquito, salvaged from wrecks left by the British in Ekron Air Force Base after the end of the British mandate in early 1948. Despite repeated attempts to repair it, this photo reconnaissance Mosquito PR Mk. XVI could not be returned to flying condition and spent the Israeli War of Independence as a training platform for mechanics. It was scrapped in June 1949.

With undercarriage down and engines throttled back, this FB.Mk.VI of the IDAF comes in for a landing.
(Israeli Air Force)

Israel's methods of acquiring aircraft at this time were not only secret but sometimes unconventional. Most aspects of the Israeli Air Force are still shrouded in secrecy, and it has proved impossible to state with any degree of accuracy the totals of aircraft purchased.

During 1950 many of the French Mosquitos were up for sale, and on 17 February 1951 Israel signed a contract with the French to purchase 69 (some sources say 59) aircraft of four different marks, 40 FB Mk.VIs. 4 PR Mk. XVIs, 20 NF.Mk.30s, but devoid of their radar equipment and three T.Mk.IIIs.

Overhaul was carried out by workers hired from Hispano and Nord Aviation, with Israeli Air Force personnel overseeing quality control. Initial crew training for Israeli aircrew was conducted in Britain after an agreement was made with the RAF to train a single Israeli airman as an experiment.

The FB.Mk.VI was to be the mainstay of the IDF/AF (Israel Defence Force/Air Force), fitted with four Browning machine-guns and four Oerlikon cannon in the fuselage, and launching rails for four 5in rockets under each wing. These could be replaced if required by racks for 250kg bombs to supplement the pair of 250kg bombs carried in the small bomb bay aft of the cannon.

First located at Ekron (Tel-Nof) Air Force Base, the Mosquitos later moved to Hazor where the 109th Mosquito Squadron was formed, comprising of three sections: operational, training and reconnaissance. A fourth section for night fighting was set up with the arrival of the Mk.30s in 1952. The large number of aircraft exceeded the storage room available at Hazor and they were parked in the sun. This had a totally negative effect on the wooden airframes and many malfunctioned until shelters were built for the entire force. The first flights of the 109th begun in February 1952 with the first reconnaissance missions taking place in May. These initial flights were conducted over the West Bank and the Sinai and enjoyed only limited success. In August the first Mosquito training course begun, including ground attacks as well as duels against the IAF's primary interceptors of the time, the Spitfire and the Mustang. On 23 August 1953 the Mosquito squadron's training section formed a new squadron, the 110th, in charge of training, and a number of Mosquitos of each variant were transfered to it.

An IDFAF Mosquito apparently crudely serialled 4X3179 is made ready for flight.
(Israeli Air Force)

Operationally emphasis placed on low-level surprise raids, very similar to 2nd Tactical Air Force operations during World War Two.

The mainstay of Mosquito operations before 1956 were reconnaissance missions, using the type's long range and high service ceiling to provide intelligence from as far as Iraq and the Egyptian-Lybian border. The weak performance initially shown during such flights was replaced by better results as the pilots of the 109th gained more experience with the type and the Mosquitos begun providing the bulk of IAF photographic intelligence. The Mosquitos routinely overflew Israel's Arab neighbours, photographing Lebanese, Jordanian, Syrian and Egyptian military installations, air bases and army camps. Although these missions provided and IAF and the IDF with much need intelligence, the IDF's high command had very little confidence in the IAF's reconnaissance capabilities. Coupled with a fear of provoking retaliation or having its aircraft shot down, it relied more heavily on its ground assets than on the IAF. After repeated requests for more reconnaissance missions were turned down, IAF personnel decided to conduct such missions on their own, without receiving any permission. On 3 and 4 September 1953 two such missions took place, one over Cairo and the other over the Nile Delta, both carried out by Mosquitos. The wealth of intelligence provided by these missions convinced the IDF top brass of the advantages in using aerial intelligence, and the number of Mosquito reconnaissance missions was stepped up. In July 1954, as the number of missions flown as well as the depth of their penetration into Arab airspace increased, the photo reconnaissance section of 109th was separated from the squadron and subordinated to Hazor's base commander. In June 1956 the section became the 115th photo reconnaissance squadron at Ekron AFB.

An Isreali Air Force PR.Mk.XVI Mosquito, apparently coded '36'
(Dr Harry Friedman Collection)

As tension in the Middle East increased in the years leading to the 1956 Suez Crisis and Israel's operation *Kadesh*, intelligence gathering was also stepped up. Dozens of missions were flown to map Egyptian air bases, the expected British and French invasion beaches and even the entire Sinai peninsula. Reconnaissance missions continued to take place even after Arab air forces begun arming with jet fighters such as the MiG-15. Despite repeated attempts to intercept the Mosquitos, none were shot down, although a number of the available PR Mk.XVIs were lost in accidents (three more Mk. XVIs were purchased in Britain in 1956).

The FB Mk. VI was the backbone of the IAF's ground attack force during its years in service. When an Israeli Navy ship run aground near Saudi Arabia in early 1954, Mosquitos and Mustangs overflew the ship to protect it from Arab forces. The FB.Mk.VI was also involved in a large number of accidents which resulted in a number of crew fatalities. On 8 August 1953 a Mosquito was lost during night bombing practice, the pilot apparently suffering from vertigo and crashing into the Mediterranean. Another Mosquito was lost the following day when it hit the sea during the search for the first missing machine. The accidents usually resulted from poor maintenance of the aircraft and problems associated with the local weather.

The most difficult machines to fly were the so-called 'Black Mosquitos', the NF.Mk.30s which were heavier and more complicated and had the larger nose radar. The black camouflage paint caused these machines to get very hot in the Middle Eastern sun and the ribs began to swell, particularly those of the tail and control surfaces.

In 1953 they formed the IAF's first night fighter squadron but the poor performance shown by the new radars, the poor maintenance and the corrosive local weather hampered their operation. Night fighter operations eventually begun only with the arrival of the Meteor NF.13s in 1955.

A further fourteen TR.Mk.33s were obtained from the Royal Navy in 1954-55, together with six PR.Mk.XVIs which were to be flown to Israel after extensive

MISCELLANEOUS PERFORMANCE DATA		
	T.III	TR/TT.33
Span	54ft 2in	54ft 2in
Length	40ft 6in	40ft 6in
Height	12ft 6in	12ft 6in
Tare weight	13,104lb	14,850lb
All-up weight	16,883lb	23,850lb
Maximum speed	384 mph	376 mph
Cruising speed	260 mph	262 mph
Initial climb	2,500 ft/min	1,820ft/min
Ceiling	37,500 ft	30,100 ft
Maximum range	1,560 miles	1,265 miles
Engines:		
RR Merlin	Mk.21 or 23	Mk.66
Armament	Nil	4 x cannon

An Israeli Air Force Mosquito FB.MkVI with bomb bay doors open. *(Israeli Air Force)*

A pleasing view of this Israeli Air Force Mosquito. Interestingly, the undercarriage fairing shows signs that there was once a 'stripe' applied here. The markings on the rear fuselage is the number '26' followed by the Hebrew letter 'koph'. *(Israeli Air Force)*

G-AOCK, the former NS753 sits at Thruxton awaiting export to Israel. It was declared no airworthy, was grounded and eventually rotted away. *(via Stuart Howe)*

refurbishment in time for the Sinai Campaign of 1956. The PR.Mk.XVIs had arrived at Thruxton airfield in England, having been allocated British civil registrations G-AOCI to G-AOCN during the early summer of 1956, but were flown to Hurn during August to be overhauled by Independent Air Travel Ltd before departing for Israel. Only six were declared airworthy - G-ACOM/4X-FDG-90, ex-Royal Navy RG174, left on 12 October, to be followed by G-AOCJ/4X-FDG-91, ex-NS742, and G-ACON/4X-FDL-92, ex TA614. The others were found to have corrosion in their elevator cables and eventually rotted away.

With advent of jet fighters in the IAF, the piston engined fighter bombers lost their seniority as Israel's frontline aircraft. Hazor AFB became home to jet aircraft and in September 1955 the Mosquitos were moved to Sirkin and Ekron AFB. In October the two Mosquito squadrons, the 109th and 110th were reunited as the 109th, and in May 1956, in anticipation of the arrival of the Dassault Mystere IVA, the 109th was disbanded and its aircraft sent into storage. The 115th photo reconnaissance squadron however, continued operating the Mosquito with ever greater fervour as tensions were rising in the Middle East. Once the Suez Crisis had broken out in 1956, the Mosquitos were withdrawn from storage and reformed the 110th squadron at Ramat David, home to all IAF bombers during operation *Kadesh,* Israel's part in the war.

The Sinai War - a joint venture between Israel, France and Britain - broke out in October of that year and was therefore well planned in advance. The Israeli Mosquito force was reinstated as a ground support squadron for the period of the conflict with two main roles in mind: to conduct long-range day and night patrols over the Suez area and the Sharm El Sheikh Strait, and to act as escort for the two IDF/AF B-17 Fortresses that were still operational. Even now, some twenty years after the design had first been mooted, the Mosquito could give a good account of itself - and hold its own when up against much more modern equipment. For the daylight hours of the first two days of the conflict, the Mosquitos were kept on the ground, as air battles were being fought out over the Sinai desert. The distant Egyptian airfields were being taken care of by aircraft from the British and French air forces, but the Israeli Mosquitos were brought into the conflict from day three onwards, and the entire squadron became engaged on operations from 31 October. The IDF/AF also used about eight PR machines to gather information on troop and equipment movements in preparation for attacks.

Three Israeli Air Force Mosquitos, with '2103' closest to the camera is seen low over the desert. (Israeli Air Force)

The initial planning for operation *Kadesh* called for the IAF to attack Egyptian airfields in anticipation of an Egyptian attack on Israeli air bases. The Mosquitos were tasked with attacking the farthest Egyptian airfields, those beyond the Suez Canal such as Cairo-West, Faid and Abu-Sweir. When fighting broke out on 29 October 1956 however, the only participating Mosquitos were the PR Mk.XVIs. The planned attack on Egyptian air fields did not take place while propellor driven aircraft were excluded from the battle zones over the Sinai Desert. Photo reconnaissance missions were flown on 29 October, Egyptian airfields photographed, but only on 31 October did Mosquitos begin to fly ground attack missions in the Sinai. Mosquitos were involved in fighting throughout the Sinai, especially in attacks on Egyptian armour and Egyptian army camps. The type was also extensively involved in the fighting around the Egyptian stronghold at Sharm-A-Sheikh at the southern tip of the Sinai, attacking the target for four consecutive days beginning on 1 November. As far as can be ascertained, 74 Mosquito sorties lasting 141 hours were flown during the operation and 2 aircraft were lost.

The end of operation *'Kadesh'* also brought about the end of the Mosquito era in the IAF. In January 1957 the 110th squadron was disbanded and the remaining Mosquitos sent to storage.

Civil Photo-Survey Work and Air Racing

An echo back to the wartime days of photographic reconnaissance and the post-war survey of Australia occurred in 1951 when a Canadian company, Kenting Aviation of Toronto, purchased KA202 and KA244, two T.29 trainers, from the RCAF. The aircraft were placed on the Canadian register as CF-GKK and CF-GKL respectively and modified for photographic survey work. 'GKL was sold to Spartan Air Services, another photographic survey company, which later acquired a number of PR.Mk.35s from the British Air Ministry; these aircraft were modified by Derby Aviation at Burnaston before delivery.

A further two Canadian Mosquitos, KA985 and KB377, both B.25s, were obtained from the War Assets Disposal department of the Canadian Government by Don McVicar of World Wide Aviation Agencies in Montreal to be used for air racing. McVicar entered KB377 (now registered CF-FZG) in the National Air Races of 1948. He was forced down in the mid-west with engine trouble on his way to Long Beach, California,the starting point of the Bendix Trophy.

The Americans also got into civilian Mosquito air racing when KB985 was

The crew of Spartan Air Services B.Mk.35 adjust their equipment before taking out CF-HML on another survey flight. Note the non-standard nose glazing and the conversion of the hinged escape hatch into an entry hatch. To operate the specialist survey equipment, a third crew member was carried.

Spartan Air Services acquired a number of PR.Mk.35s in the 1950s. Five were cannibalised for spares at Hurn, including CF-IME seen here. *(via Martin Bowman)*

Air Racing Mosquitos!

Left: N66313 *Miss Martha* ready for air racing.

Below left: NX66422 belonging to Di Ponti Aviation of Minnesota.

Below: With not only shark's mouth artwork on the nose, but also on the drop tanks, N1203V is seen before the start of the round-the-world record attempt. *(all via Stuart Howe)*

entered in the same 1948 Bendix race, registered N66313, in the hands of Jesse Stalling of Capitol Airways, but the aircraft limped into Cleveland with a dead engine in last place. The previous year Di Ponti Aviation of St Paul, Minnesota had obtained the former US Navy 91106 to enter into the 1947 Bendix, but this did not happen.

Other Mosquitos operated in the USA included N1203V, the former B.Mk.25 KA997 which was obtained by Dianna Bixby for a round-the-world record attempt which started on 2 April 1950. On take off from Calcutta, India she had to return because of a bad engine and the attempt failed. The aircraft was later sold to Flying Tiger Line and had its wooden cockpit replaced with a metal one for high-altitude photography.

Gust Research Unit

Another post-war use that in some ways reflected back to the days of meteorological reconnaissance was instigated in 1947, when N E Rowe, Controller of Research and Long-term Development of British European Airways Corporation (BEA), felt that, with higher and faster flying airliners about to enter service with

G-AJZE, the former RG231 was one of two BEA Gust Research Unit machines is seen here at Cranfield.
(British Airways)

the Corporation, flight research into clear air gust conditions was required; for only by gathering factual evidence could the whole nature of the phenomenon be understood and, if necessary, action taken to negate the effect. Rowe was by no means a stranger to the Mosquito, for while with the Ministry of Aircraft Production during the war, he had instigated the modification of the design to carry a 4,000 lb bomb, during April 1943. Rowe also played a great part in the development of the first pressure-cabin Mosquito to combat the threat of the German high-flying raider.

The Ministry of Supply agreed with Rowe's reasoning, and gave official approval for the setting up of a Gust Research Unit (GRU) by BEA. Following a survey of potential bases, it was decided that the future College of Aeronautics at Cranfield offered the best facilities to site the unit. In June 1947 two Mosquito PR.34s were allocated to the GRU by the Ministry, but these were not delivered until September, following equipment testing at RAE Farnborough. The aircraft had even more specialized equipment fitted at Cranfield before being submitted for a civil Certificate of Airworthiness (C of A) in category 'G', the category reserved for aircraft engaged on experimental work. Due to difficulties in the location of spares, the C of A clearance was held up for some while so that it was not until 1 March 1948 that the first machine, G-AJZE, was granted its C of A; G-AJZF followed on 3 June.

The GRU had a two-fold task on formation; to collect data that would assist meteorologists to forecast the position and intensity of areas of clear air turbulence; and to record the strength of the gusts so that their effect on high-speed aircraft could be judged. For the next two years the crews of these machines ranged over 90,000 miles above 15,000ft in search of these elusive regions of turbulent air, finding nineteen zones in positions ranging from the Swiss Alps to Scotland, from Spain to Denmark. The pressure-cabin PR.Mk.34s followed a 'saw-tooth' pattern, alternately climbing to 37,000ft, and then descending to 15,000ft. In this manner the possibility of discovering a turbulent region of air was increased four-fold compared with flying at a constant altitude. Broadly speaking, they found that clear air turbulence could be located anywhere, at any time and at any height above 15,000ft.

Where Are They Now?

As the turbine-powered fighters and bombers became available, the Mosquito was slowly retired. After fourteen years' service, the Mosquito dropped out of military and civil use. During the 1960s several films (factual and otherwise) were made about aviation events relating to the Second World War. The Mosquito design was not left out, for several aircraft were obtained and restored to flying condition tor '633 Squadron' and 'Mosquito Squadron', two films which served to preserve the type for future generations. Apart from the mecca of all Mosquito enthusiasts worldwide - the Mosquito Aircraft Museum housed at the aircraft's birthplace, Salisbury Hall - a small number of aircraft are preserved around the world. Perhaps the most travelled of all the survivors is RS709, a TT.35 which at one time. was a CAACU aircraft. It went to the now defunct Skyfame Aircraft Museum at Staverton, Gloucestershire, after starring in '633 Squadron'. The aircraft was then sold to an owner in New York who based the aircraft with the Confederate Air Force in Texas. It was then sold to a UK owner who sold it again - to the USAF Museum at Wright-Patterson AFB in Ohio. Thus RS709 has the claim that it is possibly the only Mosquito that has crossed the Atlantic four times under its own power.

RAF SECOND-LINE UNITS

UNIT	REMARKS
Armament Practice School	1947-50
Air Torpedo Development Unit	1944-50
Bomber Development Unit	1943-45
Bomber Support Development Unit	4/44-1945
Bombing Trials Unit	1945-51
Civilian Anti-Aircraft Co-operation Units	-
Central Bomber Establishment	1946-49
Central Flying School	-
Empire Central Flying School	-
Central Gunnery School	1944-51
Empire Test Pilots School	-
Empire Air Armament School	-
Photographic Development Unit	-
Special Installation Unit	-
Signals Flying Unit	-
204 Advanced Flying School	Disbanded 1953
Fighter Interception Unit	Became Fighter Interception Development Unit
Fighter Interception Development Unit	Also Night Development Sqn. Fighter Development Wing, Fighter Experimental Flight, Ranger Flight, Central Fighter Establishment
226 OCU Stradishall	1954
228 OCU Leeming	5/47-1954
229 OCU Chivenor	-
231 OCU Bassingbourn	1953
237 OCU Leuchars	-
237 OCU Benson	-
8 Operational Training Unit	11/42-10/46
13 Operational Training Unit	1/44-5/47
16 Operational Training Unit	12/44-3/48. Became 204 AFS
51 Operational Training Unit	7/44-6/45
54 Operational Training Unit	8/44-5/47
60 Operational Training Unit	5/43-1/45, merged with 13 OTU
132 Operational Training Unit	5/44-3/45
Pathfinder Navigation Training Unit	6/43-1945
1 Photographic Reconnaissance Unit	7/41 -Disbanded 10/42
1300 Meteorological Flight	Existed as 18 Sqn 1945-47
1401 Meteorological Flight	1942
1409 Meteorological Flight	4/43-Disbanded 1946
1655 Mosquito Training Unit	10/42. Became 11 OTU 12/44
1672 Mosquito Conversion Unit	2/44- Disbanded 8/45
1692 Bomber Support Training Unit	6/44- Disbanded 6/45

OTHER ARMED FORCES USING MOSQUITOS

Belgium, Burma, China, Czechoslovakia, Dominican Republic, France, Israel, New Zealand, Norway, Sweden, Turkey, United States of America, Yugoslavia.

FROM THE COCKPIT

When the Mosquito first flew it had a cockpit that was almost unique among RAF machines of the time, a cockpit with all the essential switches, knobs and levers located forward of the pilot, with no cunningly concealed fuel or hydraulic cocks requiring a double-jointed arm to reach backwards and downwards to locate them. On the Mosquito, the pilot's left hand worked the throttles and propeller controls while his right hand operated the rudder and aileron trim controls, together with the flap and undercarriage controls. In the fighter variant the control column was cranked over to the right; other versions used a spectacle wheel for aileron control.

The machine-guns in both the fighter and fighter-bomber versions were fired by a thumb-operated trigger and the 20mm cannon by a forefinger-operated trigger mounted on the control column. All the guns were heated with air taken from the starboard radiator; the gun heater control was on the right of the observer's seat.

The side panel of an unidentified fighter Mosquito, showing the compass, throttles and radio channel changer. (*©BAE SYSTEMS*)

View for the crew during combat was in the main good, but fighter-to-fighter combat in the Mosquito during the hours of daylight presented some difficulties because, although the forward vision was extremely good, the field of vision downwards was severely restricted by the engine nacelles, which were located so

close to the cockpit, and the side-by-side seating.

If the variant could carry bombs, a panel on the right-hand side of the instrument panel provided switching for the fuselage and wing- mounted bombs. Selection of which bomb was to be dropped could be made on this panel, being released by pressing a button on the control column after opening the bomb doors by operating the bomb-door lever situated on the left of the undercarriage lever.

Entry to the Cockpit

As the Mosquito design grew in the number of uses that it could be put to, differences occurred in cockpit layout, handling characteristics and performance figures. In versions where the navigator was provided with an attack radar, the right-hand side of the cockpit became crowded with electronics and cathode ray tubes. The changes brought about through refinement in the design, or changes in powerplants, created differences mainly in performance, so the following information has been correlated for the F.Mk.II, NF.Mk.XII, NF.Mk.XIII, NF.Mk.XVII and NF.Mk.XIX unless otherwise stated.

Entry to the cockpit was by means of a telescopic ladder leading up to a hatch in the lower starboard side of the nose, or in some variants the lower fuselage; the pilot entered first so as to be able to occupy the port seat, with the navigator following. Space was at a premium, with the two crew members sitting almost shoulder to shoulder, so care had to be taken to ensure that the various straps dangling from the crew members did not snag on any switches or levers. The crew sat with the observer/ navigator slightly behind the pilot in an attempt to provide as much room as possible, both members being in a slightly skewed position. This created the strange effect where it was possible for the seating position alone to induce a false sense of turning when flying on instruments in cloud or at night. After the crew had got themselves settled, the hatch shut and they were strapped in, the electrics were switched on and the 24-volt battery system checked to be fully charged. The pneumatic system had to show a pressure of 200 pounds per square inch, for if the aircraft was left standing on the ground for a few days, pressure would bleed away to nothing, leaving the brakes inoperative. Therefore wheel chocks had always to be in place before engine start-up. The pneumatic system also operated the radiator flaps and, if fitted, the tropical air filter and both sets of guns.

Engine Start-Up

Engines were always started port first, the pilot having previously selected outer fuel tanks, for in the event of an engine failure it was not possible to cross-feed fuel from the outer tanks from one wing to the engine on the other side. Throttle set half an inch open, constant-speed propeller control fully forward, supercharger to MOD and fuel pressure venting cock ON. Radiator flap switches OPEN. This was done for when the cockpit supercharger switch was set to AUTO, the two-speed supercharger was automatically changed to S gear by an aneroid-operated switch. when the aircraft reached a certain altitude. The switch could be set to MOD for cruising in M gear above the change gear height. Then a member of the ground crew pumped the priming pump located in each engine nacelle for a few

The cockpit of B.Mk.35 RS709, the former G-MOSI, now on display in the National Museum of the US Air Force in Dayton Ohio. The aircraft is in the markings of the 25th Bomb Group as a PR.Mk.XVI. *(author)*

strokes to prime the engine. Ignition switches *'On'* and starter and booster-coil buttons pressed. The engine would then fire, with clouds of half- burnt fuel and exhaust gases accompanying and covering the ground crew member, who could be feverishly pumping the primer to keep the engine running, for the engine-driven fuel pump was not capable of keeping fuel flowing below a certain rpm. As soon as the engine was running satisfactorily, the booster coil button was released and the ground crew member instructed to screw down the priming pump and close the panel. The whole procedure was then repeated for the starboard engine.

As soon as the engines settled down to even firing, the throttles were eased open to give 1,200 rpm for engine warm-up. Particular care had to be taken to prevent engine overheating when stationary or at a slow taxi, for the slim wing-mounted radiators offered little cooling at slow speeds. If the engine temperatures rose above 70°C it was imperative to turn the aircraft into wind and run both engines up to 2,000 rpm for a short period to force slipstream from the propellers through the radiators. After warming up the engines and before taxi- ing, checks were made to ensure the operation of each engine-driven pump. This was done by opening each engine up to 2,000 rpm individually and then raising and lowering the flaps before repeating the procedure on the other engine. While the starboard engine was running at 2,000 rpm the generator was checked to be charging at 29 volts. The engines were then opened up to +4 lb boost to ensure propeller constant-speeding, and that, with take-off boost, both engines reached 3,000 rpm. Both engines were then throttled back and the magneto 'drop' was checked (acceptable if it did not exceed 150 rpm).

Taxiing

Taxi-ing was straightforward as the view over the nose was excellent, although the later Mk.X AI-equipped night fighters with the bulky nose radome demanded fishtailing to see the track ahead. The wheel brakes were powerful and operated by a lever on the control column, differential braking being achieved by use of the

rudder-bar. During taxiing the brake pressure was checked again; if the pressure was low, it had to be checked that the pressure was building; if not the aircraft was not to be flown. The undercarriage ground locking caps were to be removed and replaced by dust caps and the flaps checked to be fully up. On arrival at the take-off point it was customary to swing into wind and then, with brakes on and the control column hard back, the engines were run up to 3,000 rpm to clear the plugs.

The pilot's panel from a B.MK.IV. From the tools and removed panels on the floor on the right, hand side of the picture, it seems that the aircraft was undergoing servicing at the time!

(©BAE SYSTEMS)

Take-Off

Take-off checks were brief. Trimmers: elevators slightly nose heavy on most versions, rudder slightly right to help counteract the torque of the engines. This could be ignored if the aircraft was fitted with 'handed' engines rotating in different directions. Ailerons were set to neutral. Propeller pitch controls fully forward, fuel cocks on outer tanks and tank contents checked. Flaps as required (usually up or about 15deg). Superchargers to '*Mod*', and radiator switches '*Open*'.

After receiving take-off clearance the throttles were slowly pushed fully forward, leading slightly with the port to counter the fairly marked swing to the left. Acceleration was immediate, with the moment that the tail could be raised varying slightly between versions. The night fighters, with more equipment in the nose, tended to assume the tail-up attitude fairly quickly, so it was necessary to check this with a slight back pressure on the stick. Lift-off was achieved at around 125- 130 mph indicated. It was essential to hold the machine level and retract the undercarriage as soon as possible after lift-off in order to build up speed quickly, to achieve the single-engine safety speed of 170 mph. The relatively small, high placed rudder coupled with the low-slung engine nacelles imposed a lack of directional control at low airspeeds that was only improved in the later marks of Mosquito which had higher power available, allowing them to reach this critical speed quicker. Raising the undercarriage produced a nose-up change of trim, with a sharp nose-down change of trim when the flaps were raised.

Once the safety speed was reached the machine could be trimmed for the climb, flaps (if used) raised and engines throttled back to 170 mph indicated to give the maximum rate of climb. If long-range fuselage tanks were fitted, but no wing drop tanks, at between 500 and 1,000ft after take-off the fuel supply was to be switched over to *'Main'*, with the immersed fuel pump switched on so that these tanks could be emptied as soon as possible. If drop tanks were fitted, it was normal to continue flying on the outer tanks until the fuel pressure warning lights indicated that the tanks were empty. It was then necessary to change over to *'Main Supply'* and turn on pneumatic pressure to the drop tanks. This would transfer fuel from the drop tanks to the outer tanks, a process taking around 20 minutes. It was not normally necessary to drop the drop tanks themselves, for the extra drag due to these tanks was very low and there would be little improvement to the speed of the aircraft. If it was operationally necessary to drop the tanks, it should only be done when flying straight and level, for damage, particularly if the tanks were metal, could occur to the airframe in other conditions of flight.

In-Flight Manoeuvring

In combat the fighter Mosquito met the two main requirements - heavy firepower and speed - but it also possessed the ability to perform manoeuvres required to press home the attack. In general flight the aircraft had good directional stability in both the lateral and longitudinal planes, but could become unstable in both the climb and glide with the centre of gravity aft. Normally the controls were light and effective, with good manoeuvrability, but care had to be taken that the rudder was not used violently at high speeds. The maximum rate of climb was achieved at 170 mph indicated from sea-level to 20,000 ft, 165 mph from 20,000 to 25,000 ft and 160 mph above.

A slow roll was reasonably difficult to execute as the speed dropped off quickly, with the nose dropping off sharply during the second half of the roll, causing the loss of a fair amount of height. It was therefore required to barrel the nose around the horizon to maintain height. There was also a risk that if the roll was too slow, one or both engines could cut out while inverted. It was usual, therefore, to enter such a manoeuvre at over 300 mph to alleviate the problem. As the speed increased, a degree of tail heaviness was experienced, requiring a good amount of nose-down trim to counter. Overspeeding of the propellers could also occur, even when constant-speed units were fitted, this being especially noticeable on later marks during high-speed dives.

Stalls in the clean condition were straightforward, indicated at the onset by slight pitching, followed by the nose, and possibly one wing dropping. Recovery was straightforward, for once the aircraft was established in the glide the speed built up very quickly. Aerobatics in any radar-equipped fighter was frowned upon for excessive G on sensitive electronic equipment and its operator was not considered conducive to the efficient operation of both. The extra weight of the radar equipment in the nose made any Mosquito so equipped sluggish in climbing and looping manoeuvres.

If an engine failure in flight was experienced, the dead propeller was to be feathered by closing the throttle immediately, holding in the feathering button for the required engine, and switching off the engine only when the propeller had stopped, and then closing the radiator flap.

Landing

Rejoining the circuit for landing was a procedure that varied according to the type of Mosquito flown. Bombers made long, flat approaches with undercarriage down, while the fighters and fighter-bombers completed a tight circuit on to the approach close to the boundary. Unless on a straight-in instrument approach, the night fighters tended to compromise with a larger circuit, straightening up for a final approach between one and two miles downwind of the runway threshold. During the downwind leg, checks were: Brake pressure 200psi, superchargers to MOD, and radiator flaps open, while reducing speed to around 180 mph. Then undercarriage DOWN, which if the landing was made on one engine only could take at least 30 seconds to lower; speed controls on the propellers fully forward; fuel cocks turned towards fullest tanks; speed reduced to 150 mph indicated before lowering the flaps FULL DOWN, trimming if required to counteract any tail heaviness. Use of the throttle was made to adjust the rate of descent, the aircraft turning on to finals at about 140 mph indicated, checking its fairly high rate of descent with engine power, and aiming to cross the runway threshold at a height of 15ft with 120 mph indicated, when the throttles could be closed and the stick eased back.

At average landing weights the Mosquito stalled at about 105 mph, the night fighters slightly higher. Special care had to be taken just on the point of touch-down for if an engine failed, the aircraft would swing violently towards the windmilling propeller, with potentially disastrous results. Landing on one engine presented no real difficulty as long as a long approach was made, enabling the speed to be kept above 160 mph, with the rate of descent being controlled by the good engine; it had also to be borne in mind that lowering the undercarriage caused a great height loss due to the high drag created. The rate of descent was much faster, and a steeper approach than normal was advisable. In the event of a missed approach and the need to go round again, it was essential to accelerate as quickly as possible, holding the aircraft down and retracting the undercarriage to gain critical speed.

Undercarriage Failure

Should the undercarriage or flaps fail to operate in the normal way, with flap failure the approach was to be made at 140 mph indicated. Action in the event of indicated undercarriage failure depended on the indications received in the cockpit. If the red indicator lights went out, but the green lights failed to show after UNDERCARRIAGE DOWN, it was possible to check that the down locks were engaged and that the lights were at fault by re-selecting DOWN. The undercarriage selector lever should return to neutral immediately if the locks were engaged. If

The cockpit of a
T.Mk.III
(©BAE SYSTEMS)

the undercarriage warning horn did not sound when the throttles were closed, it should be safe to land. If the warning horn sounded when the throttles were closed, the undercarriage was lowered but not locked. In this case the flaps should first be lowered to the landing setting; then to maintain pressure in the undercarriage jacks, the selector should be held 'Down' until the landing had been completed; the aircraft could not be taxied, nor the flaps raised until the jacks could be locked manually by ground staff.

If the undercarriage failed to lower at all on the engine-driven pumps, the selector should be left in neutral, and the emergency selector pushed down. The hand pump could then be operated until the indicator showed that the wheels were down and locked - or considerable resistance was felt on the hand pump. This would not lower the tailwheel, so the undercarriage selector was then to be placed at 'Down' and the hand pump applied to the normal system in an attempt to lower the tailwheel. If there was no indication in the cockpit that this was lowered, the landing was then to be made on grass if possible. If the undercarriage down locks failed to engage, pressure was to be maintained by pumping the hand pump until after the landing was complete. The flaps could also be lowered in the same manner.

Once the aircraft was down on the runway, deceleration caused a slight swing to the right, checked by use of left rudder. With the night fighters, and their extra weight in the nose, use of the powerful wheel brakes was not to be made until after the tail was firmly down on the ground, otherwise it was possible to stand the aircraft on its nose. After landing, and before taxi-ing, the flaps had to be raised and the engines be idled at 800 rpm for a short while, to ensure even cooling before stopping the engines; the slow-running cut-outs were then pulled and held until each engine stopped. After the engines had stopped, the ignition was switched off, fuel turned off, and electrical services switched off.

Emergencies

In the event of an emergency where the aircraft had to be abandoned, unless speed and altitude dictated otherwise, it was recommended that exit from the aircraft by parachute was preferable to ditching, no matter what mark of aircraft was being flown. Because of the weight of the engines, the aircraft showed a tendency to bury its nose in the water, with the lightweight wooden structure breaking up. If ditching was inevitable, the roof panel was to be jettisoned - through which only one member at a time could escape - and the flaps lowered to 25 degrees. If one engine had failed, the final approach was best made without power. Both crew carried 'K' type dinghies in their parachute packs and most Mosquitoes were equipped with an 'L' type dinghy and emergency pack. Release was by pulling the release control in the roof above the pilot's head; an immersion switch automatically inflated the dinghy.

Procedure for parachute exit in machines with the door on the starboard side of the fuselage was to feather the propeller on that side before operating the emergency jettison door handle (not the normal door handle). If the exit was in the belly of the machine there was no requirement to feather the propeller. On pressurized aircraft the emergency pressure release valve had first to be operated. The entrance and exit door consisted of inner and outer hatches. The inner one was operated by pulling out the hinge straps and throwing it into the nose area before operating a pedal on the left side of the hatch; this had to be pressed before the outer hatch could be released.

MOSQUITO VARIANTS

As there were so many sub-types of the DH.98 Mosquito, below is a breakdown of all the models built, or proposed to be built, over the life of the design. The main differences incorporated into the machines when they left the factory are mentioned, but no account can be made for any local modifications introduced in squadron service, or at maintenance units, and therefore should only be used as a guide to design criteria.

Prototype
Powered by two Rolls-Royce Merlin 21s. Serialled W4050. Aircraft had a wingspan of 52ft 6in.

PR.Mk.1
Powered by two Rolls-Royce Merlin 21s driving three-bladed Hydromatic fully feathering propellers. This photographic reconnaissance variant was based on the W4050 prototype, but with an increased wingspan of 54ft 2in. Nine plus the prototype were built, all with short engine nacelles. Four were modified into long-range aircraft with increased all-up weight; two of these were also tropicalized. All had three vertical and one oblique cameras. First flew 10 June 1941. These machines had a cruising speed of 255 mph, maximum speed of 382 mph and range of 2,180 miles.

Production: W4051 - Prototype. W4054-W4056. W4058-W4059; W4060-W4061 (Long-range); W4062-W4063 (Long-range/Tropicalized).

PR/Bomber Conversion
Powered by two Rolls-Royce Merlin 21s driving three-bladed Hydromatic fully feathering propellers, this was a bomber conversion of the PR.Mk.1 airframe. Nine machines were built, all with short nacelles for speed of production. They could carry a 2,000 lb bomb load. The designation was changed to B.Mk.IV Series I prior to entering squadron service. First flew September 1941.

Production: W4064-W4072.

F.Mk.II.
Powered by two Rolls-Royce Merlin 21, 22, or 23s driving three-bladed Hydromatic fully feathering

propellers, this was a day or night long-range fighter/intruder. The aircraft was armed with four 20mm Hispano cannon in the belly and four 0.303m Browning machine-guns in the nose. All had what evolved into the standard long engine nacelles. The F.Mk.II first flew 15 May 1941. Some aircraft had dual controls fitted. Twenty-five aircraft had AI radar removed and increased tankage as (Special) Intruders for 23 Sqn. Many were refurbished and re-engined in 1943/44 for use on airborne electronic counter-measures with 100 Group RAF when airborne interception Mk.IV and V radar was installed. A few were converted to PR duties. The F.Mk.II had a cruising speed of 255 mph, maximum speed of 382 mph and range of 2,180 miles.

Production: W4052 - Prototype. W4074, W4076, W4078, W4080, W4082, W4083, W4084-W4089; DD600-664, DD659-691, DD712-759, DD777-800; DD670-691, DD712-714 F.Mk.II (Special) for 23 Sqn; DZ228-DZ272, DZ286-DZ310; HJ642- HJ661, HJ699-HJ715, HJ911-HJ946, HK107-HK141, HK159-HK204, HK222-HK265, HK278-HK327, HK344-HK362.

Conversions: W4087 was fitted with a Turbinlite searchlight in its nose. DD715 was the prototype Mk.XII. DD759 was converted to Mk.XII. DZ302 was converted to NF.Mk.XII by Marshalls of Cambridge. HJ945-HJ946, HK107-HK141, HK159-K185, HK187- HK194, HK196-HK204, HK222-HK235 all went to Marshalls for conversion into NF.Mk.XII. HK186 went to Southern Aircraft, later to Marshalls, for conversion; delivered as NF.Mk.XII. HK195 went to Marshalls for conversion to Mk.XVII. HK236-HK265, HK278-HK327, HK344-HK362 went to Marshalls for conversion to NF.Mk.XVII.

T.Mk.III

Powered by two Rolls-Royce Merlin 21, 23 and 25s driving three-bladed Hydromatic fully feathering propellers. This variant was an unarmed dual-control trainer. Early designations of this variant were in fact Mk.II aircraft fitted with dual control. First flew January 1942. It had a cruising speed of 260mph, maximum speed of 384mph and range of 1,560 miles.

Production: W4053 - Prototype. W4075, W4077, W4079, W4081; HJ851-HJ899, HJ958-HJ999; LR516-LR541, LR553-LR585; RR270-RR319; TV954-TV984; TW101-TW109; VA871-VA876, VA877-VA894, VA923-VA928; VP342-VP355; VR330-VR349; VT581-VT595, VT604-VT631.

B.Mk.IV Series II

Powered by two Rolls-Royce Merlin 21 or 23s driving three-bladed Hydromatic fully feathering propellers, this was a day and night bomber. First flew March 1942. It could carry a 2,000 lb bomb load and a pair of 50gal drop tanks under the wings. Some were modified to carry a single 4,000 lb bomb on instructions of 8 Group. This was achieved with modification of bomb bay doors and reduction in fuel load carried. The variant had a cruising speed of 265mph, maximum speed of 380mph and range of 2,040 miles.

Production: DK284-DK303, DK308-DK333, DK336-DK339; DZ311-DZ320, DZ340-DZ341, DZ343-DZ363, DZ365,DZ367-DZ384, DZ386-DZ388, DZ405-DZ408, DZ410-DZ416, DZ418-DZ423, DZ425-DZ442, DZ458-DZ497, DZ515-DZ559, DZ575-DZ618, DZ630-DZ652

Conversions: DK324 was first converted to a PR.Mk.VII, then to a B.Mk.IX. This aircraft was shipped to Canada on *Oregon* 9 September 1942 to aid Downsview production. DZ434 was converted to the prototype FB.Mk.VI Series I as HJ662/G. DZ540 was the prototype pressure-cabin Mk.XVI. This variant was fitted with two Rolls-Royce Merlin 73s, then transferred to the Aeroplane & Armament Experimental Establishment. The following machines were converted to PR.Mk.IV: DZ411, DZ419, DZ431, DZ438, DZ459, DZ466, DZ473, DZ480, DZ487, DZ494, DZ517, DZ523, DZ527, DZ532, DZ538, DZ544, DZ549, DZ553, DZ557, DZ576, DZ580,

DZ584, DZ588, DZ592, DZ596, DZ600, DZ604.

DZ594 (the prototype) and DZ647 were both converted by De Havilland's. DZ599, DZ606, DZ608, DZ611, DZ630-DZ634, DZ636-DZ644, DZ646, DZ650 were converted by Vickers-Armstrongs (Weybridge) or Marshalls (Cambridge).

'Highball' Conversion

The 'Highball' conversion of the B.Mk.IV Series II airframe involved modifications to the bomb bay for the carriage of two mines in tandem with associated drives. The weights were little altered compared with standard aircraft, but the performance figures were 18mph slower at sea-level, 22mph slower at 12,000ft.

DZ471 (the prototype), DZ531/G first modified by Vickers-Armstrongs. Also DZ520, DZ524/G, DZ529, DZ530/G, DZ533, DZ534/G, DZ535/G, DZ537/G, DZ539, DZ541-DZ543, DZ546-DZ547, DZ552, DZ554-DZ556, DZ559, DZ575, DZ577-DZ579, DZ581,DZ583.

Many were later modified again by Vickers-Armstrongs (Weybridge), Marshalls and Airspeed with two Rolls-Royce Merlin 24s, new windscreen, arrester hook, armour plating and motive power for spinning up stores. These aircraft were: DZ520, DZ524, DZ529, DZ531, DZ537, DZ539, DZ541-DZ543, DZ546, DZ552, DZ554-DZ556, DZ559, DZ575, DZ577-DZ579, DZ581-DZ583, DZ585, DZ586, DZ618, DZ639, DZ648, DZ651, DZ652.

PR.Mk.IV

Powered by two Rolls-Royce Merlin 21 or 23s driving three-bladed Hydromatic fully feathering propellers, this was a day and night photographic reconnaissance aircraft. All were conversions of existing B. Mk. IV Series II machines. First flew April 1942.

Converted from B.Mk.IV Series II: DZ411, DZ419, DZ431, DZ438, DZ459, DZ466, DZ473, DZ480, DZ487, DZ494, DZ517, DZ523, DZ527, DZ532, DZ538, DZ544, DZ549, DZ553, DZ557, DZ576, DZ580, DZ584, DZ588, DZ592, DZ596, DZ600, DZ604.

B.Mk.V

Powered by two Rolls-Royce Merlin 21s, this was a projected bomber with two 50gal drop-tanks or two

De Havilland DH.98 Mosquito Geneology

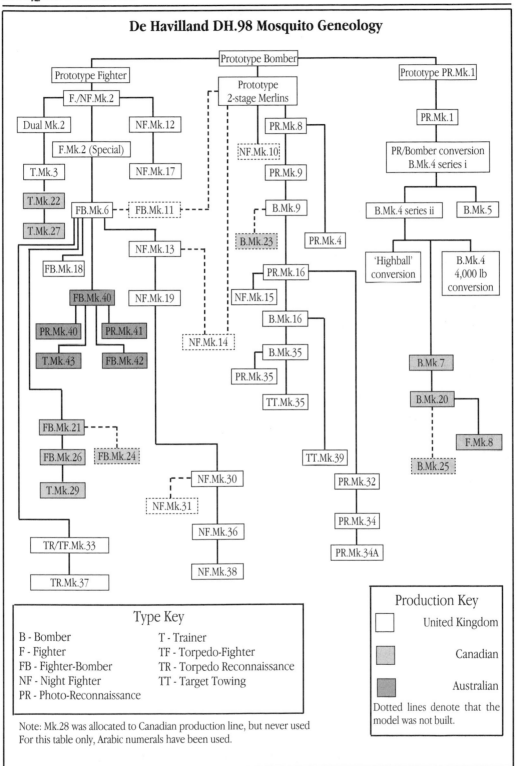

Note: Mk.28 was allocated to Canadian production line, but never used
For this table only, Arabic numerals have been used.

500 lb underwing mounted bombs. Only a single aircraft, W4057, was known as B.Mk.V prototype, and this aircraft was later used for other prototype work, including Bomber/PR conversion and B.Mk.IV.

FB.Mk.VI

Powered by two Rolls-Royce Merlin 21, 22, 23 or 25 engines driving three-bladed Hydromatic fully feathering propellers, this was a day and night fighter-bomber/intruder/long-range fighter. Provision was made for an alternative drop-tank, depth-charge, rocket projectiles or bomb under each wing. First flew 1 June 1942; first production machine flew February 1943. Cruising speed was 255mph, maximum speed 378mph and range 1,855 miles.

Production: HJ662-HJ682, HJ716-HJ743, HJ755-HJ792, HJ808-HJ833; HP848-HP888, HP904-HP942, HP967-HP989; HR113-HR162, HR175-HR220, HR236-HR262, HR279-HR312, HR331-HR375, HR387-HR415, HR432-HR465, HR485-HR527, HR539-HR580, HR603-HR649; HX802-HX835, HX851-HX869, HX896-HX901, HX905-HX922, HX937-HX984; LR248-LR276, LR289-LR313, LR327-LR340, LR343-LR389, LR402-LR404; MM398-MM423, MM426-MM431; RF580-RF625, RF639-RF681, RF695-RF736, RF749-RF793, RF818-RF859, RF873-RF915, RF928-RF966; RS501-RS535, RS548-RS580, RS593-RS633, RS637-RS680, RS693-RS698; SZ958-SZ999; TA113-TA122, TA469- TA508, TA523-TA560, TA575-TA603; TE587-TE628, TE640-TE669, TE683-TE707, TE708-TE725, TE738-TE780, TE793-TE830, TE848-TE889, TE905-TE932; VL727-VL732.

Conversions: HJ732 was converted to the prototype Mk. XVIII. LR387 was converted to a Mk.33 with folding wings and arrester hook during 1945.

B.Mk.II

Powered by two Packard-built Rolls-Royce Merlin 31s driving three-bladed Hydromatic fully feathering propellers, this was a Canadian version based on the B.Mk.IV Series II. First flew 24 September 1942. Used in North America only.

Production: KB500-KB324.

Transferred to USAAF: KB306 (43-34931), KB312 (43-34924), KB313 (43-24925), KB315 (43-24926), KB316 (43-24927), KB317 (43-24928).

PR.Mk.VIII

Powered by two Rolls-Royce Merlin 61s driving three-bladed Hydromatic fully feathering propellers, this was a photographic reconnaissance aircraft. All were conversions during manufacture of PR.Mk.IV airframes, but with two-stage engines. First flew 20 October 1942. The machine had a cruising speed of 258mph, maximum speed of 436mph and range of 2,550 miles.

Production: DZ342, DZ364, DZ404, DZ424.

PR.Mk.IX

Powered by two Rolls-Royce Merlin 72/73 or 76/77s driving three-bladed Hydromatic fully feathering propellers, this was a photographic reconnaissance aircraft. First flew March 1943. The machine had a cruising speed of 250mph, maximum speed of 408mph and range of 2,450 miles.

Production: LR405-LR446, LR459-LR474, LR478-LR481; MM227-MM236, MM239-MM240, MM243-MM257.

B.Mk.IX

Powered by two Rolls-Royce Merlin 72/73 or 76/77s driving three-bladed Hydromatic fully feathering propellers, this was a bomber aircraft based on the PR.Mk.IX. First flew 24 March 1943.

Production: LR475-LR477, LR495-LR513; ML896-ML920, ML921-ML924; MM237, MM238,MM241.

NF.Mk.X

Powered by two Rolls-Royce Merlin 61s, this variant was intended as a night fighter fitted with two-stage Merlins, but although ordered in quantity, it was not proceeded with.

FB.Mk.XI

Powered by two Rolls-Royce Merlin 61s driving three-bladed Hydromatic fully feathering propellers, this variant was to be a fighter-bomber identical to the FB.Mk.VI but with two-stage engines. The design was not proceeded with.

NF.Mk.XII

Powered by two Rolls-Royce Merlin 21, 23s driving three-bladed Hydromatic fully feathering propellers, this was a night fighter conversion of the F.Mk.II fitted with AI Mk.VIII in a 'thimble' nose. First flew August 1942. Armed with four 20mm cannon only. The machine had a cruising speed of 250 mph, maximum speed of 408 mph, and range of 2,450 miles.

Production: DZ302, HJ945-HJ946, HK107-HK141, HK159-HK185, HK187-HK194, HK196-HK204, HK222-HK235 – converted from F.Mk.II specification by Marshalls of Cambridge.

NF.Mk.XIII

Powered by two Rolls-Royce Merlin 21, 23 or 25s driving Hydromatic fully feathering propellers, this was a night fighter with a wing similar to that of the Mk.VI 'basic'. Provision for drop-tanks or underwing bomb load. Fitted with AI Mk.VIII radar in 'thimble' or 'bull' nose. First flew August 1943.

Production: HK363-HK382, HK396-HK437, HK453-HK481, HK499-HK534; HX902-HX904; SM700-SM701; MM436-MM479, MM491-MM534, MM547-MM590, MM615-MM623.

Conversions: HK364 - Converted to Mk. XIX prototype.

NF.Mk.XIV

Powered by two Rolls-Royce Merlin 67 or 72s driving Hydromatic fully feathering propellers, this was to be a two-stage Merlin aircraft based on the Mk.XIII. Not proceeded with. Superseded by the NF.Mk.XIX and NF.Mk.30.

NF.Mk.XV

Powered by two Rolls-Royce Merlin 61, 73 or 77s driving Hydromatic fully feathering propellers, this was a high-altitude fighter with two-stage engines. It was developed to combat the threat of the high-flying Junkers Ju 86P reconnaissance aircraft. Prototype conversion took just seven days, with the removal of 2,300 lb of armour and equipment. The NF.Mk.XV was fitted with extended wing-tips increasing span to 59ft and smaller-diameter undercarriage wheels. First flew in September 1942. The prototype was fitted with four Browning 0.303 machine-guns in the nose, but was later modified with AI Mk.VIII radar in the nose and the four machine-guns were moved to an underbelly pack, as were production examples.

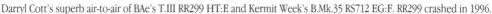

Darryl Cott's superb air-to-air of BAe's T.III RR299 HT:E and Kermit Week's B.Mk.35 RS712 EG:F. RR299 crashed in 1996.

Production: MP469 - Prototype; DZ366, DZ385, DZ409, DZ417.

PR.Mk.XVI

Powered by two Rolls-Royce Merlin 72/73 engines driving Hydromatic fully feathering propellers; later examples had Merlin 76/77 engines driving three-bladed Hydromatic propellers. This variant was a high-altitude photographic reconnaissance aircraft fitted with a pressure cabin and two-stage engines. First flew July 1943.

Production: ML925-ML942, ML956-ML999; MM112-MM156, MM169-MM179, MM181-MM205, MM219-MM226 (MM170 not delivered), MM258, MM271-MM314, MM327-MM371, MM384-MM397; NS496-NS538, NS551-NS585, NS590-NS596, NS619-NS660, NS673-NS712, NS725-NS758, NS772-NS816; RF969-RF999; RG113-RG158, RG171-RG175; TA614-TA616.

Conversions: ML935, ML956, ML974, ML980, ML995, MM112, MM117, MM142, MM156, MM177, MM192 were converted by General Aircraft into TT.Mk.39s for Royal Navy use. RG171-RG173 fitted with arrester hooks for Royal Navy. NS811/G-AIRU, NS812/G-AIRT, NS735/G-AOCK, NS639/ G-AOCI were all were all exported to Israel.

B.Mk.XVI

Powered by two Rolls-Royce Merlin 72/73 engines driving Hydromatic fully feathering propellers; later examples had Merlin 76/77 engines driving three-bladed Hydromatic propellers. This variant was a bomber with a pressure cabin and two-stage engines. First flew 1 January 1944.

Production: PF379-PF415, PF428-PF469, PF481-PF511, PF515-PF526, PF538-PF579, PF592-PF619; RV295-RV326, RV340-RV363.

Conversions: PF439, PF445, PF449, PF452, PF481-PF483, PF489, PF560, PF569, PF576, PF599, PF606, PF609 converted to TT.Mk.39; RV348-RV350 fitted with Merlin 113/114As and converted to TT.Mk.35.

NF.Mk.XVII

Powered by two Rolls-Royce Merlin 21 or 23s driving Hydromatic fully feathering propellers, this variant was a night fighter fitted with SCR720/729 radar. Some machines had AI Mk.X radar and rearward-facing radar in a Perspex tailcone.

Production: HK195/G - Prototype; HK237-HK265, HK278-HK327, HK344-HK362.

FB.Mk.XVIII

Powered by two Rolls-Royce Merlin 21, 23 or 25 engines driving three-bladed Hydromatic propellers, this variant was a ground-attack and anti-shipping fighter-bomber. First flew 8 June 1943. Fitted with Molins 6-pounder 57mm gun.

Production: HJ732 - Prototype. Converted from FB.Mk.VI Series I; MM424-MM425; NT200, NT224, NT225, NT592-NT593, PZ251-PZ252, PZ300-PZ301; PZ467-PZ470.

NF.Mk.XIX

Powered by two Rolls-Royce Merlin 25s driving three-bladed Hydromatic propellers, this variant was a night fighter fitted with AI Mk.VIII or SCR720 and SCR729 radar in a 'thimble' or 'universal' nose and was based on the NF.Mk.XIII.

Production: MM624-MM656, MM669-MM685;

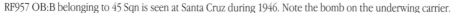

RF957 OB:B belonging to 45 Sqn is seen at Santa Cruz during 1946. Note the bomb on the underwing carrier.

TA123-TA156, TA169-TA198, TA215-TA249, TA263-TA308, TA232-TA357, TA389-TA413, TA425-TA449.

B.Mk.XX

Powered by two Packard-built Rolls-Royce Merlin 31s driving three-bladed Hydromatic fully feathering propellers, this variant was the Canadian version of the B.Mk.IV Series II. Provision was made for the carriage of a bomb or drop-tank under each wing.

Production: KB100-KB299, KB325-KB329.

Conversions: KB130-KB132 as 43-34932 to 43-34934 for USAAF as Mk.F-8; KB 138-KB141 as 43-34936 to 43-34939 for USAAF as Mk.F-8; KB145 as 43-34935 for USAAF as Mk.F-8; KB146-KB152 as 43-34940 to 43-34946 as Mk.F-8; KB154-KB159 as 43-34946 to 43-34953 for USAAF as Mk.F-8; KB171, KB180-KB189 as 43-34954 to 43-34963 for USAAF as Mk.F-8; KB190 as 43-34947 forUSAAF as Mk.F-8; KB328 for USAAF as Mk.F-8; KB132, KB138, KB140, KB146, KB148, KB156, KB158, KB182, KB185, KB188, KB189 transferred to RAF.

FB.Mk.XXI

Powered by two Packard-built Rolls-Royce Merlin 31s driving Hydromatic fully feathering propellers, this variant was the Canadian version of the FB. Mk. VI. It was superseded by the FB.Mk.26.

Production: KA100-KA102.

T.Mk.22

Powered by two Packard-built Rolls-Royce Merlin 33s driving Hydromatic fully feathering propellers, this variant was the Canadian version of the T.Mk.III. Developed from the FB.Mk.21.

Production: KA873-KA876, KA896-KA897.

B.Mk.23

Powered by two Packard-built Rolls-Royce Merlin 69s driving three-bladed Hydromatic fully feathering propellers, this variant was the projected Canadian bomber similar to the B.Mk.IX. It was not proceeded with.

FB.Mk.24

Powered by two Packard-built Rolls-Royce Merlin 301s driving three-bladed Hydromatic fully feathering propellers, this variant was to be the Canadian high-altitude fighter-bomber based on the FB.Mk.21, but was not proceeded with.

Production: KA928-KA929 allocated, but order cancelled.

B.Mk.25

Powered by two Packard-built Rolls-Royce Merlin 225s driving three-bladed Hydromatic fully feathering propellers, this variant was the revised B.Mk.XX with improved single-stage Merlins.

Production: KA930-KA999; KB370-KB699.

Conversions: KB409, KB416, KB490, KB561, KB625 converted to 4,000 lb bomb bay.

FB.Mk.26

Powered by two Packard-built Rolls-Royce Merlin 225s driving three-bladed Hydromatic fully feathering propellers, this variant was the Canadian version of the FB.Mk.XI and a revision of the FB.Mk.21.

Production: KA103-KA773.

Conversions: KA117, KA120, KA121, KA122, KA137, KA138, KA139, KA141, KA149, KA150, KA158, KA166, KA167, KA172, KA173, KA174, KA202, KA203, KA206, KA207, KA221, KA232, KA233, KA234, KA242, KA243, KA280, KA281, KA290, KA297, KA298, KA299, KA300, KA301, KA312, KA313, KA314 all converted to T.Mk.29.

T.Mk.27

Powered by two Packard-built Rolls-Royce Merlin 225s driving three-bladed Hydromatic fully feathering propellers, this variant was the Canadian-built dual-control trainer developed from the T.Mk.22 with improved powerplants.

Production: KA877-KA895, KA898-KA927.

Mk.28

Mark allocated to de Havilland Canada - not used.

T.Mk.29

Powered by two Rolls-Royce Merlin 225s driving three-bladed Hydromatic fully feathering propellers, this variant was the dual-control trainer developed from the FB.Mk.26. All aircraft were conversions from FB.Mk.26s.

Production: KA117, KA120, KA121, KA122,

KA137, KA138, KA139, KA141, KA149, KA150, KA158, KA166, KA167, KA172, KA173, KA174, KA202, KA203, KA206, KA207, KA221, KA232, KA233, KA234, KA242, KA243, KA280, KA281, KA290, KA297, KA298, KA299, KA300, KA301, KA312, KA313, KA314.

NF.Mk.30

Powered by two Rolls-Royce Merlin 72 or 76 engines driving three-bladed Hydromatic fully feathering propellers, this variant was a development of the NF.Mk.XIX fitted with two-stage engines and Mk.X airborne interception radar. First flew March 1944.

Production: MM686-MM710, MM726-MM769, MM783-MM822; MT456-MT500 (MT480 not delivered); MV521-MV570; NT241-NT283, NT295-NT336, NT349-NT393, NT415-NT458, NT471-NT513, NT526-NT568 NT582-NT671; RK929-RK954.

NF.Mk.31

Powered by two Packard-built Rolls-Royce Merlin 69s driving Hydromatic fully feathering propellers, this variant was planned as an American version of the NF.Mk.30, but was not built.

PR.Mk.32

Powered by two Rolls-Royce Merlin 113/114 engines driving Hydromatic fully feathering propellers, this was a high-altitude photographic reconnaissance aircraft with two-stage engines, pressure cabin and extended wingtips. Based on the PR.Mk.XVI. First flew August 1944.

Production: NS589.

TF/TR.Mk.33

Powered by two Rolls-Royce Merlin 25 engines driving Hydromatic fully feathering propellers, this variant was a torpedo-reconnaissance fighter/fighter-bomber for carrier operations. It was equipped with upward-folding wings, arrester hook, four-bladed propellers, Lockheed oleo-pneumatic landing gear, ASH radar and rocket-assisted take-off equipment. Armed with four 20mm cannon.

Production: TS444, TS449 - prototypes for service trials; TW227-TW257, TW277-TW295.

Conversions: TW240 - prototype TR.Mk.37.

PR.Mk.34

Powered by two Rolls-Royce Merlin 114s driving Hydromatic fully feathering propellers, this variant was a very-long-range reconnaissance aircraft developed for Air Command South-East Asia. It had a range of over 3,500 miles, obtained by fitting an overload tank in the bomb bay and doubling the size of the wing tanks to raise the total fuel load carried to l,255gal.

Production: VL613-VL625; PF620-PF635, PF647-PF680.

Conversions: VL625; PF652, PF656, PF662, PF669-PF670, PF673, PF678-PF680 were converted to PR.Mk.34A.

PR.Mk.34A

Powered by two Rolls-Royce Merlin 114A engines driving Hydromatic fully feathering propellers, this variant was the same as the PR.Mk.34 but with different engines.

Production: VL625 converted from PR.Mk.34; PF652, PF656, PF662, PF669-PF670, PF673, PF678-PF680 converted from PR.Mk.34.

B.Mk.35

Powered by two Rolls-Royce Merlin 113/114s (fitted with cabin blowers for cabin pressurization) driving Hydromatic fully feathering propellers; later aircraft had a pair of Merlin 114As, additional equipment and a slightly modified cabin layout. This variant was the final Mosquito bomber.

Production: VP178-VP202; VR792-VR806; RS699-RS723; RV364-RV367; TA617-TA618, TA633-TA670, TA685-TA724;TH976-TH999; TJ113-TJ158; TK591-TK635,TK648-TK656.

Conversions: VR793 was converted to banner-towing TT.Mk.35 prototype for trials at Cambridge; RS701, RS702, RS704, RS706- RS710, RS712-RS713, RS715, RS717, RS719, RS722, RV365-RS357, VP178, VP181, VP191, VP197 were converted to TT.Mk.35; RS700 converted to the first PR.Mk.35; TA650, VP183, TJ124, TJ145, TH985, TH989, TK615, TK632, TK650 were converted to PR.Mk.35; TA633-TA634, TA637, TA639, TA641-TA642, TA647, TA649, TA651, TA660-TA662, TA664, TA669, TA685, TA688, TA699, TA703, TA705, TA710-TA711, TA718-TA720, TA722, TA724;

TH977-TH978, TH980-TH981, TH987, TH989-TH992, TH996, TH998; TJ113-TJ114, TJ116, TJ119, TJ120, TJ122- TJ123, TJ125-TA128, TJ131, TJ135, TJ136, TJ138, TH140, TJ147-TJ149, TJ153-TJ157; TK591-TK594, TK596, TK599, TK603-TK610, TK612-TK613, TK616 converted to TT.Mk.35.

PR.Mk.35

Powered by two Rolls-Royce Merlin 113A and 114A engines driving Hydromatic fully feathering propellers. All were photographic reconnaissance conversions of B.Mk.35 aircraft, the work being done at D.H. Leavesden.

Production: RS700; TJ124, TJ145, TH985, TH989; TK615, TK632, TK650; TA650.

TT.Mk.35

Powered by two Rolls-Royce Merlin 113A and 114A engines driving Hydromatic fully feathering propellers. All were target-towing conversions of B.Mk.35 aircraft, the work being done by Brooklands Aviation Ltd. Early conversions were fitted with an external M.L.Type G winch and high-speed target-towing equipment; but a much larger number had the winches installed inside modified bomb bays. They were intended for use mainly by Civilian Anti-Aircraft Co-operation Units.

Production: VR793 converted from B.Mk.35 to banner prototype for trials at Cambridge; RS701, RS702, RS704, RS706-RS710, RS712-RS713, RS715, RS717, RS719, RS722; RV365-RV367; TA633-TA634, TA637, TA639, TA641-TA642, TA647, TA649, TA651, TA660-TA662, TA664, TA669, TA685, TA688, TA699, TA703, TA705, TA710-TA711,

TA718-TA720, TA722, TA724; TH977-TH978, TH980-TH981, TH987, TH989-TH992, TH996,TH998; TJ113-TJ114, TJ116, TH119, TJ120, TJ122-TJ123, TJ125-TJ128, TJ131, TJ135, TJ136, TJ138, TJ140, TJ147-TJ149, TJ153-TJ157; TK591-TK594, TK596, TK599,TK603-TK610, TK612-TH613, TK616.

NF.Mk.36

Powered by two Rolls-Royce Merlin 113/114 or 113A/114A engines driving Hydromatic fully feathering propellers, this variant was a night fighter and later had airborne interception radar fitted.

Production: RK955-RK960, RK972-RK999; RL113-RL158, RL173-RL215, RL229-RL268.

Conversions: RL248 - prototype NF.Mk.38.

TF.Mk.37

Powered by two Rolls-Royce Merlin 25 engines driving Hydromatic fully feathering propellers. This variant was a torpedo-fighter/bomber with ASV Mk.XIII radar in an enlarged nose, otherwise similar to the Mk.33. First flew during 1946.

Production: VT724-VT737.

NF.Mk.38

Powered by two Rolls-Royce Merlin 114A engines driving paddle-bladed fully feathering Hydromatic propellers, this variant was similar to the NF.Mk.36 but with different engines.

Production: RL248 - prototype; VT651-VT683, VT691-VT707; VX860-VX879,VX886-VX916.

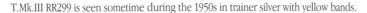

T.Mk.III RR299 is seen sometime during the 1950s in trainer silver with yellow bands.

TT.Mk.39

Powered by two Rolls-Royce Merlin 72/73 engines driving Hydromatic fully feathering propellers, this variant was a target-tug conversion of the B.Mk.XVI for the Royal Navy to Specification Q. 19/45 to replace the Miles Monitor. The work was undertaken by General Aircraft Ltd, Hanworth. It saw service in the United Kingdom and overseas.

Production: PF439, PF445, PF449, PF452, PF481-PF483, PF489, PF560, PF562, PF569, PF576, PF599, PF606, PF609.

FB.Mk.40

Powered by two Packard-built Rolls-Royce Merlin 31 or 33 engines driving Hydromatic fully feathering propellers, this variant was the Australian-built fighter-bomber similar to the FB.Mk.VI. First 100 aircraft fitted with Merlin 31s with needle-blade propellers. The remainder had Merlin 33s and paddle-blade propellers.

Production: A52-1 to A52-212.

Conversions: A52-2, A52-4, A52-6, A52-7, A52-9, A52-26 converted to PR.Mk.40.

PR.Mk.40

Powered by two Packard-built Rolls-Royce Merlin 31s driving Hydromatic fully feathering propellers, this variant was a photographic reconnaissance machine converted from the FB.Mk.40.

Production: A52-2, A52-4, A52-6, A52-7, A52-9, A52-26.

PR.Mk.41

Powered by two Packard-built Rolls-Royce Merlin 69 engines driving Hydromatic fully feathering propellers, this variant was the Australian-built photographic reconnaissance aircraft similar to the PR.Mk.IX and Australian PR.Mk.40.

Production: A52-300 to A52-327.

Conversions: A52-300 - converted to FB.Mk.42.

FB.Mk.42

Powered by two Packard-built Rolls-Royce Merlin 69s driving Hydromatic fully feathering propellers, this variant was an Australian-built fighter-bomber fitted with two-stage powerplants. Prototype only. Production: A52-300.

T.Mk.43

Powered by two Packard-built Rolls-Royce Merlin 33s driving Hydromatic fully feathering propellers, this variant was an Australian-built dual-control trainer similar to the T.Mk.III.

Production: A52-1051 to A52-1071.

AOC's Inspection at Tangmere in April 1951. The aircraft behind is thought to be NT596, a NF.Mk.30 of 29 Sqn. (Author's Collection)

TEST AIRCRAFT

A significant contribution to the Mosquito's success as a weapons delivery system was made by the research and test establishments that were involved in refining the basic design, rapidly clearing the fitment of existing and new weapons for service use on the aircraft, and solving any problems that arose.

By far the largest amount of work was done by the de Havilland Aircraft Company, working closely with the Aeroplane and Armament Experimental Establishment (A & AEE) at Boscombe Down. However, other centres also tested and developed the design. Much of the research for this book has been derived from the use of such reports, issued at the time. Detailed investigation of these reports are of the greatest use for future historians, engineers and designers alike to gain an overview of how, even at a time of extreme crisis, there was no substitute for precise research and development by impartial bodies, working closely with the manufacturer. There follows a list of all known Mosquitoes used for trials and tests, together with known report numbers for reference.

W4050 Mk.I A & AEE for prototype trials, 19/2/41. Damaged 24/2/41. Preliminary performance and handling trials, Report AAEE767/1 issued 5/3/41. Returned to Boscombe Down 19/3/41 to complete initial handling trials. Brief handling trials with extended nacelles. Report AAEE767/2 issued 19/4/41. Handling trials. Report AAEE767/3 issued 6/6/41. Fuselage static vents trials, Report AAEE767/4 issued 17/6/41. Cooling trials and take-off trials, Report AAEE767/5 issued 22/6/41.

W4051 PR.Mk.I A & AEE. Preliminary radio, Report AAEE767b/1 issued 6/6/41. Camera and cabin temperatures. Report AAEE767b/2 issued. Accident, Report AAEE767/F1 issued 14/7/41 following tailwheel retraction damage 28/6/41.

W4052 F.Mk.I A & AEE for longitudinal stability trials, Report AAEE767a/1 issued 23/8/41. Gun heating trials, Report AAEE767a/2 issued 30/9/41. Performance of night fighter version trials, Report AAEE767a/3 issued 18/9/41. Calibration of air thermometer trials, Report AAEE767a/4 20/10/41. Flame-damping trials, Report AAEE767a/5 issued 4/11/41. Increase in tailplane area from 88 to 98.5sq ft area trials, Report AAEE767a/6 issued 13/2/42. Airbrake around fuselage trials, Report AAEE767a/12 issued 24/9/42.

W4054 PR.Mk.I A & AEE for fuel consumption trials, Report AAEE767b/3 issued 19/9/41.

W4057 Prototype B.Mk.V A & AEE for carbon monoxide contamination trials. Report AAEE767a/9 issued 20/5/42. Take-off test trials, Report AAEE767c/1 issued 5/11/41.

W4060 PR.Mk.I A & AEE for oil cooling trials, Report AAEE767b/4 issued 17/11/41. Cabin and camera heating, Report AAEE767b/5 issued 19/12/41. Tailwheel shimmy trials, Report AAEE767b/6 issued 24/1/42. Overload fuel system trials. Report AAEE767b/7 issued 22/1/42. Stability trials, Report AAEE767b/8 issued 16/2/42. Oil cooling trials, Report AAEE767b/9 issued 8/3/42.

W4073 A & AEE for dual-control system trials, Report AAEE767d/1 issued 4/3/42.

W4076 F.Mk.II A & AEE for handling and stability CG 6.3in aft trials, Report AAEE767a/7 issued 1/4/42. Speed trials - smooth and matt finish, Report AAEE767a/8 issued 28/4/42. Carbon monoxide contamination trials. Report AAEE767a/9 issued 20/5/42. Static longitudinal stability trials, Report AAEE767a/10 issued 2/6/42. Static longitudinal elevator stability trials. Report AAEE767a/11 issued 13/6/42.

W4096 A & AEE for performance efficiency trials,

Left: this was how FB.Mk.VI MM401 SB:J of 464 Sqn came back from a raid on the Pas de Calais area on 21 February 1944. Not surprisingly, the aircraft was later written off. *(© BAE SYSTEMS)*

Below: T.Mk.III VA893 RO:Q of 29 Sqn following a crash-landing at Tangmere in April 1951. *(Paddy Porter Collection).*

Report AAEE767a/13 issued 11/12/42. Single-engine flying trials. Report AAEE767a/ 14 issued 22/12/42. Effect of air cleaner on range trials. Report AAEE767a/16 issued 10/4/43. Speed performance trials using different cowlings. Report AAEE767a/17 issued 3/1/44.

DD613 NF.Mk.II Airborne interception radar clearance at Royal Aeronautical Estab- lishment.

DD635 F.Mk.II A & AEE for propeller test trials. Report AAEE767a/18 issued 27/6/45.

DD664 NF.Mk.II To Australia to assist production. Became A52-1001 with Royal Australian Air Force.

DD668 NF.Mk.II Fighter Interception Unit for Mk.V airborne interception radar trials.

DD723 NF.Mk.II To Rolls-Royce for Lancaster 'Power Unit' engine installation trials, including fitment of 'chin' radiators for performance comparison trials with a standard NF.Mk.II (DD736).

DD735 NF.Mk.II Tailplane incidence and stick load tests at De Havilland

DD736 NF.Mk.II Rolls-Royce Flight Test Establishment, Hucknall, Notts. Received 28/8/42. To be used for performance calibration, coolant system investigation following reports of top joint failures on NF Mosquitoes. Vibration investigation and development of the Consus engine mounting, and flame- damping trials. Departed 26/1/43. To 'C' Flight, Performance Testing Squadron, A & AEE. Received 26/1/43. Used to test efficiency of a modified exhaust system which terminated under the leading edge of the wing using four fishtail exhausts and ducts to damp the exhaust flame. On one night test this was assessed as unsuitable as the flames from the exhaust system were visible at ranges up to 1,000 yards behind the aircraft. Report AAEE767a/15 issued 28/2/43. Departed 1/1/43. To Rolls- Royce Flight Test Establishment, Hucknall. Received 1/1/43. Used for vibration and performance testing of Consus engine mounting, engine reliability flying and performance investigation. Performance calibration was flown in comparison with DD723 used to test Lancaster powerplants with underslung 'chin' radiators. Damaged on landing 5/7/43.

DZ286 Mk.IV (Hatfield-built). To A & AEE for flight tests following high rate of structural failure in squadron use. Report AAEE767n/l issued 23/7/44.

DK290 B.Mk.IV A & AEE for handling and stability in dive trials, Report AAEE767c/2 issued 26/8/42. Flame damping using multiple fishtail ejectors trials. Report AAEE767c/4. Speed trials. Report AAEE767c/12.

DK290/G B.Mk.IV Handling without stores (special duties - each store to weigh l,1001b) trials, Report AAEE767c/5 issued 22/4/43. Handling with storcs trials, Report AAEE767c/6 issued 15/4/43. Speed and performance with/without stores trials, Report AAEE767c/7 and 8 issued 20/5/43. Fuel consumption at 2,000ft trials. Report AAEE767c/9 issued 20/6/43.

DK300 Mk.IV (Hatfield-built). To A & AEE for flight tests following high rate of structural failure in squadron use. Report AAEE767n/l issued 23/7/44.

DK324 B.Mk.IV Series II, converted to PR.Mk.VII A & AEE for weights and loading trials, Report AAEE767f/l issued 8/2/43.

DK327 B.Mk.IV Series II A & AEE for performance efficiency trials. Report AAEE767c/10 issued 25/7/43.

DZ294 NF.Mk.II Stability investigation by de Havilland's and Royal Aeronautical Establishment.

DZ345 B.Mk.IV Telecommunications Flying Unit, Defford.

DZ350 F.Mk.II Research aircraft for Royal Aircraft Establishment.

DZ412 B.Mk.IV Telecommunications Flying Unit, Defford.

DZ434 B.Mk.IV Royal Aircraft Establishment.

DZ540 PR.Mk.XVI A & AEE for weights and loading data trials, with Merlin 72 fitted port, 73 fitted starboard, Report AAEE767j71 issued 8/10/43. Carbon dioxide contamination trials (pressure-cabin version). Report AAEE767J/2 issued 3/11/43. Performance, brief handling trials (pressure-cabin version), Report AAEE767J/3 issued 11/11/43.

NT306/G ZD:D following a crash at Odiham on 11 September 1946. From the position of the prop-blades on the starboard engine it looks as if they are feathered, indicating an engine problem. *(Simon Peters Collection)*

DZ541 B.Mk.IV Research and Development at Vickers-Armstrongs.

DZ590 B.Mk.IV Series II A & AEE for CG with metal elevator trials. Report AAEE767c/14 issued 10/5/44.

DZ594 B.Mk.IV Series II A & AEE for light- load landing trials. Report AAEE767c/ll issued 22/8/43. Performance efficiency trials, Report AAEE767c/13 issued 10/3/44. Handling with 4,000 lb load trials. Report AAEE767c/15 issued 23/7/44.

DZ637 Mk.IV Series II (Hatfield-built). To A & AEE for flight tests following high rate of structural failure in squadron use. Report AAEE767n/l issued 23/7/44.

DZ679 B.Mk.IV Series II Initially fitted with Rolls-Royce Merlin 21s. Fitted with SCR720 and SCR729 radar at Fighter Interception Unit, named *'Eleanora'*. Also fitted with trial installation of universal radar nose.

DZ700 B.Mk.IV Series II For Royal Navy. HJ659 NF.Mk.II Fitted with trial installation of bomb gear.

HJ662/G FB.Mk.VI Prototype. To A & AEE 13/6/42 for weights and loading trials, Report AAEE767e/l issued 24/8/42. Handling and diving trials (intruder version), Report AAEE767e/2. This aircraft crashed 10/7/42 while on trials, but was repaired for take-off trials. Report AAEE767e/3 issued 25/9/42.

HJ663 FB.Mk.VI A & AEE Boscombe Down for handling and drop tests of auxiliary tank trials, Report AAEE767e/4 issued 23/5/43. Performance efficiency trials, Report AAEE767e/5 issued 20/5/43.

HJ666 FB.Mk.VI To Air Fighting Development Unit for trials 1943.

HJ672 FB.Mk.VI To 60 Squadron, South African Air Force.

HJ679 FB.Mk.VI A & AEE for performance efficiency trials. Report AAEE767e/6 issued 9/6/43. Performance

trials. Report AAEE767e/7 issued 19/9/43. Engine cooling trials. Report AAEE767e/8 issued 8/10/43. Radiator suitability and oil cooling trials, Report AAEE767e/9 issued 5/11/43. Drop tests with underwing fuel tank trials, Report AAEE767e/13. Diving with underwing bomb trials. Report AAEE767e/14 issued 30/4/44. Later used for radar research. To Hatfield, Air Sea Warfare Development Unit.

HJ732/G FB.Mk.VI A & AEE for G45 camera gun installation trials, Report AAEE767k/2 and 4 issued 19/11/43.

HJ858 T.Mk.III (Hatfield-built). To A & AEE for flight tests following high rate of structural failure in squadron use. Report AAEE767n/l issued 23/7/44.

HK196 F.Mk.II converted to NF.Mk.XII A & AEE for suitability of Hamilton propellers with American constant-speed unit trials, Report AAEE767i/l issued 26/8/43.

HK369 NF.Mk.XIII Trials for airborne interception radar Mk.VIII at Fighter Interception Unit.

HR135 FB.Mk.VI A & AEE for handling with Mk.XI depth-charge and Mk.VII mines trials. Rcport ΛAEE767e/15 issued 1/10/44. HR303 FB.Mk.VI A & AEE for weights and loading trials, Report AAEE767e/l 9 issued 26/7/45. Navigation/torpedo-carrying trials, Report AAEE767e/20 issued 27/8/45.

HX809 FB.Mk.VI A & AEE for performance efficiency of static vent trials, Report AAEE767e/10 issued 15/12/43. Level speed with increased boost trials. Report AAEE767e/12 issued 1/2/44.

HX902/G FB.Mk.VI A & AEE for weights and loading data in relationship to 'Tstetse' installation of 6-pounder, 7cwt Mk.IV gun minus carriage and special Molins feed trials, Report AAEE767k/l issued 3/10/43. Altitude measurements FB.Mk. XVIII trials. Report AAEE767k/5 issued 5/12/43.

HX903/G Mk.XVIII A & AEE for brief handling

tests at overload trials. Report AAEE767k/3.

HX918 FB.Mk.VI A & AEE for altitude and performance efficiency with eight rockets trials. Report AAEE767e/1 1 issued 26/4/44. Mk.la rocket projectile trials. Report AAEE767e/16 issued 24/2/45.

KA201 FB.Mk.26 A & AEE for check trials and bombing installation trials. Report AAEE767r/1 issued 5/12/45.

KB202 B.Mk.XX (Toronto-built). To A & AEE for flight tests following high rate of structural failure in squadron use. Report AAEE767n/1 issued 23/7/44.

KB205 B.Mk.XX (Toronto-built). To A & AEE for flight tests following high rate of structural failure in squadron use. Report AAEE767n/1 issued 23/7/44.

KB328 B.Mk.XX A & AEE for climb performance trials. Report AAEE767i/1 issued 8/12/43. Performance efficiency of static vent trials. Report AAEE7671/2 issued 3/1/44. Level speed performance trials, Report AAEE7671/3 issued 5/3/44. Brief handling trials, Report AAEE7671/4 issued 1/4/44.

KB352 A & AEE for Mk.III and Mk.IIIG 'Identification Friend or Foe' trials. Report

AAEE7671/5 issued 31/3/45. Radio compass communications trials. Report AAEE7671/6 issued 16/6/45. Determination of most acceptable aft position of centre of gravity trials, Report AAEE7671/7 issued 15/10/45.

LR359 FB.Mk.VI Modified into semi-naval aircraft, used for first deck-landing trials. Fitted with experimental four-bladed non- feathering D.H. propellers and strengthened rear fuselage. First twin-engined aircraft to land on an aircraft-carrier.

LR387 FB.Mk.VI Modified into semi-naval aircraft. Used as back-up aircraft for deck- landing trials. Later modified into first full Sea Mosquito TR.Mk.33 with manually folding wings. To A & AEE for cockpit layout trials, Report AAEE767p/1 issued 10/10/45. Weights and loading trials, Report AAEE767p/2 issued 30/10/45. Handling trials. Report AAEE767p/2 issued 31/5/46.

LR410 PR.Mk.IX Rolls-Royce.

LR418 PR.Mk.IX Royal Aircraft Establishment.

LR475 Mk.IX (Hatfield-built). To A & AEE for flight tests following high rate of structural failure in squadron use. Report AAEE767n/1 issued 23/7/44.

LR495 B.Mk.IX First trials aircraft, to A & AEE for

NT220, a FB.Mk.VI of the Royal Aircraft Establishement at Farnborough with a pair of anti-aircraft missiles slung under it's belly in October 1945.

heights and loading trials. Report AAEE767n/l issued 25/5/43. Performance efficiency of static vent trials. Report AAEE767h/2 issued 31/5/43. Cooling without external bombs/tanks trials, Report AAEE767h/3 issued 9/6/43. Performance without external bombs/tanks trials. Report AAEE767h/4 issued 11/6/43. Performance and cooling with two externally mounted 500 lb bombs trials. Report AAEE767h/5 issued 13/10/43. Climb performance with two externally mounted 500 lb bombs trials, Report AAEE767h/6 issued 26/11/43. Level speed with two externally mounted 500 lb bombs trials, Report AAEE767h/8 issued 2/4/44. Fuel consumption with two externally mounted 500 lb bombs trials, Report AAEE767h/10 issued 13/5/44.

ML897 Mk.IX. (Hatfield-built). To A & AEE for flight tests following high rate of structural failure in squadron use, Report AAEE767n/l issued 23/7/44.

ML913 Mk.IX (Hatfield-built). To A & AEE for flight tests following high rate of structural failure in squadron use. Report AAEE767n/l issued 23/7/44.

ML914 B.Mk.IX Used for trials with 4,000 lb bomb and six store Avro carrier.

ML926/G PR.Mk.XVI H2S, 'Oboe', repeater and radar bombsight trials at Defford. To A & AEE. Handling trials with 'Oboe' repeater equipment fitted to modified bomb doors. Report AAEE767J/10 issued 23/4/44.

ML932 B.Mk.XVI A & AEE for weights and loading trials. Report AAEE767J/4 issued 12/4/44. Rogue aircraft trials. Report AAEE767J/5 issued 16/4/44 following a flight from Marham when the aircraft was discovered unstable at 32,000ft. Pilot diverted to Woodbridge. A letter was sent to A & AEE from HQ PFF requesting investigation. No faults were found, and it was thought that the problem was with an ASI blockage coupled with some low-speed engine vibration.

ML937 B.Mk.XVI A & AEE for take-off trials at 24,750lb, Report AAEE767J issued 8/4/44. Performance and efficiency trials (first production aircraft with large bomb doors - fixings for 1 x4,000 lb or 4x500lbs+50gal drop-tanks), Report AAEE767J/12 issued 20/9/44. Handling trials, Report AAEE767J/13 issued 27/12/44.

MK987 Mk.XVI (Hatfield-built). To A & AEE for flight tests following high rate of structural failure in squadron use, Report AAEE767n/l issued 23/7/44.

ML991 Mk.XVI (Hatfield-built). To A & AEE for flight tests following high rate of structural failure in squadron use, Report AAEE767n/l issued 23/7/44.

ML994 PR.Mk.XVI Used for 200gal drop- tank tests and Mk.VIII development aircraft. To A & AEE for handling with 2 x 200gal underwing drop-tanks trials, Report AAEE767J/15 issued 11/12/44, Release of 500 lb mine A Mk.VIII trials. Report AAEE767J/18 issued 22/3/45. Drop tests of 43gal metal underwing tank trials, Report AAEE767J/23 issued 19/2/46.

MM174 A & AEE for diving characteristic reduced inertia weight trials. Report AAEE767J/14 issued 19/12/44.

MM175 PR.Mk.XVI H2S trials aircraft. To A & AEE for handling with/without H2S blister trials, Report AAEE767J/19 issued 29/4/45.

MM229 PR.Mk.IX Fitted with Merlin 67s for installation trials.

MM230 PR.Mk.IX Exhaust shroud tests at D.H. and Fighter Interception Unit for trials installation. To A & AEE for flame-damping exhausts trials with six fishtails and two ducts, Report AAEE767h/9 issued 2/4/44.

MM235 PR.Mk.IX A & AEE for suitability of Hamilton paddle-blade propellers with British constant-speed unit trials. Report AAEE767h/7 issued 20/2/44.

MM258 PR.Mk.XVI Trials installation aircraft.

MM328 PR.Mk.XVI Fitted with four-bladed propellers for Westland Welkin.

MM363 PR.Mk.XVI A & AEE for handling with 2xl00gal underwing drop-tank trials, Report AAEE767J/6 issued 23/4/44. Drop tests with 2xl00gal underwing drop-tank trials. Report AAEE767J/7 issued 29/4/44. Handling with asymmetric load trials, Report AAEE767J/8 issued 4/4/44. Brief diving trials when fitted with 2xl00gal underwing drop- tanks, Report AAEE767J/11 issued 29/7/44. Handling with reduced aileron balance tab gear trials. Report AAEE767J/16 issued 5/1/45. Level speed and performance effi- ciency trials, Report AAEE767J/17 issued 25/3/45.

MM686 NF.Mk.30 A & AEE for preliminary handling trials. Report AAEE767m/l issued 3/7/44.

MM748 NF.Mk.30. To A & AEE for weights and loading data trials. Report AAEE767m/2 issued 18/8/44. Handling trials, Report AAEE767m/3

issued 22/3/45. Performance efficiency and level speed performance trials. Report AAEE767m/4 issued 12/12/45.

MP469 NF.Mk.XV A & AEE for short performance and handling trials. Report AAEE767g/l issued 3/2/43.

MT446 NF.Mk.30 Fitted with Merlin 113s for NF.Mk.36 programme.

NT220 FB.Mk.XVIII Fitted with B.Mk.IV nose, torpedo rack and rocket projectiles. Used at Royal Aircraft Establishment.

NS586 PR.Mk.32 To A & AEE for weights and landing data trials, Report AAEE767o/l issued 6/1/45.

PF459 A & AEE performance handling of 69th Percival-built aircraft. Report AAEE767J/20 issued 13/5/45. Weights and loading data trials. Report AAEE767J/21 issued 7/6/45. Handling trials. Report AAEE767j722 issued 17/9/45.

The Vickers/Miles Aircraft rocket-propelled supersonic model slung under the belly of the RAE Mosquito Mk.XVI PF604 at St Eval, with pilot Sqn Ldr D A Hunt and Mr G B Lochee Bayne in October 1947. (via Martin Bowman)

PF489 Prototype TT.Mk.39 A & AEE for performance efficiency correction trials, Report AAEE767u/2 issued 14/6/49. Handling trials, Report AAEE767u/3 issued 11/1/50.

PF606 TT.Mk.39 A & AE for TT.Mk.39 radio trials. Report AAEE767u/l issued 3/2/49.

PZ202 FB.Mk.VI A & AEE for 2xl00gal drop tanks and Mk.IIIA rocket projectile installation trials. Report AAEE767e/17 issued 15/4/45. Speed measurements when carrying 2x l00 gal drop-tanks and Mk.IIIa rocket projectile installation trials. Report AAEE767e/18 issued 26/7/45.

RG176 PR.Mk.34 To A & AEE for handling trials, Report AAEE767q/l issued 14/2/46.

RG178 PR.Mk.34 To A &AEE for handling trials, Report AAEE767q/l issued 14/2/46.

RK945/G NF.Mk.30 Vickers aircraft RL114 NF.Mk.36 A & AEE for comparative trials with VT658, Report AAEE767V2 issued 28/10/48.

RL136 NF.Mk.36 A & AEE for comparative trials with VT706, Report AAEE767V3 issued 10/11/49.

RS719 A & AEE for TT.Mk.35 towing 2ft and 4ft low-drag target sleeve trials, Report AAEE767v/T/l issued 20/8/52. Radio acceptance trials. Report AAEE767v/3 issued 12/11/51.

TA488 FB.Mk.VI Air Sea Warfare Development Unit camera tests.

TK615 PR.Mk.35 A & AEE for F52, K19B and F61 camera trials. Report AAEE767v/4 issued 20/12/51.

Radio acceptance trials, Report AAEE767v/5 issued 7/1/52.

TK634 A & AEE for TT.Mk.35 towing 2ft and 4ft low-drag target sleeve trials, Report AAEE767v/T/l issued 20/8/52.

TK650 B.Mk.35 A & AEE for bombing installation trials. Report AAEE767v/l issued 22/11/49. Pyrotechnics trials, Report AAEE767v/2 issued 11/4/51, Report AAEE767v/2 addendum issued 11/7/52.

TS444 TR.Mk.33 A & AEE for rocket projectile installation trials. Report AAEE767p/4 issued 9/9/46. Triplex rocket projectile trials, Report AAEE767p/5 issued 31/8/46. Bombing installation trials, Report AAEE767p/6 issued 2/1/47. Performance efficiency trials, Report AAEE767p/7 issued 19/6/47.

TS449 TR.Mk.33 Special TR.Mk.33 prototype. Used for RATOG tests at Farnborough. To A & AEE for performance efficiency trials. Report AAEE767p/8 issued 10/3/49. TW228 TR/TF.Mk.33 Trials of 'Card' - a 'Highball' development. TW230/G TR/TF.Mk.33 'Highball' trials. TW240 TR.Mk.37 To A & AEE for performance efficiency and critical speed trials, Report AAEE767s/l issued 15/4/48. Carbon monoxide contamination trials. Report AAEE767s/2 issued 22/6/48. VT654 NF.Mk.38 A & AEE for static vent performance efficiency trials. Report AAEE767t/l issued 6/9/48. Experimental hydraulic system trials. Report AAEE767t/4 and 4 addendum issued 30/11/49. VT658 NF.Mk.38 A & AEE for comparative trials with RL114, Report AAEE767t/2 issued 28/10/48.

VT706 NF.Mk.38 A & AEE for comparative trials with RL136, Report AAEE767t/3 issued 10/11/49.

IN CONCLUSION

The DH.98 design is now over 70 years old, and it seems as good a time as any to reflect on Sir Geoffrey de Havilland's 'Wooden Wonder'. That nickname in itself is still used by some as a derogatory phrase, as if something made from wood should not be that good.

Far from being a 'Wooden Wonder' the DH.98 was what, in modern parlance, be called a 'composite structure' - basically a combination of two or more materials, each of which retains it own distinctive properties. The fundamental design concept of composites is that the bulk phase accepts the load over a large surface area, and transfers it to the reinforcement material, which can carry a greater load. The significance here lies in that there are numerous matrix materials and as many fiber types, which can be combined in countless ways to produce just the desired properties. The Mosquito was a composite of wood, metal - and in the later years of production - epoxy adhesives. This is can be said that the Mosquito was the forerunner to all todays modern aerospace structures.

It is clear that the Mosquito was a superb fighting machine, one that could be, and was, honed into a marvellously adaptable weapons system. History, however, shows us that the Mosquito design so nearly became just a 'paper aeroplane' - one that never got off the drawing board.

We are well aware that in the DH.98 Geoffrey de Havilland and his team 'got it right' from the start and produced a multi-role aircraft that in its time could not be bettered - a forerunner perhaps of the Tornado of the 1980s. But were the Air Council as short-sighted as history makes them appear in rejecting the Mosquito design for so long? To answer this question, one has to consider the mood of the aeronautical industry at the time, together with that of the British Air Council and what the air force they oversaw was tasked against.

During the mid-1930s the aircraft industry had just moved into an era that many still regard as the 'golden days of flying'. New discoveries were being made almost daily, with a better understanding of aerodynamics, structures, stresses and engine technology. Construction of aircraft had, in the main, previously been of wood (with the notable exception of Dr Hugo Junkers and his company who had established the design of an all-metal monoplane as early as 1915). In the 1930s all-metal construction - as opposed to fabric-covered metal airframes - was just coming into vogue,

with many of the European aircraft manufacturers looking across the Atlantic towards America, where the Douglas Airplane Company were producing the first of the 'Douglas Commercial' family of airliners that peaked in the pre-war years with the famous DC-3. Around the same time Boeing were rolling out the four-engined Model 299, bristling with guns. The *Seattle Daily Times* ran an article on the new aircraft, along with a photograph caption that read '15-ton Flying Fortress'. The photo and its caption were flashed around the world, the name stuck, and the 299 evolved into the famous B-17 Flying Fortress. The Germans, restricted by the Treaty of Versailles, were building fighting aircraft in secret or under the guise of large, metal transport aircraft; while the British aircraft industry was producing mainly tubular metal structured aircraft for fighters clad with light alloy or fabric.

One has only to browse through copies of *Flight* and *The Aeroplane* for the mid-1930 period to understand that everyone in the industry thought that the future of the aeronautical development lay in aircraft built from metal, no matter what the requirement - fighter or bomber, commercial or military transport.

This underlying feeling must have been picked up by members of the Air Council. The Royal Air Force, although tasked with a peace-keeping role throughout the British Empire, was badly in need of new aircraft and equipment for, due to severe cut-backs in the 1920s, it was slipping behind the rest of the world. This need, with the war clouds looming on the horizon, had to be filled fast.

When Specification 13/36 was drafted, it must have been in the back of everyone's minds that no matter what aircraft finally appeared, it would be of metal construction. From the defensive armament part of the specification, there must also have been thoughts of twin-engined aircraft bristling with guns, similar in concept to the Boeing 299.

All this created what can only be called in retrospect a blinkered instead of an open-minded outlook, but one that was completely understandable for the time, considering all the indications contained in research papers that were emanating from the aircraft industry.

At the height of all this, Geoffrey de Havilland went knocking on the Air Council's door with a proposal for a fast unarmed wooden bomber. It is no wonder, therefore, that he appeared out of step with current thinking. If this aircraft had just been unarmed and built of wood, then the design would have been a non-starter from the beginning; but it had one saving grace - its speed. Because of it, there was no need for armament, gunners or structure to carry them. By getting rid of all this excess weight, the team at De Havilland had thus created a 'minimal' bomber - the minimum number of engines pulling along the minimum number of crew needed to do the job, which exposed them to the minimum amount of danger for the minimum amount of time. Here was an aircraft, to paraphrase an old joke, that '...could get out of trouble faster than it got into it'.

The Air Council, however, were highly suspicious of the estimated performance figures, for they were a quantum leap ahead of anything currently in service. They were also rightly worried that the enemy would produce an even faster fighter to nullify the Mosquito's speed advantage.

Eventually, of course, this did happen, with the later versions of the piston-powered Fw.190 and Me.410, and the Me.262 jet fighter; but even when ranged against this first generation of jet aircraft, the Mosquito still had several advantages to its credit. The interference in production of these jets by Hitler kept the numbers pitted against the Mosquito down, and further improvements by Rolls-Royce in reciprocating engine technology - and therefore power output - meant that the Mosquito could at least partially maintain its speed advantage.

History shows us that the DH.98 was incredibly adaptable, but had it always been intended that way? De Havilland had initially planned the aircraft - and submitted the design to the Air Council - as simply an unarmed bomber; but Richard Clarkson ensured that, from the outset, there would be space for armament in the nose and thus the aircraft could easily be changed into a fighter.

The photographic reconnaissance version was a very simple conversion of the bomber, just swapping bombs for cameras, therefore producing the three main versions of the Mosquito. Once De Havilland and the Air Ministry realized that the design was so adaptable, a whole series of modifications was introduced into the airframe to suit the changing requirements of war. These changes resulted in an incredible 51 distinct 'official' variants produced to suit different purposes - a further number of specialized conversions were done at squadron level - and so take advantage of the latest advances in technology and equipment as it became available. A further nine versions were planned, but for various reasons were never built. Production eventually reached a worldwide total of approaching 8,000, and it says much for the flexibility of the aircraft that it took all this in its stride.

Many of the uses that the DH.98 was put to could never have been foreseen when the design was conceived before the war. Much of the electronic equipment used to navigate to distant targets, or to track and intercept the enemy, had not been developed when the Mosquito was first planned and only came about through the desperation of having to find ways to beat the enemy. Yes, all this additional equipment resulted in a cluttered, overcrowded working environment for the aircrew. Boxes of electronic gear were placed in awkward places and a long unbroken row of switches meant that the pilot had difficulty in telling which was which in the dark; but remember, this was before the days of ergonomically designed cockpits, ensuring that the interface between man and machine was as good as it could be.

The aircraft was, however, supremely fast, nimble and very, very strong. Pilots were known deliberately to do a high speed flick stall to escape enemy interception. Possibly the highest praise for the Mosquito in wartime use came from the German night fighter command who allowed any German pilot who shot down a Mosquito to count it as two victories.

In combat the aircraft stood up well to punishment. The wooden structure withstood shell damage, both from ground fire and attacking aircraft well. If there was a weakness in the Mosquito design, it lay in the use of liquid-cooled engines and the associated cooling radiators which were vulnerable to puncture by the smallest shell fragment. However, the weakness of the close-cowled, slim-frontal-area Merlins must be viewed against the undoubted higher drag generated if larger diameter air-cooled radial engines had been used. De Havilland and the Air Ministry stuck with liquid-cooled engines and thus aircrew were forced to learn to live with the problem. Even then, there were still benefits of the slim Merlins, for less drag was caused by a dead engine and it was therefore easier for an aircraft to return to base on one engine.

In the immediate post-war years the Mosquito compared favourably with the first generation of jet aircraft for, although its speed was not quite as high, the Merlins offered much better fuel economy than the thirsty gas-turbine engines, affording greater range.

So was the Mosquito created and, after a somewhat painful gestation period, developed into a superlative multi-role combat aircraft that could not be matched by any other aircraft design of its time. Although the phrase 'composite structure' may have been more accurate and modern, somehow and without doubt it truly deserved the soubriquet 'The Wooden Wonder'!

INDEX

BIBLIOGRAPHY

Andrade, J. *US Military Aircraft Designations and Serials since 1909,* Leicester, 1979.
Bishop, Edward. *The Wooden Wonder,* London 1959.
Borovik, Y. *Israeli Air Force,* London, Melbourne, Harrisburg, Cape Town, 1984.
Bowman, Martin,*The De Havilland Mosquito,* Marlborough 1997
Bowman, Martin, *The Reich Intruders,* London 1997
Bowyer, C. *Mosquito Squadrons of the Royal Air Force,* London, 1984.
Bowyer, M. & Sharp, C. *Mosquito,* London, 1971.
Bowyer & Phillpot, B. *Classic Aircraft No. 7 Mosquito,* Cambridge, 1980.
Bowyer, Michael J, *2 Group RAF,* London 1974
Curtis, L. *The Forgotten Pilots,* London, 1982.
de Havilland, Sir Geoffrey, *Sky Fever,* London, 1979.
Freeman, R. *Mighty Eighth War Manual,* London, New York, Sydney, 1984.
Flintham, V & Thomas A, *Combat Codes,* London 2003
Hall, Richard, *The Making of Molins,* London, 1978
Halley, J. J. *The Squadrons of the Royal Air Force*, Tonbridge, 1980.
Harvey-Bailey, A. *The Merlin in Perspective - The Combat Years,* Derby, 1983.
Hastings, M. *Bomber Command,* London, Sydney,1982.
Howe, S. *Mosquito Portfolio,* London, 1984.
Jackson, A. J. *De Havilland Aircraft since 1909,* London, 1978.
McKee, A. *The Mosquito Log,* London, 1988.
Ministry of Defence, *The Mosquito Manual,* London,1988.
Robertson, B. *British Military Aircraft Serials 1878-1987,* Leicester, 1987.
Robinson, A. *Night Fighter,* London, 1988.
Smith, D. *De Havilland Mosquito Crash Log*, Leicester, 1980.
Streetly, M. *The Aircraft of 100 Group,* London,1984.

Pilots Notes - NF.Mk.II
Pilots Notes - B.Mk.IV
Pilots Notes - PR.Mk.IV
Pilots Notes - F-8, USAAF 1944
Pilots Notes - FB.Mk.VI, FB. Mk. XVIII, FB. Mk.26.
Pilots Notes - PR.Mk.34 & B.Mk.35
Pilots Notes - NF.Mk.38
Pilots Notes - TT.Mk39